GEOGRAPHY AND POLITICS IN ISRAEL SINCE 1967

GEOGRAPHY
AND POLITICS
IN ISRAEL
SINCE 1967

ELISHA EFRAT
*Department of Geography,
Tel Aviv University*

FRANK CASS

First published 1988 in Great Britain by
FRANK CASS & CO. LTD.
Gainsborough House, Gainsborough Road,
London, E11 1RS, England

and in the United States of America by
FRANK CASS & CO LTD.
c/o Biblio Distribution Centre
81 Adams Drive, P.O. Box 327, Totowa, N.J. 07511

Copyright © 1988 Elisha Efrat

British Library Cataloguing in Publication Data

Efrat, Elisha
  Geography and politics in Israel since 1967
  1. Israel. Politics 1967–1987. Geographical
  factors
  I. Title
  320.1'2'095694

  ISBN 0-7146-3303-8

Library of Congress Cataloging-in-Publication Data

Efrat, Elisha.
  Geography and politics in Israel since 1967 / Elisha Efrat.
    p.   cm.
  Bibliography: p.
  Includes index.
  ISBN 0-7146-3303-8
  1. Israel--Politics and government. 2. Israel–Arab War, 1967–
  –Occupied territories. 3. Land settlement--West Bank.
  4. Palestinian Arabs--Israel. 5. Israel--Geographical, Historical.
  6. Israel--Ethnic relations.   I. Title.
  DS126.5.E344 1988
  956.94'05--dc19   88–4319
                                            CIP

Printed and bound in Great Britain by
A. Wheaton & Co. Ltd, Exeter

Contents

List of Figures

List of Tables

Preface

The 1984 election campaign in Israel and its outcome have high-lighted among other things the difference of opinion among Israelis on the future of the Occupied Territories, on the desirable geo-graphical dimensions of the country and on the possibility of Jewish–Arab coexistence in the various regions of the Land of Israel. At no other time in the history of the country has the population been so aware of territorial matters and their political significance. While in the 1920s and 1930s, under conditions of a State in the making without territorial sovereignty, territory and government were abstract concepts, today they have become very concrete and acquired great importance.

Politics, including its passing aspects, has become part of the people. Political information is speeded to it hourly, and the population's preoccupation with the many aspects of Israeli politics is one of its special attributes. The vast interest in local political matters is explained by their importance for the survival and future of the country; the combination of small territory, long borders, regional isolation, and a difficult security situation and regional strategic status results in a special situation that may well arouse the concern of every one of its citizens.

The outcome of the Six Day War and the activities of the Likud government in the seven years from 1977 to 1984 brought to the fore new political and territorial matters that the State was compelled to deal with. The conquest of territory and its occupation; the settle-ment of areas across the borders for the purpose of controlling them or turning them into a bargaining card in peace negotiations; the emergence of Jewish national and religious ties with the Greater Land of Israel Movement; all of the massive investment in the physical infrastructure of the new areas to the detriment of develop-ment in Israel within the so-called Green Line, that marked the boundary of Israel as determined by the Armistice Agreement of 1949; and certain political acts such as the creation of Greater Jerusalem, the settlement of and subsequent military withdrawal from Sinai or the annexation of the Golan Heights – all these exemplify how geography and politics interact in the current period.

Israel today is characterized by many unusual features, very different from those with which political leaders in the Western world have been familiar. Consequently most of them, contemplating Israeli politics and seeking to understand it, are surprised by the rapidly changing political situation.

Some of the factors contributing to Israel's special situation and having considerable political impact are extremely complex. Among them is the nature of the Jewish people and its long peculiar history, and the short history of the State and the consequent lack as yet of a governmental tradition. Characteristic of Israel are the many traumatic, dramatic, unexpected events the populaton has experienced. Three great traumas, each unique, underlay the establishment of Israel: the Holocaust; the actual establishment of the State and the years of the War of Independence; and, for most of the population, immigration to Israel. In addition there were among other things the outcome of the Six Day War and the Yom Kippur War, Sadat's peace initiative, the political change in 1977, the rampant inflation, the bank share crisis, the Jewish terrorists, etc.

Now the result of such repeated traumatizaton is the disappointment of expectations previously relied on and a feeling of great confusion and helplessness, which lead to certain political developments: lack of confidence in the establishment, particularly in the parties believed responsible for the confusion, and loss of a sense of security; a search for an unambiguous message and doctrine supplying a clear solution to the confusion; a yearning for a strong leader the identification with whom might remove the feeling of helplessness; a search for scapegoats to blame; and withdrawal from societal concerns into immediate satisfactions, sometimes with political support.

Living with a feeling of constant danger leads to important political developments exemplified by the ecological anti-nuclear movements such as the 'Greens' of Germany, which arose against a background of the fear of ecological holocaust and nuclear war. In Israel the persistence of the conflict with the Arab countries in recurring confrontations, the reserve army service required of most of the population and the constant menace of terrorist acts combine to produce a feeling of constant danger presented by a definite outside enemy.

Such a feeling leads to hatred of the foe and a tendency to escape from reality, whether in the belief that a lasting peace can be speedily attained, or in the belief that absolute security can be ensured by military and settlement means and through the annexation of territories.

Despite the prominence of politics in Israeli life, it has not been properly taken into account from the professional geographical point of view. Social and economic matters have naturally been deemed more relevant to politics, but geography has not always constituted a recognized dimension. A study of political events against a spatial background and all that this implies has not so far been undertaken, and for that reason there is no period as fitted as the recent past to facilitate a proper investigation of this aspect of politics.

This book, dealing with geography and politics in Israel since 1967, is the first attempt of its kind to analyse current political events against the background of the geographical space in which they took place, and is based on a follow up, record and study of the events of recent years. The book highlights the physical background as a factor in the development of the political events as well as their relative importance. The various chapters therefore treat subjects of great interest and importance for life in Israel today, such as the future of Greater Jerusalem, the problematics of settlement in Judea–Samaria, the fate of the Gaza Strip and its relations with Israel, the status of the Golan Heights, the withdrawal from Sinai and establishment of the Shalom region, and also the problems within Israel proper: the Judaization of Galilee, the populating of the Negev, land as a political problem and border settlement in Israel.

CHAPTER ONE

The New Settlement
Map of Israel

The boldest expression of the geographical–political changes taking place in Israel is undoubtedly the acceleration of settlement in the Occupied Territories. Since the accession of the Likud in 1977, the process has exemplified a number of the elements of geography and politics: the importance of territory as an arena for political confrontation; the application of political power for the realization of nationalist and religious interests; decision-making of dubious legitimacy in territorial issues; the influence of central government on accelerated development and implementation; emphasis on identifying religious and nationalist values with territory in order to attract people to deliberate action; and above all, the power of political decisions to create faits accomplis and change the geographical layout of territories.

The settlement map of Israel today is very different from what it was in the 1950s and 1960s, and it is continually being further altered by the development of additional new settlements throughout the area, by the internal migration of population to them, and by new priorities of regional development. No other period in the history of the State of Israel has witnessed such rapid and significant changes in the settlement map. The decade of the 1970s was perhaps crucial, for it was then that Israel's ties were strengthened with the occupied territories beyond its political borders – the Golan Heights, Judea and Samaria, the Gaza Strip and the Sinai Peninsula. A new map of Israel was drawn during that decade, influenced by the new political situation resulting from the Six Day War. Israel then gained control of territories of different economic, social, and demographic character, which for political and security reasons dictated a new settlement endeavour in the 'Green Line'* area and in particular beyond it.

This new geopolitical situation gives rise to a number of questions: how do settlement characteristics of the 1970s differ from those of

*see Glossary of Terms

the two preceding decades? How has settlement in Israel been affected by the establishment of new borders? Which regions were given preference for settlement in the 1970s, and which were not? Who authorised the settlement map during the decade? What is Israel's future settlement map likely to be in the wake of the political and settlement developments of recent years?

SETTLEMENT AND DEVELOPMENT IN THE FIRST TWO DECADES

In the 1950s, national goals revolved around absorbing thousands of new immigrants, settling and establishing them economically, and strengthening the security borders of the State. In the 1960s the goal became the consolidation of the economy and settlement pattern within the country's sovereign territory, which needed to be quickly populated and provided with a great many development projects, particularly in the arid Negev, mountainous Galilee, and the Jerusalem corridor, and along the meandering 'Green Line' that was the partition line agreed upon between Israel and Jordan, Syria and Egypt.

The measures adopted during these two decades to attain the national goals were, among others, the establishment of Nahal border settlements along the 'Green Line'; the organization of new development regions, such as the Lakhish, Besor, Ta'anach and Korazim regions; and the settlement of the Arava region, mainly for the purpose of reinforcing the border strips. At the same time, development towns were founded in peripheral areas in order to disperse the population throughout the country, to create an urban alternative to counter the attraction of the large cities, and to establish a new pattern for the distribution of population and settlements. These measures were in part meant to 'correct' the settlement geography of the country that had resulted from the pre-State British mandatory government's policy of freezing Jewish settlement, from the territorial consequences of the War of Independence, and from the need to provide a speedy solution to the settlement and security problems that arose when the State was established; and to find new and original settlement patterns befitting a sovereign state. These measures were adopted in response to the demographic changes that took place over the years of mass immigration to Israel, to the accompaniment of continual study and experiment with new ways of developing the country's infrastructure.

In the early 1970s, however, due to the outcome and achievements of the Six Day War, Israel's national goals changed. Mass immigration diminished, no longer creating demographic pressure. The development districts in outlying areas near the 'Green Line' lost much of their importance. They were now devoid of significance for security, and there was no need to set up more development towns, especially since the existing ones had not yet reached their planned population targets. In addition, priorities previously applied to the Negev and Galilee regarding development, settlement and investment in infrastructure gave way to new priorities related to the territories occupied in the Six Day War.

SETTLEMENT AND DEVELOPMENT IN THE 1970s

The new geopolitical goals of the 1970s were: the occupation as rapidly as possible of areas beyond the 'Green Line' by the establishment of numerous settlements; the creation of new security belts beyond the 1967 borders; continued socioeconomic consolidation of previously established settlements within those borders; and further expansion of the infrastructure.

The ways in which these were to be achieved were basically unchanged. In this period too, border settlements were founded, although the borders were now in the Golan Heights, the Jordan Rift Valley and the northeast of the Sinai Peninsula. Development districts were set up on the Golan Heights, in the Rafah area, in the Jordan Valley, and at selected and more restricted spots between Elat and Sharm el-Sheikh. Now too new towns were established – Qatzrin on the Golan Heights, Yamit and Ofira in Sinai, and Qiryat Arba, Qarne Shomron, Ari'el, etc. in Judea and Samaria. All of them received priority in development and infrastructural investment.

Most of the development in this decade thus took place not within the sovereign domain of Israel, but far beyond it. This new development did not form a continuum with the settlement complexes established during the two previous decades. Moreover, the change in the priority in basic investment and the diversion of resources to the occupied territories left insufficient funds for the socioeconomic consolidation of the settlements established in the past. In the 1970s, in fact, a new settlement geography began to take shape, with comprehensive political and security interests beyond the original border. This peripheral area was triple the size of the State itself,

GPI—B

which was compelled to function as a small settlement and economic core for a large territory.

THE NEW GEOGRAPHICAL DIMENSIONS OF ISRAEL

The sovereign territory of Israel as established by the 1949 armistice amounted to 8,017 sq. miles. The zones occupied by Israel after the Six Day War added a periphery of 26,476 sq. miles, which is 3.3 times the area of Israel proper. After the withdrawal from Sinai there remained 2,854 sq. miles, or about one-third of the area of Israel.

Israel's territorial extension through the newly occupied territories can be summarised as follows: the Sinai peninsula (23,622 sq. miles) – very few rural and urban points, and no sovereignty over the area; the Golan Heights (444 sq. miles) – planning and implementation of regional settlement throughout the entire area, establishment of a new town and more than 30 new settlements, with Israeli law applied to the region in 1981; Judea and Samaria (2,270 sq. miles) – comprehensive, intensive rural and urban settlement against the background of a dense Arab settlement configuration, and without sovereignty over the area; the Gaza Strip (140 sq. miles) – limited Jewish settlement in the Qatif Bloc, against a background of a dense Arab population, and here too without sovereignty.

From north to south, Israel was 256 miles long before the Six Day War and 406 before the withdrawal from Sinai. Before 1967 there were 2,750,000 people in Israel with many areas sparsely populated, while today there are more than four million on territory just a third larger, with a distribution no better than the earlier one, and 1,340,000 additional Arabs in Judea, Samaria and the Gaza Strip. Consequently the limited 'settlement energy' of Israel has been spread over a very large expanse, a situation not likely to ensure the consolidation and stabilization of a settlement pattern.

Furthermore, past settlement was organized in sovereign territory within fixed borders recognized internationally or according to the armistice lines which were about 625 miles long. The occupied territories created a border that is 1,349 miles long, 523 miles on land and 826 miles along water. This involved the elimination of the 'Green Line' which had been so dominant for 19 years, and Israel's unilateral recognition of the Jordan River as the eastern border, the unilateral conversion of the Golan Heights armistice line into a political border, and the creation of a de facto border between Israel and Lebanon along a narrow security zone beyond the recognized international border between the two countries. Thus since 1967 the settlements have been established within four types of borders: a recognized and accepted border (Sinai, the Arava), a unilaterally recognized border (the Jordan River), a border whose existence is disregarded (Judea, Samaria and the Gaza Strip), and a de facto border (southern Lebanon). No other country in the world has so many types of borders as Israel. It is hard to believe that such borders can create the proper conditions for the development of a stable settlement configuration.

SETTLEMENT PRIORITIES IN THE PAST

Before the establishment of the new national goals in the settlement of the occupied territories, another order of priority applied in Israel, which related mainly to the Negev, Galilee and Jerusalem. Yet it must be borne in mind that that priority notwithstanding, the desired goals have not yet been achieved. The settlement of the Negev is still in its inception, despite having been the focus of the national vision for many years. Many difficulties were encountered in overcoming the desert so far as water and soil are concerned, so that settlement in the Negev mountains, for instance, or in the Arava is quite sparse. The population increased in a number of urban locations in the northern Negev, especially in Beersheba which in 1987 had a population of about 120,000. A considerable scattering of settlements marks the northwestern Negev, which contains a concentration of new immigrant cooperative settlements (moshavim). All in all, however, the entire Negev and Judean desert, which constitutes 60 per cent of Israel, accounts for just 250,000 inhabitants, 6 per cent of the Israeli total. If that area had had any chance of developing in the future, this was scotched by the Sinai expansion with the Rafah region, Yamit, Ofira and extensive military arrangements, which left the Negev and Judean desert area marking time. The hope that the withdrawal from the Sinai would restore its priority proved vain, for the redeployment of the army there did little to increase its population or settlements.

Recently there has been a tendency to favour the Galilee in the development initiative, because of the serious demographic problem presented by the constant diminution of the Jewish sector there compared with the Arab, in particular in mountainous central Galilee. Yet the aim of Judaizing Galilee has not been accomplished, the development towns still call out for settlers, and many of the rural settlements require economic assistance. For despite the admitted importance of developing Galilee, in the last decade priority has been accorded to the Golan Heights, and its reinforcement by a dense network of settlements to promote the security of the border with Syria.

Development priority has also been accorded to Jerusalem throughout the years, despite the 30 or so development towns founded when the State was established to attract urban settlers and scatter the population. The motivation was the desire to transform the city into a large capital, for nationalist and religious reasons, although this was not justified on objective geographical grounds. In most historical periods, Jerusalem was not a large city, and its mountainous location makes it unsuitable for a metropolis. Its mountainous environs make traffic difficult, its economic agricultural hinterland is quite limited, it is far from the centres of economic activity in the coastal plain, and any artificial enlargement of the city is likely to impair its special historical and architectural character. Throughout the years Jerusalem was favoured for development while most of the development towns did not receive the help and encouragement needed to establish them solidly, and old cities like Tiberias, Safed, Ramla, Lod and Acre did not develop at the expected pace. The change in Jerusalem's geopolitical status, due among other things to its location in the heart of Judea-Samaria, made the city even more important after the Six Day War. As a result, its priority (at the expense of the Negev and Galilee) was augmented for the purpose of making it a large metropolis, yet in a geographical situation which restricted its ability to function as a large city.

Thus development priorities within the 'Green Line' fluctuated from one pole to the other. Neither the Negev, Galilee, the Jerusalem corridor nor the southern lowland, not to speak of any region in the Arab sector, enjoyed any great development. In the 1970s they were all neglected, in favour at times of Sinai, at times of the Golan Heights, and at times of Judea and Samaria; and only Jerusalem was the gainer. The part of Israel within the 'Green Line' did not benefit from much investment on the regional level and, except for isolated places such as Ramat Hovav in the northern Negev or the Tefen region in Galilee, most of the settlements that flourished before 1967 did not make much progress.

ISRAEL CHANGES DIRECTION

Instead of solving substantive and physical problems within the sovereign territory of Israel, accelerated development activity is being directed to sites outside it. As the longitudinal dimension of the country was shortened, development activity turned in a new direction, on the east–west axis, given the political blockage to the north and to the south. In the wake of the frustrations of the withdrawal from Sinai, and the enforced territorial shrinkage, the declared policy of the government gave greater impetus to the east–west direction, turning its attention to the occupied territories for reasons of security, strategic depth, and territorial integrity. The three objectives of this expansion are naturally the Golan Heights, the Gaza Strip, and Judea and Samaria. The Golan Heights have a great deal of unoccupied land and a small local population; the Gaza Strip has little unoccupied land and a large local population; while Judea and Samaria have both considerable unoccupied land and a large population. On the Golan Heights the acquisition of physical control had been relatively easy and was already accomplished; in the Gaza Strip there is no possibility of expansion, because there are about 542,000 people in an area of 140 sq. miles, or 3,871 per sq. mile, one of the highest population densities in the world. There thus remains one possible objective for expansion – Judea and Samaria.

With this objective, an expansion in width was expressed in the junction of two longitudinal axes, that of the coastal plain and that of the Jordan Valley, by means of new cross-sections, exemplified in practice by a set of roads, such as the Samaria bisector, the Jerusalem–Ma'ale Edumim axis, the Judea bisector, in strengthening and 'thickening' the Etzion bloc, in the continued population increase in Qiryat Arba, in the establishment of new townlets, in the development of the industrial zone of Ma'ale Edumim, in the founding of dozens of holdings in reaction to political measures inconvenient to Israel, and in the widening of Jerusalem's periphery beyond the surroundings and the desert to the east.

It must be borne in mind that this latitudinal direction is beset with considerable difficulty, facing an 837,000 strong Arab population in dense concentrations throughout Judea and Samaria, facing a continuum of villages and towns, facing difficulties in acquiring land, and facing a hostile population that does not make things at all easy for the civil administration in the areas.

This latitudinal expansion is based on a number of phenomena characteristic of the present-day Israeli population. The Jewish population has a definitely urban mentality and is therefore prepared for non-agricultural settlement involving industry and services; it is interested in places of residence of improved environmental quality devoid of pollution; and it wishes to abandon disorderly urban crowding even for places beyond the 'Green Line'. The motivation derives from the fact that in Judea and Samaria it is possible to find relatively easy solutions to all the defects so glaring in Israel and for which no reasonable solutions were planned in a changing territorial situation. While in Israel proper building lots are extremely expensive, in Judea and Samaria they are almost gratis; in Israel housing is very costly, there it is for the most part subsidized. Here the roads are jammed, and there new wide roads are being constructed that bring every settlement closer to Israel territory and Jerusalem. Here urban pollution and overcrowding are on the increase, there development is implemented with priorities and preferential treatment. Here it may be hard to find a place for suburban living, but there every settler is eagerly awaited. Here space is unavailable for the expansion of various services, and there it is abundant. And finally, if in Israel the realization of nationalist goals no longer carries much weight, there everything becomes more pioneering, more Zionistic, more security-oriented, and even earns great admiration.

CONTRACTION VERSUS EXPANSION

The withdrawal of the Israel Defence Forces (IDF) and civilian settlers from Sinai, which was the first territorial change since the faits accomplis following the Six Day War, created a new situation in the geography of Israel within the 'Green Line' which has affected those involved in planning and development who had considered Sinai a site for essential economic and military activity. The arena for action was now considerably reduced in both area and length compared with what the people of Israel had become accustomed to during the preceding 17 years.

The IDF withdrawal from Sinai, which entailed the transfer of many military installations to the Negev, the construction of camps and an airfield, and the reservation of new areas for training and manoeuvres, actually required the use of a third of the Negev area, especially from Mitzpe Ramon southwards, for military purposes. Thus another 1,367 sq. miles of territory – 35 per cent of the Negev or 17 per cent of Israel within the 'Green Line' – was written off. In addition to all this, there was a change in the spatial configuration of certain functions; the Red Sea bathing beaches for tens of thousands of holiday-makers were truncated, civilian air space was restricted in favour of the military, and pressures are growing regarding the use of the Mediterranean shore for port and fuel facilities, naval bases, power stations, etc. Thus in fact shrinkage and reduction of the country is even greater than its purely territorial limitation.

It was reasonable to assume that, in the wake of these changes in the geographical facts, the authorities would draw the logical conclusions and try to solve spatial problems within Israel's sovereign territory: prepare new bathing beaches for summer holiday-makers, develop new recreational facilities, improve and expand the road system to increase mobility in the increasingly crowded country, ameliorate the infrastructure in cities and towns to enable them to handle larger populations, encourage urban construction in height and depth to economize on land area, utilize unoccupied and uncultivated land more efficiently and to a greater extent, prepare development plans for new population concentrations around industrial projects, implement plans for public transport by train, in order to reduce road traffic, improve communication to eliminate unnecessary travel, put urban land to multi-purpose use, create new sources of employment near urban concentrations, promote regional development in settled areas on the basis of growth points and reciprocal relations between centre and periphery, and, in sum, adopt drastic measures to improve the environment and the quality of life in the centre of the country to make life easier for the population in conditions of increasing density and territorial diminution.

However, the authorities made a different response to the new geographical conditions. The changed direction they took disregarded the principles that had underlain the upbuilding of the country in the past. There is no doubt that the settlement map of the 1970s was influenced primarily by political, military and security factors, subject to pressure from the United States, Egypt and Syria which dictated various measures in Israel. Yet there were also various domestic nationalist motives and political party interests that contributed to the settlement activities and the change in the map of Israel. In the course of the process various social and economic pressure groups arose which were very much interested in having Israel change direction so that they could derive some benefit.

Thus the 1970s differ from all earlier decades in the emphasis on political motivation for settlement going beyond economic considerations, on mass settlement rural and urban, public and private, in areas whose ultimate fate is not yet known, involving the penetration of a crowded Arab settlement fabric, on new types of settlement – and all this with a daily political struggle. Israel's new borders led to a regrettable diffusion of the new settlements; it created too few consolidated areas such as the Golan Heights and the Jordan Valley, and left many sparsely settled ones. In the past the Negev was chief focus of the settlement, later replaced by Galilee, and in the 1970s by Sinai, the Golan Heights, Judea and Samaria, and the Jerusalem environs. The Likud government fostered extreme politicization in the settlement of Judea and Samaria, in order to change the map of the country within a short period and strengthen it toward the east. It is doubtful whether it is a map within which it will be possible to maintain uni-national sovereignty and a democratic society.

In any case, anyone interested in a different government and a different development policy based on the geographical structure of Israel and its sovereign area will have to take into account a different order of priorities in the development challenges, and to focus efforts internally so as to give the inhabitants of Israel a chance to enjoy a reasonable quality of life in a country whose geographical area contracted in the course of the 1970s.

CHAPTER TWO

Jerusalem as a Metropolitan City

Among the geopolitical changes that have taken place from the establishment of the State up to the present, those in Jerusalem are particularly salient; nowhere else have so many complicated political, security, planning, demographic, historic and architectural problems been combined as in that city. The special importance of Jerusalem for the Jewish people and the nations of the world set it in a different light from other cities, and therefore planning and construction for it have always been accompanied by sensitivity to public and international reaction.

This sensitivity grew after the Six Day War, when for the first time Israel had the opportunity to alter the geopolitical status of Jerusalem. The world followed what was being done in the city with concern for the fate of the holy places and the balance of political power that might develop between Jews, Arabs, the Christian minority and the Kingdom of Jordan. The Israeli government then adopted an unequivocal position, and with no differences of opinion a consensus developed in the nation regarding the need to unify Jerusalem and turn it into a large city populated mainly by Jews. Considerable resources were poured into the city in order to create in it, and in its environs, a new urban-political situation that would compensate for past frustrations and establish a new settlement fabric which it will be impossible to change. And indeed, since 1967, the city has experienced rapid, intensive construction against a political background both tacit and open, in the presence of an apprehensive Arab population. The signs of this accelerated construction are discernible in the formation of a very large urban system that does not exactly fit forms of construction in mountainous regions. As it looks to us today, Jerusalem is a tangled urban fabric, the result of historical, religious, nationalist and political desires imprinted on a given geographical expanse whose ability to encompass the new system in the making is doubtful.

Jerusalem as an urban-geographical phenomenon differs from

every other city. There are some 180 capitals in the world today, and, not surprisingly most are not at a great topographic elevation, most are not contiguous with a desert, and most are not away from the centres of economic activity and population concentrations in their countries, as Jerusalem is. Only 25 (14 per cent) of capitals are situated, like Jerusalem, 2,400 feet or more above sea level; of these, only 15 (8 per cent) have populations of more than 300,000; and only seven (4 per cent), such as Mexico City, Nairobi, Salisbury and Kampala, for example, have suburbs around them. Thus a mountain capital at a considerable elevation, with suburbs around it, is not at all a normal urban situation. Capitals tend to be located on plains, or near sea coasts, with the possibility of industrial development, an agricultural hinterland and convenient transportation arteries.

Furthermore, in addition to this unusual urban manifestation, in the course of the past 40 years Jerusalem has undergone serious vicissitudes in planning and construction; it has functioned as a city divided between two nations, and subsequently has become an expanded city, encouraged increased population, had government institutions transferred to it, developed new roads, absorbed an Arab population constituting 28.4 per cent of its total − all projects that require many decades in an ordinary city. The constant political changes, the desire to avert any future division of the city, the fear of its again becoming a city at the end of a corridor, the goal of achieving a Jewish majority within it and the aspiration to maintain its status as the national capital are what seem to have led to such intensive development and construction that there has been no opportunity to formulate a conception regarding its structure and nature. Taking action has often preceded overall planning, so that basic problems still remain unsolved. Should its centre be developed rather than the periphery? Is the aim a consolidated Jerusalem or a spread out one? Jewish or mixed? A union of sub-cities, or a continuous agglomeration? Development toward the east, north or south? In a continuous ring or in separated holdings? Clearly, in the absence of a basic infrastructure for a large Jerusalem, and so long as no clear policy has been formulated regarding the crucial questions, accelerated development is being carried out extending towards the city outskirts in difficult topography, far from the centre and in inconvenient geographical conditions eastward and westward, colliding with existing Arab towns to the north and south and constituting a sporadic urban structure which has no relation to the organic construction of a mountain city.

Up to now the establishment has not considered Jerusalem's spatial ring in any systematic manner. Various approaches on what should be done in the space have been proffered intermittently by planners, but most have not yet been approved.

The development of Jerusalem actually reflects the conflict between the political–nationalist approach that favours a metropolitan Jerusalem, and the local objective approach which sees in the geographical conditions a chance for a medium-sized city, with special characteristics unsuited for a metropolis. We shall, therefore, endeavour to analyse the features of Jerusalem as a future metropolis based on the various political approaches to this matter.

JERUSALEM AT THE END OF THE SIX DAY WAR

The development of Jerusalem after 1967 was considerably influenced by political decisions that led to the establishment of new neighbourhoods in the areas added to it, which were thenceforth included in the municipal domain, now totalling 27,025 acres compared with the previous 9,525 acres. The location of the neighbourhoods was determined primarily by political factors, intended to demonstrate Israeli control of the close environs of the city.

The two parts of the city were united by a government decree that extended Israeli jurisdiction and administration to east Jerusalem. This was supplemented by a government decision to begin to settle Jews beyond the 1967 borders. These measures could be interpreted as correcting the distortion produced during the War of Independence (1948) when the Jewish quarter in the Old City fell, Mount Scopus was isolated, and Jerusalem divided between Israel and Jordan. Israel's response to that situation was the creation of a series of housing projects between Jerusalem and Mount Scopus, and the construction of the neighbourhoods of Ramot Eshkol, Givat Hamivtar and Ma'alot Daphna. The neighbourhoods filled up rapidly because they enabled many Israelis to improve their living conditions. Talpiyot to the east and Gilo to the south were also targets for increased population. In addition, Neve Ya'aqov was established to create a continuum of buildings between Jerusalem and the Atarot airfield. With the construction of these neighbourhoods, each containing between 300 and 5,000 units, Jerusalem diverged for the first time from the compact historical structure it had been in the past. Here the Ministry of Housing and Construction was the executive arm of the government, which favoured rapid construction, despite objections by elements in the Jerusalem municipality and other planning institutions who urged limiting construction so as not to damage the architectural and aesthetic values of the city (Figure 1).

The construction of the new neighbourhoods achieved the political goal of a municipal spread throughout the area within the new city limits of Jerusalem. The neighbourhoods also control peripheral roads from all sides. At the same time they are far from the city centre, have no local sources of employment, are separated from the central institutions of the city and in a sense are a manifestation opposing the character of the city.

THE JEWISH–ARAB STRUGGLE FOR THE ENVIRONS OF JERUSALEM

Since the Six Day War unprecedented building activity has been conducted in the Jerusalem area with Arab financing and co-ordination between landowners, former mayors, heads of village councils and 'mukhtars'. Areas that were neglected are now cultivated, and every month dozens of houses are erected in the vicinity of the city.

The demand for workers from among the Arabs of the occupied territories grew in the course of time and the inhabitants of Judea, especially from Mount Hebron, began streaming to the building sites in Jerusalem, and gradually moved into the Old City of Jerusalem with their families, despite its crowded conditions. The original residents then moved into the Old City suburbs. Today only 15 per cent of those who lived in the Moslem quarter of the Old City before 1967 are still there. It is estimated that the Arab population of Jerusalem has doubled since 1967 and now amounts to about 126,800.

At the same time the demographic balance in the city has changed. The annual increase in the Jewish population is about half that of the Arab and the ratio of 73.3 per cent Jews to 26.7 per cent Arabs in 1967 shifted to 71.6 per cent Jews and 28.4 per cent Arabs in 1985. This trend has obtained since 1969, and according to 1985 figures has accelerated with the government-assisted move of Jerusalem residents to nearby towns beyond the 'Green Line'.

In recent years Arab construction in Jerusalem has also acquired a political tinge. The National Guidance Committee of the Arabs of the occupied territories has urged the inhabitants to plant trees and erect buildings in every place designated for Jewish settlement. The Arab villagers of Judea and Samaria make no distinction between State land and private land. For them both are Arab lands to which

FIGURE 1
GREATER JERUSALEM AND ITS NEW RESIDENTIAL SUBURBS

Key: 1. Municipal boundary. 2. Main road. 3. Central Avenue. 4. Tunnel. 5. Railway line. 6. Old City. 7. Urban residential area. 8. Rural residential area. 9. Commercial centre. 10. Central business district. 11. Government offices. 12. Institutions. 13. Industrial area. 14. Communications. 15. Public open space. 16. Cemetery. 17. Hotels. 18. Central area zone. 19. Special open space.

the occupation authorities have no right. The areas never operated according to an overall plan, have a long tradition of unauthorized building, and lack awareness of planning, so that the application of construction regulations there is extremely difficult.

Northwest of Jerusalem, in the villages of Beit Iksa, Nebi Samuel, Beit Hanina, Bir Naballa, el-Jib, Jedira, Kalandia and Rafat, more than a thousand new buildings have been erected since 1967. On the mountainside north of Jerusalem, at el-Bire, Shuafat, er-Ram, and Kafr Aqeb, more than 2,000 have been added in those years. East of Jerusalem in el-Ezeriyye, Abu Dis and et-Tur the spread of Arab construction and the acquisition of land for building purposes is obvious. The number of houses has doubled during the period under discussion. South of Jerusalem, at Sur Bahir, Beit Sahur, Beit Safafa, Sharafat and Beit Jalla, the pace of growth has been smaller, but there too amounts to several hundred units.

This accelerated Arab construction has implications for the future planning and development of Jerusalem. The route of the national lateral road at the Bet Horon–Jerusalem axis was changed several times due to these constructions. Speedy Arab construction on the eastern slopes of Mount Scopus may stop the expansion of Ma'ale Edumim toward Jerusalem. Arab building at the Hizme–Beit Hanina road junction prevents the uninterrupted continuity of construction between Neve Ya'aqov and the French Hill. Furthermore, this Arab construction has spatial and political implications, involving the occupation of considerable territory by a relatively small population, control of important roads connecting Jerusalem with its environs, the placing of obstacles between sites of Jewish development, and the creation of difficulties in providing services. The centres of Arab building between Ramallah and Shuafat to the north in the villages east of Jerusalem's municipal boundaries, in the area of Arab es-Suachra to the southeast, and at Beit Sahur and its environs to the south may in the future produce insoluble physical difficulties. Continuous Arab development may take place between Ramallah, Kafr Aqeb and er-Ram, spatial options around the Atarot airfield will be closed, a barrier may be created between Jaba and er-Ram, Hizme and Beit Hanina and between Anata and Shuafat, and Neve Ya'aqov and French Hill may be cut off from each other, so that eventually contiguous construction between er-Ram in the north and Arab Suachra in the south will isolate Jerusalem altogether from the Judean desert. Uninterrupted building between Bethlehem and Beit Safafa, and a greater density of building at Beit Sahur, will cut the Etzion Bloc off from Jerusalem and may in the future prevent the paving of a road between Arad and Ma'ale Edumim. These developments impelled the authorities to take preventive measures in the form of confiscation of land. South of Neve Ya'aqov 1,175 acres were confiscated, in the Giv'on area a narrow corridor to ensure the possibility of a road in the future, near Beit Hanina several thousand acres to allow for the paving of a highway which has to cross Jerusalem from north to south, and several thousand acres to expand Ma'ale Edumin in the future.

Jewish private individuals and public bodies have been acquiring hundreds of acres of land, occupying as much territory as possible in order to ensure orderly construction and development of the region in the future. The settlement and development authorities claim that within one or two decades the settlement policy of the government will prove to be a solution to the establishment of rural and semi-urban settlements, based on a comprehensive regional plan to the east of the Arab population. It will be effective and be able to compete in size with the Arab concentrations.

In regard to the Jewish areas of settlement in the region, in three places in the Giv'on area there are about 3,000 settlers. The townlet of Givat Ze'ev, now being built, will house hundreds more families. Further north is Bet Horon with only a few hundred people. East of Jerusalem is the town of Ma'ale Edumim, now being rapidly populated, and planned to absorb thousands of settlers. South of that town a settlement bloc is being planned, to be called Mevo'ot Edumin. This Jewish expansion over the region is designed to ensure control of access to Jerusalem, there being no desire to return to the pre-1967 situation when Jerusalem was a cul-de-sac, cut off from its environs and from Mount Scopus, and Jewish settlements in the Etzion Bloc, Neve Ya'aqov and Atarot were entirely destroyed.

The Arab–Jewish struggle for the Jerusalem area has a demographic aspect as well. In 1984 the Jewish population increased by 5.0 per cent compared with 2.9 per cent in 1979, while the Arab population increased by 5.1 per cent compared with 3.4 per cent in 1979. At the end of 1984 Jerusalem had 446,500 inhabitants, 13,500 more than in 1981. The Jews numbered 320,000 (297,600 in 1981) and the non-Jews 126,500 (115,400 in 1981). Furthermore, the Jewish population of the city is aging, while the Arab population is becoming younger.

These facts indicate that the Jerusalem region is the site of a demographic and physical competition between two populations aiming at substantive achievements with the clear political purpose of holding and controlling the environs of the city. It may be assumed that without a comprehensive regional plan and rapid systematic implementation of important aspects of such a plan, Israel will not be able to safeguard the region of its capital.

A PLETHORA OF PLANS FOR CONTROL OF THE REGION

Since the Six Day War, development and planning bodies in Israel have been trying to grapple with the problem of the Jerusalem region. Various approaches have emerged in the course of the years in plans which have not been approved, except for a plan for the city of Jerusalem and one for the Jerusalem district that covers only the western part of it.

Among the planning approaches suggested, the following should be noted:

1. The 1968 master plan for Jerusalem envisages urban and suburban residential areas and industrial zones beyond the city's municipal boundaries, in a concentric consolidated formation to the north, east and south, and in a linear alignment, particularly along the Shuafat–Ramallah axis. The plan proposes spatial expansion as absolutely essential for the solution of municipal problems, the addition of suburban residential areas for Jews, residential neighbourhoods for Arabs, new industrial zones to the east and southeast, all this keeping as close as possible to the existing municipal boundaries (Figure 2). This master plan was drawn up by a special team appointed by the municipality of Jerusalem. So far the plan has not been approved or received any official status.

2. The Zionist Settlement Unit of the Jewish Agency sees the solution in rural settlements in the region – small ones of about two hundred families, in blocs to avert isolation. Such settlement, this approach contends, could be carried out at the Ofra-Beth El and Kokhav Hashahar–Mikhmash bloc, in the Givon–Bet Horon bloc, in the Etzion bloc and Mevo Edumim and Qidron to the east. These would be supplemented by three urban centres, Bet Horon to the northwest, Ma'ale Edumin to the east, and Teqo'a to the south. Such an alignment of industrial villages with centres in selected places could be carried out within a short time, would provide control of the region, and would not adversely affect the population of Jerusalem. Industrial villages could also be based on a limited number of families, so that the investment

FIGURE 2

OUTLINE SCHEME OF GREATER JERUSALEM 1967

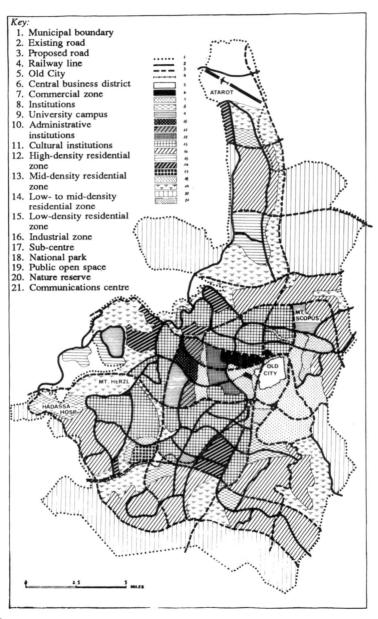

Key:
 1. Municipal boundary
 2. Existing road
 3. Proposed road
 4. Railway line
 5. Old City
 6. Central business district
 7. Commercial zone
 8. Institutions
 9. University campus
10. Administrative
    institutions
11. Cultural institutions
12. High-density residential
    zone
13. Mid-density residential
    zone
14. Low- to mid-density
    residential zone
15. Low-density residential
    zone
16. Industrial zone
17. Sub-centre
18. National park
19. Public open space
20. Nature reserve
21. Communications centre

in infrastructure for each such place was smaller than for an urban settlement (Figure 3).

FIGURE 3
EXISTING AND PLANNED SETTLEMENT BLOCS AROUND JERUSALEM

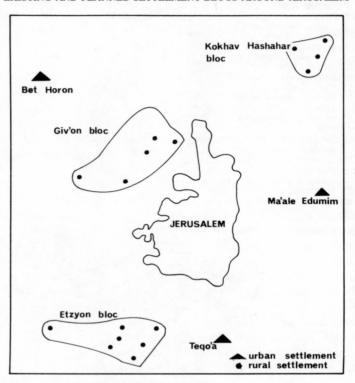

3. The Israel Land Authority is endeavouring to enlarge the Jerusalem corridor north and southwards by establishing settlements along main roads, and by founding towns at Bet Horon and Eshtemo'a, even if these turn out to be outside the Jerusalem city limits. It aims to set up villages along the Bet Horon road, and the Teqo'a–Hafurit axis. Bet Horon would be located in the remote periphery of the Tel Aviv conurbation and Eshtemo'a in the remote periphery of Beersheba. In addition, the Authority favours populating those neighbourhoods of Jerusalem within the city limits which contain few Jews, in order to prevent the repartitioning of Jerusalem. It envisages development priority

being given to the approaches to Jerusalem, while safeguarding the communication with other parts of the country.

4. The Ministry of Construction and Housing proposes the establishment of three towns — Giv'on, Efrat and Ma'ale Edumim — at strategic intersections of the region, each having a population of from 25,000 to 50,000. Between them villages would be set at important points. Control of the region according to this approach means large population concentrations in towns, which might serve for metropolitan expansion in the future. Towns of this size, with settlement communities in their hinterland, would guarantee the dispersal of Jewish population throughout the region (Figure 4).

5. The Judea and Samaria command have prepared a partial regional plan for the Jerusalem environs with the aim of restraining Arab construction around the city, in order to safeguard security areas and roads to and from Jerusalem. Villages north and east of Jerusalem were designated as places where no construction could be extended, some north, south and north-west villages were marked for limited building, and a group of villages to the north-west were to be allowed planned expanded construction. In the absence of any statutory plan, this plan would make it possible to prevent the closure of the region by Arab construction, with supervision and authorization of building within the existing villages.

6. The Etzion regional council is working on the enlargement of the bloc toward the towns of Efrat and Teqo'a to the east, and unification with Jerusalem to the north. The purpose is to exert spatial control over Mount Hebron, reinforce the lateral axis from the lowland to the Dead Sea, and transform the Etzion Bloc into a dominant urban centre between Hebron and Jerusalem.

7. The Ministry of Transport together with the Public Works Department has prepared a plan for proposed roads in Jerusalem and its environs. The new roads it proposes are: a fast road through the Bet Horon Ascent to Jerusalem; the continuation of that road eastward from Atarot to Ma'ale Edumim and its junction with the Allon road; a road from Atarot in the north to Solomon's Pools and the Etzion Bloc in the south; a junction between the Etzion Bloc and Gilo, and from there parallel to Jerusalem's western boundary along the Hadassah–Bet Zayyit–Abu Gush–Anata line; bypassing Ramallah and el-Bire to the south; and a road bypassing Shuafat (Figure 5).

8. In addition to all the plans noted above, the Ministry of Defence

FIGURE 4
URBAN SITES ERECTED BY THE MINISTRY OF HOUSING

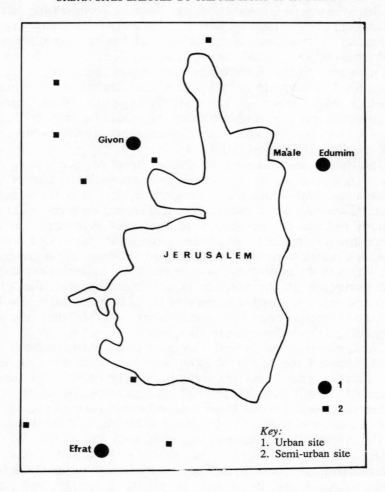

Givon

Ma'ale   Edumim

JERUSALEM

1

2

Efrat

Key:
1. Urban site
2. Semi-urban site

and the Settlement Department of the Zionist Organization
have prepared detailed building plans for settlements like
Giv'on, Mevo Edumim, Efrat, the Etzion Bloc and Ofra.
9. Various national and regional plans relevant to the Jerusalem
region have been drawn up by various planning institutions.
They deal with the Jordan valley, with the location of security
installations and military camps, with water, sewage and water
pipes, population, satellite towns, land, minerals, mines, etc.

FIGURE 5
ROAD NETWORK IN AND AROUND THE GREATER JERUSALEM AREA

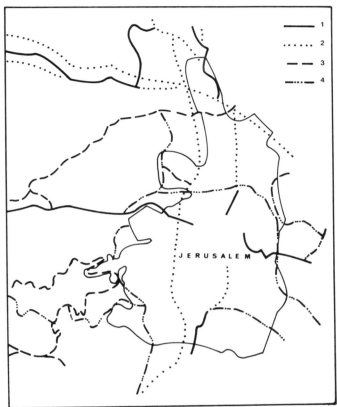

Key:
1. Existing motorway　　3. Proposed motorway
2. Existing main road　　4. Proposed main road

It thus transpires that many matters are being dealt with by planning, development and security interests, each subject constituting just a small fragment of planning thematically, sectorally, or spatially. They do not add up to a unified planning fabric capable of directing development based on a comprehensive view. The only approved plans are the 1959 plan for Jerusalem within the 'Green Line', and the 1960s plan for Jerusalem District within the 'Green Line' borders of the 'Corridor'. Because these two plans are included in the boundaries of the State of Israel, they could be approved according to the Town Planning Law which covers the sovereign territory only. All the other plans which have been prepared after 1967 were master plans, full of proposals and ideas, but which could not be given a legitimate status, because planning in Judea and Samaria took place according to the Jordanian laws as occupied territories.

The implications of all the plans for Jerusalem bring us back to the demographic problem. According to the government's policy, Jerusalem must increase its Jewish population by 3.7 per cent annually in order to maintain the ratio between Jews and Arabs. It is doubtful whether such an increase can support the establishment of three towns in the Jerusalem area. Nor is the natural increase in the city large enough to fill the demographic need. As the Arab natural increase is greater than that of the Jews, the Arab population will constantly grow if there is not enough Jewish migration into the city. Today, the migration balance is against the Jews. In order to maintain a favourable balance, the three new towns proposed will require 67,000 inhabitants by 1990. And to maintain a population increase of 3.7 per cent annually with a natural increase of only 2.2 per cent in the next decade Jerusalem and its region will have to have an additional 120,000 inhabitants, or 12,000 net per annum, three times the size of the average annual increase between 1968 and 1975. The settlements in the suburbs too, as proposed by the Land Authority, would require a large population, and as long as the new suburbs have trouble filling up, it is doubtful whether population could be found for most of the proposals outlined above.

POSSIBLE MODELS FOR METROPOLITAN JERUSALEM

Before determining guidelines for the planning of the Jerusalem metropolitan region, a decision needs to be taken as to the desirable model for such a metropolitan structure. There are various theoretical possibilities for urban development of this kind, the critical aspects being the size and population density, the capacity of the services, the inner movement patterns of the population in obtaining them, and all the characteristics of its functioning.

It may be assumed, as those taking the maximalist approach assume, that for Jerusalem a population of 600,000 would be optimal, as the geographical conditions of the town would not permit convenient circulation beyond that figure, and the capacity for services and employment would be limited because of its location. On the other hand, the existing layout, and the presence of administrative, economic and cultural functions in its old centre do not allow for far-reaching changes in its urban structure.

There are five common basic models for the structure of metropolitan cities in the world (Lynch, 1968): the dispersed model, the galaxy model, the core model, the star model, and the ring model (Figure 6).

FIGURE 6

BASIC MODELS FOR METROPOLITAN DEVELOPMENT

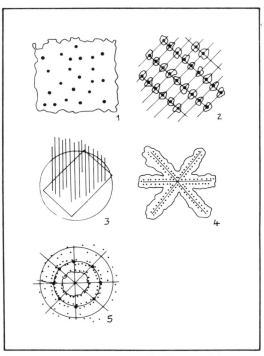

Key: 3. Core model
1. Dispersed model   4. Star model
2. Galaxy model   5. Ring model

1. *The dispersed model.* The main aspect is freedom for urban dispersal beyond the fringes, leaving the city centre relatively uncrowded, and the scattering of services, functions and institutions in all directions throughout the area. Its advantages are in allowing the propinquity of dwellings to work places, and in easy access to services, without recourse to a crowded city centre. The model does not cause overloaded transport, and provides open spaces near at hand. Its disadvantages are that the substructure is

expensive, it requires a great deal of territory, and must rely on private transportation.

2. *The galaxy model.* This model too allows for urban scattering beyond the fringes, but in small centres of equal size which concentrate selected population and functions, such as banking, commerce, culture, etc. Transport is easy and free but drains into these centres. The model allows for the proximity of residential and work areas and even community independence from the city centre. It has advantages over the previous model as it requires less territory and more easily prevents unplanned development, but may create a monotonous set of neighbourhoods.

3. *The core model.* This model aims for maximum city centre development, high-rise building, is based on public transport, on access at short distances, creates segregation for pedestrians, makes possible more economical services, but on the other hand produces a life of over-crowding, noise and pollution, with a high population density.

4. *The star model.* This model preserves a dominant city centre with basic functions, but allows linear construction development in various directions where there is land, and along the axes where secondary centres will develop, with lower level functions than those of the city centre. A concentric transport network will develop between the axes. The important urban functions remain in the city centre and secondary ones are distributed along the selected axes. The model can be enlarged by lengthening and thickening the axes. The difficulty arising here is the long concentric connections and the distance between one axis and the next.

5. *The ring model.* This model forgoes the intensive development of the city centre and transfers most of the development to rings around it that have a high population density. Between the city centre and rings the empty area is crossed by roads. Beyond each ring is open territory. Each ring contains small secondary centres with internal annular connection. In this model it is hard to preserve the empty areas between the rings, and development in the outer rings is costly.

It is obvious from the above descriptions of the metropolitan models that the unique conditions in the Jerusalem region make it impossible to develop any one of the classic models completely. The dispersed model is impossible because of land and the cost of services, and the core model is impossible for political reasons requiring comprehensive development. Because the region contains too many established facts, including the presence of many Arab villages around the city, it will be necessary to adopt a combination model. That model will need to preserve the character of the city centre and functions of Jerusalem as noted in the core model; adopt the ring model as regards the close environs of the city, particularly just beyond the municipal boundaries, in order to foster the development of extensions along the important road links with leading settlements along them, such as in the star model; and to seek to secure the edges of the region through a ring of urban settlements as part of a ring model.

THE JERUSALEM METROPOLITAN REGION AND ITS
DEVELOPMENT POINTS

On the basis of a proposed combination model it is possible to set the boundaries of the region for planning purposes – of course granted the political pressure that sees the necessity for the development of that region. Making use of spatial criteria such as the existing municipal boundaries, topography, commuting, density and links with Jerusalem of the population, three geographical units can be distinguished for planning and development purposes: the city of Jerusalem within its official boundary, the second ring that encircles the close environs of the city and the immediate settlement hinterland, and the third ring, which is the city's broader zone of influence. If the first ring is established by the official boundaries of the city, the second may be identified by the concentrations of Arab towns and villages close to Jerusalem spread over the plateau at a high topography, stretching from Beth El in the north and the Judean desert on the east to the passage to the Judean hills on the south and the centre of the Jerusalem corridor on the west. This ring will include towns such as Ramallah and el-Bire on the north, Bethlehem, Beit Jalla and Beit Sahur on the south, the series of villages between them and the Jewish settlements on the west, up to the Ma'aleh Hahamisha–Abu Gosh–Mevo Betar axis. The third ring is composed according to the zone of influence of the villages north of Ramallah that still have some relation to Jerusalem – the first step of the plateau that drops towards the Judean desert with Ma'ale Edumim on the east, the Etzion Bloc as a relatively dense Jewish concentration on the south, and the fold line of the Judean hills on the west on the Shoresh–Ramat Razi'el axis (Figure 7). The area within the first urban circle is 27,000 acres, that in the

FIGURE 7

DEVELOPMENT RINGS IN THE JERUSALEM METROPOLITAN AREA

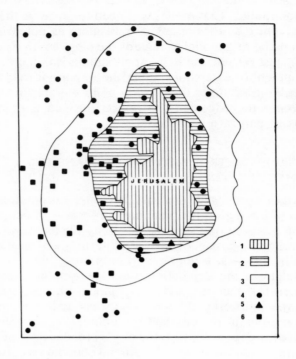

Key:
1. First Ring
2. Second Ring
3. Third Ring

4. Arab settlement
5. Arab town
6. Jewish settlement

second ring is 25,000 acres, and that in the third 70,000 acres. The only official boundary is that of the city of Jerusalem; the other two are purely development limits. They bound regions that differ in development and construction characteristics. While the first bounds urban building and the intensive growth of a capital city, the second exemplifies accelerated Arab rural construction, rapid increase in the number of houses and inhabitants. The third is more purely rural, with agriculture on the north and south, desert and grazing land on the east, and new immigrant settlements in the Jerusalem corridor on the west.

POSSIBLE DEVELOPMENT WITHIN THE REGIONAL
BOUNDARIES

According to the ring model, which means expansion of urban
construction in a ring linked to the city, the entire Nebi Samuel ridge
northwest of the city should be developed, as well as the area
between Qatana and Bidu beyond the city limits and Ramot. The
development around the Atarot airfield needs to be increased and a
continuum established between Atarot, Neve Ya'aqov and French
Hill in the rear of the Arab settlements. Also the area east of Mount
Scopus, east of the 'High Commissioner's Residence' and between
el-Ezeriyye and Beit Sahur should be developed and built up.

According to the star model, which involves the development of
linear extensions, the axes to Ma'ale Edumin, Gilo–Etzion Bloc,
Etzion Bloc–Efrat–Teqo'a, Bet Horon Ascent, Shuafat–Ramallah,
Qalandia–Ma'ale Edumim and Giv'on–Ramallah all need to be
developed and thickened.

The ring model on the edges of the Jerusalem region can take the
form of development areas north of Neve Ilan and Sha'ar Hagai on
the western extensions between Giv'on and Ramallah, around
Mount Ba'al Hatzor, the eastern edges of the mountain between
Ba'al Hatzor and Ma'ale Edumim, and the mountain edges and
desert border on the Ma'ale Edumin–Teqo'a axis.

Another attempt to define the boundaries of the Jerusalem
metropolitan region was made by a research team of the Jerusalem
Institute for Israel Studies, in order to understand the reciprocal
effects of activity in the city and what happens around it (Kimhi,
Reichman, Schweid, 1984). As the team's main interest was the
reciprocal relations in the region, they worked out a gradual
definition of the boundaries of Jerusalem's metropolitan region by
distinguishing between the centre – the organic, functional part of
the city – and the fringes, which are the other parts of the area related
to the centre.

The study established four criteria for the determination of
Jerusalem's metropolitan boundaries. The first proposes setting the
line of greater Jerusalem according to present and past district and
sub-district lines. The conclusion according to this criterion is that
the attachment of the Hebron sub-district to the Jerusalem metropolitan area would be natural because of the close employment
connections between it and Jerusalem, and because of the close
social and family relations obtaining for many years between the
populations of the two cities.

Another criterion proposed is to set the metropolitan boundary on the basis of equal transport time in private cars – specifically, that most rides for work, purchases or study can be accomplished within 45 minutes. Most of the area concerned, which extends northward and westward, is actually in the Tel Aviv metropolitan zone of influence, and in order to change this situation the road system around Jerusalem must be improved.

A third criterion proposed is the place of residence of people working in Jerusalem who do not live there. There appear to be 24,000 such, 15,000 of them Arabs from Judea and Samaria, and 8,000 of them Jews from other parts of Israel. On this basis the boundary could be set 9.3 to 11.2 miles from the centre of Jerusalem. The enclave in the south, toward Hebron, is considerably larger than the northern one, and this suggests that the interrelationship between the southern region and Jerusalem extends to a larger area.

A fourth criterion proposed is the range of service to Jewish settlements, their need for commercial and public services such as health, education, etc. To establish this, a line was marked halfway between Jerusalem and Tel Aviv, and halfway between Jerusalem and Beersheba, and the relations of settlements close to the line on both sides, and between the lines and Jerusalem, were examined. According to this criterion Jerusalem's metropolitan area extends to Shilo on the north, close to Bet Shemesh on the west, to Hebron on the south, and to the Jordan Valley on the east.

The main conclusions from that survey are, therefore:

a.   The metropolitan area of Jerusalem is not all of one piece, and there are various differences and characteristics in each of its developmental directions. The border on the west and north-west is a line halfway between Jerusalem and Tel Aviv, and special measures are needed to ensure that part of the area maintains a link with Jerusalem. In the south the border stretches from Hebron to the southern end of the Hebron district, and it may be possible to extend the influence of Jerusalem to the limits of that district. On the east and northeast the border is less definable. Although the territory of the Jordan region is only marginally within the Jerusalem area, as long as the border with Jordan is more or less closed that area has close ties with Jerusalem.

b.   As long as there is no competing urban centre east of Jerusalem, the eastern area's link to the city is ensured. Consequently, any investment and any additional population in it will remain in the domain of the services of Jerusalem. On the other hand, any development on the west, northwest and southwest is likely eventually to be a contribution to the strengthening of the Tel Aviv area or the Beersheba area.

c. The access from Jerusalem to the areas in the southwest, southeast and northeast is relatively limited. Improvement of the road system in those directions is likely to enlarge and consolidate a broader service area for Jerusalem.

d. The commuting area of greater Jerusalem extends from the Shilo region in the north to the southern part of Hebron in the south. The area is elliptical due to the competition and attraction of Tel Aviv northwestwards, and the absence of settlements to the southeast. Within the commuting area a centre was defined with a diameter of 15 miles and very strong employment ties with Jerusalem. The broader commuting area extends to the Jewish settlements in Judea–Samaria.

e. Because of the physical structure of the region, the absence of a large urban centre near Jerusalem, and the attraction of Tel Aviv, a number of the features of greater Jerusalem (such as its diameter and the degree of activity in the centre) will continue to obtain for a long time. On the other hand, the nature of the ties with Jerusalem on the margins of the area is likely to change shortly, owing to developments in the settlement picture because of activity within that area or in the neighbourhood, or to a change in the nature of the border with Jordan. It is also clear that it is possible to affect the strength of these links, and thus Jerusalem's economic situation, through a development policy that will direct investments and determine administrative frameworks.

The goal, as most of those involved see it, is, under whatever verbal camouflage, the annexation de facto of quite a large area to Israel. The unconcealed desire is that, whatever the eventual political solution for Judea and Samaria, the Jerusalem region will retain a special status, and, even if not under Israeli sovereignty, will have a special relationship with Jerusalem in practice.

DEVELOPMENT POINTS AND THEIR SITES

Those favouring maximum development of the Jerusalem metropolitan region see possibilities for industry, urban and rural construction, tourism and agriculture (Figure 8).

FIGURE 8

DIFFERENT BORDERLINES AROUND JERUSALEM

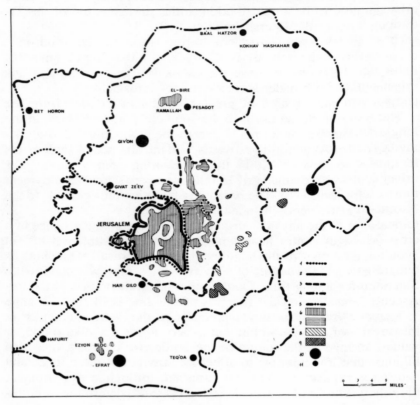

Key:
1. The 'Green Line'
2. Municipal Borderline before 1947
3. Present Municipal Borderline
4. Master Plan Municipal Borderline
5. Metropolitan Borderline

6. Built-up area
7. New residential area built after 1967–8
8. Proposed semi-urban area
9. Industrial zone beyond Municipal Borderline
10. Proposed urban settlement
11. Proposed rural settlement

As to industry, they believe that non-polluting light industry that is labour-intensive is best for the hilly region, in addition to workshops that can take advantage of the potential labour force in the Arab sector. There would even be room for industrial zones between towns in industrial parks. An area of light, sophisticated industry could be developed around the Atarot airfield, at Ma'ale Edumin, along the Hizme–Anata axis, and southeast of Bethlehem.

Additional urban and rural construction would depend on the availability of State land or land owned by Jews. Urban settlement is already being carried out at Ma'ale Edumim to the east, Efrat to the south, and to a more limited degree at Giv'on to the north. Semi-urban settlements could be established between Arab concentrations and Jerusalem or between other Jewish concentrations, such as Mount Gilo near Bethlehem, Teqo'a near Efrat, Hafurit between the Etzion Bloc and the villages of western Mount Hebron, lower Bet Horon, between el-Bire and Qalandia, etc. Rural or semi-urban settlements could be added at Ba'al Hatzor, around Giv'on, and between the Etzion Bloc and Teqo'a.

The Jerusalem region will in the future also require several main longitudinal and lateral roads to facilitate movement from the lowland to Jerusalem and from Samaria to Judea. Local and regional roads will be needed to connect rural settlements or semi-urban centres in the second and third settlement rings. One of the most important of the lateral ones would be the Bet Horon Ascent–Atarot–Ma'ale Edumim road. The most important longitudinal one is the Ramallah–Solomon's Pools route, which would cross west Jerusalem and make it possible to traverse the city while avoiding the city centre. Other important longitudinal roads are the one designed to connect Neve Ya'aqov and French Hill east of the Shuafat road, and one from the Hadassah Hospital to the Bet Horon Ascent.

Tourist attractions on the west would be located around religious, historical and archeological subjects, scenic and recreational values, and would include national parks, nature reserves, springs, hiking paths, antiquities, field schools, etc. National parks and nature reserves are proposed for the eastern edges of the hills and the desert boundary; the river beds such as that of the Qidron, the flora of the Um-Tsafa forest and Mount Ba'al Hatzor. Archaeological and historical sites include all those in Jerusalem itself plus outstanding ones such as Mount Herod, the Wadi Qelt monasteries, Mar Saba, the monasteries of Theodosius, Latrun, etc. Observation points would need to be prepared at Mount Scopus and the Mount of Olives, Mount Ba'al Hatzor, Nebi Samuel, Mount Gilo and Mizpah. Hotels could be developed at Bethlehem, Ramallah, and of course, Jerusalem.

Agricultural development could only be rather limited, because of the proximity of the desert on the east and because of the mountainous topography in the centre. Agricultural areas should be retained primarily in the Etzion Bloc and around the rural settlements to be established in the second and third rings, in accordance with land preparation possibilities. It is thus evident that the Jerusalem environs face an Arab–Jewish struggle for territory, for spatial control and for population. Intensive Arab construction coupled with high natural increase may cause the city of Jerusalem gradually to lose its Jewish majority, so that territories it cannot make use of will accumulate within it, and the urban planning options will contract. Today the region has some urban and rural settlement points which are steps toward saving the region and maintaining its Jewish character, but it is as yet difficult to view them as the basic solution to the problem. The many physical plans prepared by government and planning institutions indicate that the region has aroused great interest and ways are being sought to find reasonable solutions, but so far no plan has been found to merit adoption because all have to be partial, areal, local or sectorial. There is no doubt that Jerusalem requires a regional plan, even if some planners, politicians or governmental bodies consider the metropolitan plan the best one. As topographical limitations do not allow for the development of Jerusalem according to any classical metropolitan model, it is necessary at best to adapt parts of models, and to surround the city with development rings of various stages of urgency, filling them with planning and functional content with regard to industry, homes, transport, tourism and agriculture.

There is no doubt that the present situation requires the future of the Jerusalem region to be reconsidered. The question is, is there really a need for such a large metropolitan Jerusalem, which would have few counterparts in the world? Would it not be better to be content with its present size, of about 420,000 people on 27,500 acres, concentrating development on the existing neighbourhoods and retaining the city's historical and architectural characteristics? Are there no easier solutions for the security of the area around the city than continuous urban development? Is there no danger that Jerusalem might become an ordinary large city of 600,000–700,000 people by the 1990s? If what is wanted is another, different Jerusalem, the time has come to say what kind, and to submit the various proposals regarding the region to general criticism.

CHAPTER THREE

The 'Allon Plan' and Settlement in the Jordan Valley

The echoes of the Six Day War had just faded. While Israel was still having trouble digesting the magnitude of its victory over the Arab armies, in July 1967 the government was presented by one of its ministers, Yigal Allon, with a plan for the future borders of the country, and with proposed principles concerning peace arrangements with neighbouring countries. The plan was never accepted as Israel's official plan, and consequently continued to be known by the name of its proponent as the Allon Plan, but even so it had considerable effect on Israel's settlement map throughout the period that the Alignment was in power.

In 1967 the government of Israel was prepared to return territories it had conquered in return for peace. Therefore, when Yigal Allon submitted his plan, they considered that it embodied a hawkish element because it stipulated the addition of certain areas to Israel. After the Khartoum Conference and the world's reaction to the Israeli conquest, the government changed its mind and informed the U.S. that it would hold discussions with any Arab government on essential matters. At that stage the plan became 'dovish'.

This first political plan for Judea and Samaria, the 'Allon Plan', applied mainly to the eastern part of Judea and Samaria and the Jordan Valley. Its value lay in the fact that it was the first comprehensive attempt to formulate a clear territorial stand regarding Israel's most problematic border, that with Jordan; the boundaries of the plan, derived from topographic and demographic considerations, were set between two longitudinal axes, one along the Jordan river, and the other along the eastern slopes of the Samarian hills. Between these two axes there is land suitable for cultivation, and the area is rather sparsely populated. The approach regarding the Jordan Valley was based on a regional settlement concept of development, with agricultural settlements around a regional centre, as was the practice in other development areas within the 'Green Line'.

To his proposal of July 1967 Allon attached explanatory material which included three assumptions:

a. that Israel needed an immediate decision regarding the political future of the territories conquered during the Six Day War;
b. that Israel must have the assurance of the integrity of the country from the strategic standpoint, and of the Jewish character of the State from the demographic standpoint;
c. that an Israeli initiative to solve the refugee problem was both a human and political matter and an Israeli necessity no less than an Arab one.

In regard to the first assumption Allon pointed out the harm and possible loss of prestige that would be caused Israel internationally by indecision (especially in view of the U.S. position), on the level of relations with the Arabs in those territories on the one hand, and the Arab countries on the other, and also on the domestic level.

In respect of the second assumption Allon presented various possibilities, but recommended as follows:

> I suggest setting, even unilaterally, the Jordan river and the line going down the middle of the Dead Sea as the border between Israel and the Hashemite Kingdom of Jordan. In order to make the border effective and not just formal, in my opinion a strip six to ten miles wide along the Jordan Valley up to the Dead Sea should be attached to Israel. The western edge of this Jordan Valley strip should be based on a series of suitable topographic strongholds making the greatest effort to avoid including any large Arab population, and indeed the population of the Jordan Valley is very sparse and it is possible to establish an acceptable border separating Israeli territory from the Arab enclave. North of the Dead Sea the border should be set further west (perhaps deliberately skirting Jericho) toward the northern border of new Jerusalem, with the Dead Sea–Jerusalem road included in Israel. From the Ramallah suburbs the border should be pulled westward so that the Latrun–Bet Horon–Jerusalem road is within Israel ... connect all of the Judean desert and the uninhabited parts of Mt. Hebron in territorial

continuity with the Jordan Valley, but more deeply to the south to Dahariyye and Samoa so that there will be an Israeli territorial continuum from the Bet Shean Valley to the Negev. The Arab inhabitants in Hebron, Bethlehem and a small number of townlets, villages and encampments will constitute a kind of second enclave which will have the right of access to the enclave in Samaria through a road (not a corridor) and be an inseparable part of it from the standpoint of its political status (Figure 9).

Allon stressed that despite its disadvantages – the possibility that in the future the residents of the area would demand the status of a state, with no economic or security connection with Israel, and might even wish to merge with the Hashemite Kingdom of Jordan or join some other Arab framework – this proposal was preferable to any others because of its security advantages: 'A solid military and settlement foothold in a rather broad strip along the Jordan Valley, the Jerusalem area and the Judean desert removes any real military danger in advance from the Arab area.'

As to the status of the local residents, Allon proposed

to establish in close cooperation with the leaders, representatives and functionaries of the Arab population an autonomous Arab district with an independent political government bound to Israel in a common economic framework, a mutual defence pact, and agreements regarding the absorption of some of the refugees from the Gaza Strip ... and technical and cultural cooperation.

Israel would place at the disposal of the Arab district 'a free wharf in the Haifa port and transit privileges on the Jenin–Megiddo–Haifa road (not a corridor) ... Similar transit rights are also possible on one of the Jordan river crossings to Jordan.'

Although Allon spoke of 'an autonomous Arab district with an independent political government' in the overall peace plan, he evidently envisaged the district as belonging to the Hashemite Kingdom of Jordan as a permanent solution.

As to the Gaza Strip, his proposals in 1967 were as follows:

naturally it is not to be returned to Egypt, nor is it to be annexed to the autonomous Arab district. It should be joined, without the refugees, to Israel. As the solution of the refugee problem will take a long time, the union of the Gaza Strip to Israel should not in the meantime be announced and a military government

FIGURE 9
THE ALLON PLAN

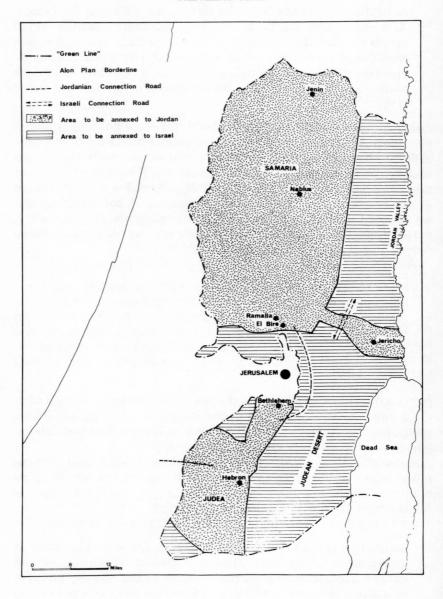

[should be] maintained there as occupied territory till a solution to the refugee problem outside the Strip is found. The joining of the Strip to Israel will add some hundred thousand permanent Arab residents to the country, but because of the importance of the Strip we must assume that responsibility. Until the merger with Israel UNWRA will be responsible for the refugees and government ministries for the permanent residents.

Allon viewed his plan as a peace plan, and therefore included the refugee problem among his three basic assumptions. He stressed that 'planning the desired solution and beginning its actual implementation should not await the advent of peace, which may be delayed'. In his view a start should be made immediately because it was first and foremost a human problem. 'Such action will even bring peace closer and create a salutary atmosphere around Israel ... a political argument based on moral grounds has great force, and we felt that personally and from our national experience.'

He proposed beginning immediately to plan a model settlement

on the West Bank or in Sinai at Israel's expense, in order to prove to the refugees and interested parties the world over what could be done and how to solve the problem, so tragic from the human standpoint and dangerous politically.

At the same time he emphasized that the maintenance and rehabilitation of the refugees was the responsibility of UNWRA, and in order to coordinate plans and activities proposed the establishment of a 'single special government authority'.

The Allon Plan, as noted above, was never formally approved by the Israeli government, but in the years after 1967 the government acted in Judea–Samaria and Gaza in accordance with the principles of the plan. Allon himself acquiesced in the government proposals intended to amend and realize his plan. In February 1968 he submitted a bill regarding the Jordan Valley providing for the following:

(a) the immediate creation of an Israeli presence – in addition to the military presence – in the Jordan Valley through the establishment of security settlements along the valley; (b) a ministerial committee composed of the prime minister and the ministers of defence, agriculture and labour in consultation with the commander-in-chief, will decide on the timing and location of the new sites.

In his explanation of the bill he insisted on the need to establish 'facts of security and political importance by territorial modifications essential to the security of the State within the framework of any possible solution'. Claiming that 'a military and civilian Israeli presence in the Jordan Valley is a border adjustment that has no alternative', he stressed that the settlements should be located in such a way that 'all options for various solutions should remain open'.

In speaking to the government at the beginning of 1969 Allon again stressed that his proposal left 'all the options for political solutions open, because it does not require the annexation of areas densely populated by Arabs, but provides for a more massive Israeli presence at points of military and political value'.

A few months later Allon submitted a proposal to the government calling for '(a) the immediate expansion of the town planning area of united Jerusalem; (b) the extension of Israeli law and municipal authority to the merged areas at a time deemed suitable'.

In his explanation Allon noted the attraction Jerusalem had for Israelis and new immigrants in particular who wished to settle there, and claimed that

> in order to ensure the proper development of greater Jerusalem its master plan must be based on a sufficiently large area and a start must be made on locating new projects in Jerusalem according to that expanded master plan.

Allon explained his plan by outlining the principles of the future map of Israel:

1. The future map of the borders of Israel that will be determined as part of the peace treaty must be based on four principles:

   a. They must be strategically defensible.
   b. They must be anchored in the Jewish people's historic rights to the Land of Israel from the moral standpoint.
   c. They must ensure the Jewish character of the State of Israel.
   d. They must be politically realistic.

   It is not essential for every bit of territory on the map to comply with all the principles, but every border must take strategic requirements into account as a first priority.

2. It is superfluous to stress that so long as there is no peace pact between Israel and its neighbours, Israel will continue to maintain the armistice lines.

3. Instability in the occupied territories and the danger of the penetration of the influence of hostile powers might produce conditions that would prevent us from maintaining military bases or conducting patrols in areas under Arab sovereignty. Thus for that reason as well such arrangements cannot be relied on to endure.

4. Controlled demilitarization of areas of strategic importance can and must serve as one of the bases in security arrangements, but the demilitarization of such areas cannot substitute for truly defensible borders in the possession of Israel from the standpoint of legal sovereignty as well as military control.

5. The borders must be based on a topographical system constituting a permanent obstacle for the deployment of motorized land forces on the one hand and a base for a counter-offensive by our forces on the other. They must provide the State with a reasonable strategic depth and ensure an early warning system, as far as possible, of the approach of enemy planes. The possibility that guerilla warfare, terror and sabotage will develop must also be taken into account.

6. The defence system planned must embody an element of deterrence by making it difficult through its very existence to foster delusions of an easy victory in the Arab camp, and also to ensure that possible aggression is repelled with the greatest efficiency and the least casualties.

BORDERS AND TOPOGRAPHY

The northern border in the 'Allon Plan' in its broad scene begins at the Gilboa ridge and continues southward west of the Jordan Valley to the eastern suburbs of Hebron, and also includes part of the Judean desert. The security strips within the plan are the Jordan with is meanderings on one side and the eastern extensions of the Samarian hills on the other. The Jordan Valley was set aside for settlements and agricultural areas. The eastern security strip of the Jordan Valley was to be 6–9 miles wide, stretching southwards along the eastern end of the Judean desert to the flanks of Mount Hebron where the average width is 15 miles. The security strip was to join Israeli sovereign territory by a broad strip of several miles along the Jerusalem–Jericho axis. In these areas, according to the Plan, it was possible to acquire vital territory with a minimum of Arab inhabitants. These borders added new vital territory to Israel, which would eventually become sovereign territory of Israel.

The Arab population naturally chose the best conditions for agricultural settlement, and it is thus understandable that it did not extend to the east of the Samarian hills and the desert, or to most of the Jordan Valley, which is arid and poor in natural water sources. The 1967 census showed no more than 15,000 inhabitants in the entire Valley, 5,000 of them in Jericho.

Againt the background of these geographical conditions, the plan posited a large Jewish population in many settlements along the Jordan and the slopes of the Samarian hills. The 'Allon Plan' was never formally adopted by any Israeli government, but it was agreed on and accepted as an ideological and territorial consensus. It represented a sort of compromise between the maximalists and minimalists among Israelis, and was given some support by both. As past experience had shown that agreements with the Arabs were not to be relied on too much, it was necessary to ensure a security strip east of Judea and Samaria. Control of the security strip and, in its wake, of Judea and Samaria as a whole, had to be achieved by a combination of agricultural settlement and military surveillance.

SETTLEMENT IN THE JORDAN VALLEY

As the Jordan Valley is in effect a border area, it was settled to begin with, like other development areas within the 'Green Line', with agricultural villages. The basis for this was the relative ecological advantage of the Jordan Valley for early ripe winter crops and tropical items. It was divided for planning purposes into two areas, the Adam region stretching south from Bet Shean to the Jerusalem–Jericho road, and the Dead Sea area from that road southwards to En Gedi. Settlement was dependent on the availability of land and water, so settlements could be located only in places where there were concentrations of State-owned land with reasonable water sources in the vicinity. To this was added also the consideration of continuity of settlement to avoid undue isolation of any one site. The land and water potential determined the number of agricultural units that could be established. Yet the process of settling the Jordan Valley was accomplished through trial and error as local problems were encountered.

The settlement of the Jordan Valley was of course influenced by the climate, the amount of water found locally, and the frequency of its availability, as well as the topographical features of the land. The Rift climate is dry and hot, characterized by summer temperatures as high as 100°F and little precipitation throughout the year. The high temperatures make it possible to raise autumn and winter crops and tropical produce for export. The eastern slopes of the Samarian Hills are relatively suitable climatically for human habitation, so settlements can be established there. As to land, it should be noted that out of 375,000 acres only 37,500 were found to be arable, and only 12,500 of these in the hilly area. The State-owned land within that potential amounted to only 16,500 acres – 10,000 acres in the Adam region and only 6,500 in the area just north of the Dead Sea. Recently, a beginning has been made on the preparation for agriculture of a few thousand acres of the Jordan area never previously cultivated. In general, most of the good land was cultivated by Arabs, and was close to flowing water sources as well.

The Arab population in the Jordan Valley amounts today to about 26,000 people who own 13,500 acres of land, 10,000 acres of it under cultivation. Most of this land is in the area stretching between Wadi Fari'a and the Giftlik, and in the Jericho area. In the central Jordan Valley there is Arab-owned land in Patza'el and Auja et-Tahta. Larger concentrations of Arab-owned land are to be found on the eastern slope of the Samarian Hills. Jewish settlement in the Jordan Valley at first utilized Arab-owned agricultural land. In the northern part there were greater difficulties in the concentration of land than in the centre and the south.

THE JEWISH SETTLEMENT ALIGNMENT IN THE JORDAN VALLEY

Jewish settlement in the Jordan Valley follows two axes, one along the Jericho–Bet She'an road, and the other further west along the slopes of the Samarian Hills. This linear alignment is connected by lateral axes.

The first settlement took place in 1968 with the establishment of Mehola in the north, not far from the Bet She'an settlements. Thereafter Argaman, Masuah and Gilgal were set up in the central Jordan Valley in order to establish a presence there. During the first years, 1968 to 1970, political and security considerations were paramount. The influential factors were: proximity to the Jordan river to secure the eastern border, proximity to the longitudinal road so as to maintain continuity between settlements; maximal populating of uninhabited areas; and avoidance of occupying land cultivated by Arabs. The concentration of settlements in the northern Jordan Valley was designed to establish continuity with the Bet She'an Valley (Figure 10).

FIGURE 10

JEWISH SETTLEMENTS IN THE JORDAN VALLEY

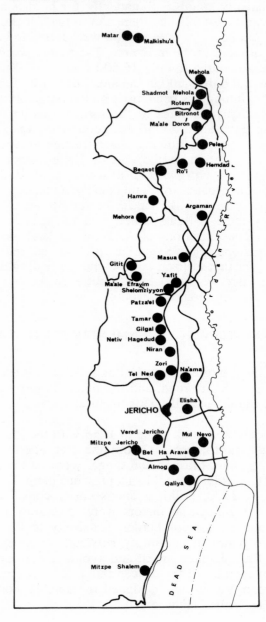

In the second phase, 1971 to 1974, the settlement of the western axis was begun as a security belt to prevent the penetration of Arab population in the wake of Jewish settlement in the Jordan Valley. It was at that time that the settlements of Beqa'ot, Gitit and Hamra were established, as well as Kibbutz Yitav.

In the third phase, 1975 to 1976, five settlements were founded in order to amplify the existing alignment and strengthen the weak places, and also to prevent the development of isolated settlement blocs.

In the fourth and last phase, 1977 to 1981, seven new points were settled, three of them in the northern Dead Sea area and the other four in the Adam region. The southern sites were designed to be the beginning of new settlement in a desert area, and the northern ones to buttress the existing settlement alignment.

The plan called for 15 settlements in the Adam region, which requires two sub-regional centres, each serving five to seven agricultural villages. One of these was set at Hamra and the other at Shelomziyyon. Services at a higher level were planned for the regional centre at Ma'ale Efrayim. That centre was established on the eastern slopes of the Samarian Hills, quite high up, because of the superior climatic conditions there compared with the Jordan Valley, though the result was a considerable distance between villages and centre. Actually neither the sub-regional centres nor the regional centres are as yet operating to the full extent planned, because close ties did not develop between them and the villages. The Hamra centre functions somewhat better than the others. The regional hierarchy in general operates less well than expected because in the course of time many of the settlements made reciprocal arrangements, particularly in regard to education, culture and health, and did not always need the sub-regional or regional centre.

Functional difficulties have appeared in the regional centre of Ma'ale Efrayim. On the one hand, it does not have enough stores, and on the other, its large school building is underpopulated. Access to it is difficult because of the topography, so some of its residents work in Jerusalem and only spend the weekends at Ma'ale Efrayim. The kibbutzim in the Jordan Valley tend to operate in a separate system and obtain services through the national kibbutz organization. Besides, it must be borne in mind that Ma'ale Efrayim and Shelomziyyon were established later than the other Jordan Valley settlements, which by then were already connected with centres outside the region. The longitudinal road system and high frequency of public transport make it possible to seek services outside the Jordan Valley. Furthermore, the relative proximity of Jerusalem prevents the development in the Jordan Valley of services with a high entrance threshold. Thus the hierarchical settlement development in the Jordan Valley has failed, and without a change of approach and government investment the region will not be able to function as a separate independent unit.

THE POLITICAL BACKGROUND TO SETTLEMENT IN THE JORDAN VALLEY

The Settlement Department of the World Zionist Organization planned and carried out the construction in the Jordan Valley, while the population was recruited by the political party settlement movements, which influenced the character and form of each place. The types of settlement in the Jordan Valley resemble those elsewhere in the country and include kibbutzim, moshavim, co-operative moshavim, and village communities. Today the Jordan Valley has thirteen moshavim, three kibbutzim and one co-operative moshav, besides a number of 'Nahal' settlements.

The kibbutzim and cooperative moshavim are located in the areas that present physical difficulties, while the moshavim and individually populated urban and rural units are in places that are relatively easy to settle. The northern part of the Jordan Valley is convenient for settlement, which becomes progressively more difficult the further south one proceeds. Jordan Valley settlement began in the north, from the connection with the Bet She'an Valley, to more distant places in the Judean desert. The HaKibbutz HaMeuchad federation established three centres – Gilgal, Niran and Yitav – in an area considered difficult to settle since the agricultural land allotments are far from the residential areas. The Moshav movement established a bloc of moshavim north of these kibbutzim. The Betar movement founded two settlements, Gitit and Argaman, even before the Likud rose to power, but none thereafter, since later its greatest efforts were concentrated on the Judean Mountains. The main settlement endeavour in the Jordan Valley has been made by movements connected with the Labour Party, such as the HaKibbutz HaMeuchad and the Moshav movement. Among Alignment supporters a decision was taken to settle the area as early as 1967, which fitted in with the 'Allon Plan'. The HaKibbutz HaArtzi Federation did not establish any kibbutzim in the Jordan Valley because they opposed the Greater Land of Israel

Movement; and the 'Amana' movement of Gush Emunim preferred to locate its settlements in the hills in the midst of concentrations of Arab population. Thus when the Alignment, which favoured the Allon Plan, was in power, a large number of settlements were established by movements connected with it politically, while subsequently Betar and Amana, which are connected with the Likud, did not settle the Jordan Valley.

The settlers in the Jordan Valley are a heterogeneous band, including former city-dwellers, people who came from agricultural settlements, and members of youth movements. In 1984 that population totalled 5,000, of whom 3,000 live in the Adam region. The 'Allon Plan' envisaged a population of 20,000 on the basis of the physical potential of the region, assigning 4.5 acres of land to a family, with 30,000 cu.m. of water per annum. Such a potential would provide for 2,000 agricultural units. In fact, however, there is quite a difference between the potential and actual population. The physical hardships of a semi-desert region make it difficult to settle following the patterns obtaining in Israel proper. Then some of the land is too saline for agriculture, and the expectation that the area would become a hothouse from which early crops could be exported to Europe was not realized either. Increased population of the Jordan Valley is apparently feasible only through the establishment of urban settlements. It should also be borne in mind that the Camp David agreements sowed confusion among Jordan Valley residents, who do not clearly see what their future will be. Table 1 shows the 1987 population of the Adam region of the Jordan Valley.

TABLE 1
ADAM REGION 1987
POPULATION ACCORDING TO NUMBER OF FAMILIES

Mehola	39	Gitit	24	Tomer	42	Na'aran	65
Ro'i	27	Argaman	27	Netiv Hagedud	30	Yitav	21
Beqa'ot	36	Masu'a	35	Na'ama	14		
Hamra	36	Yafit	23	Shedemot Mehola	34		
Mehora	31	Patza'el	50	Gilgal	51	Total:	585

The average number of people per family is 4.8. Apparently limits to water and land, which do not allow the settlement of the entire population on an agricultural basis, have led to the gap between a proposed population of 20,000 and the existing one. Yet it should be noted that the steps taken to implement the 'Allon Plan' were a political necessity despite the geographical difficulties.

The settlement in the Jordan Valley can thus be deemed geo-political, displaying the following features: attempting to settle a semi-desert area as a border region; basing the settlement on regional rural settlements, following the example of the 1950s; establishing a settlement complex under the pressures of climate, topography, land and water limits and Arab ownership. The north-central Jordan Valley complex actually consists of 17 settlements, two sub-regional centres and one regional centre. The transfer of settlement intiative to the Samarian and Judean mountains resulted in a conflict of interests between the settlers and settlement movements on the one hand, and the Settlement Department of the World Zionist Organization which on government instructions concentrated on settling the hills in Judea and Samaria, on the other.

The Allon Plan was based on obtaining a territorial compromise which would meet Israel's security requirements and at the same time take into account the nationalistic aspirations of the Arab population in Judea, Samaria and Jordan. It proposed to include 40 per cent of the area of Judea and Samaria under Israeli sovereignty, following the conception of the Labour Party which favoured the settlement of the Jordan Valley as a security belt. The plan was not officially discussed, in order to avert its rejection on the fall of the government. The religious elements objected to participating in a government that would announce its willing-ness to give up parts of the 'Greater Land of Israel'. On the other hand the Arabs were not willing to accept the plan as a basis for negotiations. For those reasons the plan was simply made known to government ministers with the understanding that they might make it an official government proposal if there was Arab willingness to consider it.

The principles that should guide Israel in determining its future map, in Allon's opinion, are defensible borders that are anchored morally in the right of the Jewish people to the Land of Israel, that ensure the Jewish character of the country and that are politically practical. Three aspects governed Allon in his plan: geography, demography and sovereignty. The plan endeavoured to emphasize those three aspects. It is no secret that the plan was made known to many Arab leaders and elements through the United States and in direct meetings with representatives of Israel. The response of the Arabs was, as is well known, that they could not accept the plan because it involved giving up territory. Allon was not disappointed, because he believed that the Arabs would not be able to accept the plan unless the proper conditions developed. He was disappointed by the Jews who would not allow him to implement his plan.

The Allon Plan was at the time a most important innovation in Israeli strategic thinking. But in rapidly changing circumstances there is nothing more dangerous than cleaving to past notions and turning them into doctrines that block future thought. From at least three viewpoints the Allon Plan is today outmoded:

a. Technological change in means of warfare and the composition of the force likely to operate against Israel in the future require Israel's security control over very broad areas. From the military viewpoint, a strip along the Jordan River does not suffice even if eastern parts of the mountain region are included.

b. For the same reasons the security and strategic value of settlements establishing a fait accompli is very small; they become a two-edged sword in that they restrict the Israeli government's own room for manoeuvre.

c. It is impossible to ignore the change in Israel's domestic political situation. To this must be added changes in the Jewish settlement deployment in Judea–Samaria as well as the doubts about the willingness of Jordan's present rulers to reabsorb their Palestinian brethren residing in the West Bank.

CHAPTER FOUR

The Settlement Geography of Gush Emunim

Settlement as a means of attaining political aims is not a new device. The Crusaders in the Holy Land, the Chinese in Manchuria, and the British in India, for instance, took such action in countries they conquered in order to deepen their hold. Thus the rise in the Judea–Samaria region, of a group of religious nationalists called Gush Emunim, reflecting aspirations of circles in Israel interested in rapid settlement of the territories conquered in 1967 should be regarded as part of a geopolitical process and current condition of conquest obtaining in part of 'the Land of Israel' (*Eretz Yisrael*). Political and settlement activity flourished in the region because of the ambiguous nature of Israel's borders. Concepts such as 'Zion' or 'the Land of Israel' are not clearly defined in the political sense. They are quite vague and open to differences of opinion on their meaning, and of course present different challenges for political action.

THE POLITICAL BACKGROUND OF GUSH EMUNIM'S SETTLEMENT ACTIVITY

Settlement activity in Judea and Samaria has been carried out, in the past 20 years, by the two large parties, the Alignment with its secular, socialist approach and the Likud with its religious, national-istic one. While the Alignment took a pragmatic stand on settlement, adopting as a basis the Allon Plan's notion of defensible borders, the Likud took a more broadly nationalistic position based on a terri-torial ideology and what is known as the Greater Land of Israel Movement.

After the Six Day War, the view that the Jews have full territorial rights over the 'Greater Land of Israel', even beyond essential security needs, found considerable support. A new sort of pioneer Zionism emerged at that time which exhorted Israelis to exercise historic rights in their homeland, and incorporated religious justifications as well. While in the first two decades of the State the pioneer Zionist ideology concentrated on the settlement of the Negev and Galilee, this pioneer settlement was directed at Judea and Samaria. The settlers had to be highly motivated because the region in question was mostly populated by Arabs, and settlement there might be dangerous.

Those years also saw the emergence of the Greater Land of Israel Movement, which attracted many diverse elements. It had a maximalist doctrine with a nationalist mission, and uncompromisingly insisted on all territory of the Land of Israel being settled. Its extremists demanded intensive urban and agricultural settlement with economic integration in the occupied territories, the application of Israeli law there, and the territorial annexation of the areas to Israel. In contrast there arose the 'Peace Now' movement which demanded withdrawal from the occupied territories, their release in return for peace, abstention from ruling a foreign people, and the initiation of a dialogue between Jews and Arabs aimed at finding a political solution. The two movements became more and more extremist in the course of time, representing diametrically opposed views on the Israeli political scene.

Two additional facts form part of the background. Moshe Dayan as Minister of Defence was influential in those years in developing settlements in Judea and Samaria which maintained complete economic ties with the State of Israel. He favoured Jewish urban settlement in the occupied areas, and the right of Jews to purchase land there. He did not fear the demographic spectre brandishing an Arab majority versus a Jewish minority, for he envisaged the existence in the occupied territories of two separate settlement complexes having economic relations. He did not claim Israeli sovereignty for all of Judea–Samaria, but approved military supervision and control of places vital for Israel from the point of view of security.

Yisrael Galili's celebrated political statement of 1973 constituted a kind of ideological platform for the Alignment regarding the occupied territories. It supported the continuation of 'security' settlement along the borders, and in fact encouraged the settlement trends proposed by Moshe Dayan. The document also asserted that there would be no returning to the 1967 borders, and no Palestinian state in Judea–Samaria. Later differences of opinion reduced the influence of the document, however.

The Yom Kippur War (1973) and its outcome made the Alignment supporters sceptical about the utility of agricultural settlements on the defence lines in the occupied territories. The conclusions drawn by the Likud people were much more dogmatic: they claimed that settlements were a deterrent and impeding factor for any enemy that might attack, and therefore there was a need for rapid, intensive settlement in Judea–Samaria and the other occupied territories so that there could be no repetition of what happened in 1973.

THE NATURE OF GUSH EMUNIM

Gush Emunim was founded in 1974 with the aim of accelerating the settlement of the 'Greater Land of Israel', and of Judea–Samaria in particular. Its members aspired first and foremost to settle on the mountain crest and the areas of dense Arab population, a view opposed to the settlement policy of the Alignment government and to the Allon Plan. The members also worked energetically to get government ministers to adopt a new settlement policy which would change the settlement map of Israel. This radical political movement emerged against the background of the low morale in the Jewish population after the Yom Kippur War. The Gush Emunim approach to the problem of the occupied territories was clearly religious, based on 'ancestral right' and the insistence that Jerusalem, Hebron, Nablus, Beth El, Shiloh etc. should be Israeli. The movement adopted an ideology that taught the sanctity of the people and the land as chosen by God (Newman, 1984).

Gush Emunim combined religious faith with secular vision and argued that the return of the Jews to the Land of Israel was in effect the redemption of the Jewish people, and the settlement of Judea–Samaria amounted to a religious precept. Practically, this meant the need to settle the Greater Land of Israel, and the creation of territorial continuity between Judea–Samaria and the State of Israel. It was the religious idea behind the settlement of the Greater Land of Israel that became the prime aspect, while the security angle was merely an appendage. The settlement in the occupied territories was perceived as the implementation of the entire philosophy. The movement adopted the pioneer spirit that had animated the Jewish people in the past and inspired the establishment of the State of Israel. However, in contrast to the past when the pioneer settlement took place in a Jewish-populated region along the coast and in other places where land had been purchased in time, there was now a desire to settle in the midst of Arabs, since the pioneer settlement of the past had not managed to occupy much new territory. The tradition that had developed in Israel whereby settlements never abandoned their land gave the movement the confidence to seek the realization of its aims through this effective way. Up until 1973 the Greater Land of Israel Movement, which aimed at reviving the Etzion bloc of settlements and reinstating Jews in Hebron by establishing the suburb of Qiryat Arba, was quite active. Gush Emunim was represented in it through the young guard of the National Religious Party. They even wished to make their participation in the coalition government conditional on its acceptance of settlement throughout all of Judea–Samaria. The growing influence of this young guard in their party and among religious people in general led to the unequivocal demand that the government should annex the occupied territories to the State of Israel.

THE HISTORY OF GUSH EMUNIM SETTLEMENT

The first Gush Emunim settlement attempts were made in 1974, with the establishment of Qeshet near Quneitra on the Golan Heights, Qadum near Nablus, near the railway station of Sebastia, at Shiloh, in Kefar Edumim and near Jericho. As the Alignment cabinet was unable to come to an agreement on what measures should be taken against Gush Emunim, the latter were in the meantime left undisturbed. The Ministry of Defence gradually even began to help them, with housing, water and electricity. By the end of 1976 there were 220 Gush Emunim settlers, and it was already clear that the government would not remove them. After setting up Qadum, Gush Emunim took a further step and established Ofra, which quickly attracted a population of 150. Qadum and Ofra were important milestones in the movement's rapid settlement programme. That year Gush Emunim prepared an overall settlement plan aimed at settling a million people at a hundred points in Judea–Samaria in the course of a decade. The points were located mainly in the centre of the mountain ridge, very close to historic places and archeological sites, near important roads, and primarily on State-owned land. The plan accorded priority to places on the Jerusalem–Nablus axis, the Jerusalem–Hebron axis, and on two or three lateral axes traversing the mountain region as well. The plan even noted for the first time the functional ranking of settlements: kibbutzim or moshavim designed for several hundred people each, larger rural settlements for several thousand, and towns with populations of 10,000 or more.The principles underlying the plan were: maximum spread of settlements in the areas as a whole, transfer of resources from the coastal plain to the hills in order to accelerate the settlement process, the establishment of a company to invest in industrial enterprises in Judea–Samaria, rapid development of profitable projects in the settlements established, and seizure by the State of land whose ownership was unclear. The Gush Emunim plan contained new geographical elements unusual in that it proposed rural, semi-rural and urban settlement on the mountain slopes on the site of an age-old Arab settlement that could not be moved. It was a kind of emergency plan that did not, of course, include the Allon Plan settlements in the Jordan Valley. While this plan received no official response, what happened was that Qadum, Ofra and Kefar Edumim benefited in practice from gradual development, and permission was later given to settle Elqana in the heart of Judea–Samaria. By 1977 Gush Emunim had succeeded in setting up 12 settlements in the hills, some in military camps, in addition to the first three that had gained post factum government support (Figure 11).

The accession to power of the Likud in 1977 resulted in a new approach to settlement in Judea–Samaria and to Gush Emunim. It was now easier to implement ideological and religious desires regarding the Greater Land of Israel. The new government claimed that the territories had been liberated and there was no longer room for negotiation about them. Settlement there now acquired the justification of historic right, and the need to settle the heart of Judea–Samaria was especially stressed. Gush Emunim began to operate with greater legitimacy.

Some unexpected external factors also affected the situation that developed. The visit of President Sadat of Egypt to Jerusalem was designed among other things to soften the Likud's adamancy regarding the occupied territories. It was a visit that eventually led to the Camp David agreements and towards the goal of reaching political agreements in the near future on Sinai and Judea–Samaria. Now the Israeli circles that welcomed such agreements and those that opposed them began to gird their loins for a confrontation. The opponents of such agreements claimed that historic right and ancestral right superseded any compromise. Minister of Defence Ariel Sharon, holding maximalist views, encouraged the settlement activities of Gush Emunim. Many outsiders objected, chief among them the Americans who, hoping to strengthen their position in the Middle East, held to Sadat's peace campaign.

In July 1978 Gush Emunim prepared a second master plan, providing for the settling of 750,000 Jews in Judea–Samaria, 100,000 of them by 1981. The movement had begun to feel that the

FIGURE 11
GUSH EMUNIM SETTLEMENTS

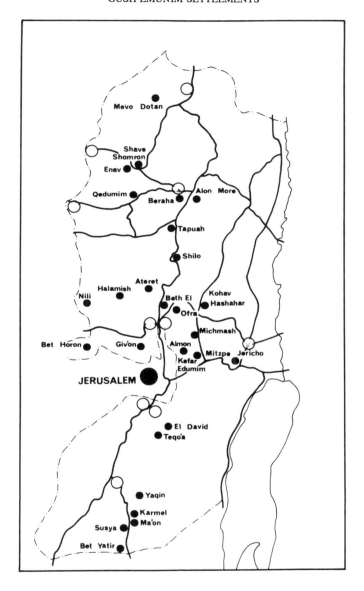

plan had to have a professional planning basis rather than merely a political one, and the new plan was supposedly more realistic than its 1976 predecessor. Yet, though Israel's population was then only 3.5 million with emigration exceeding immigraton, the master plan called for two towns of 60,000 people each (Qiryat Arba and Ari'el), four of some 20,000 each (Dotan, Shimron, Shiloh and Eshtemo'a) plus 20 urban centres with 10,000 people each, and 25 concentrations of community settlements. The Amana company was then set up by Gush Emunim to construct settlements in Judea–Samaria.

After 1978 Judea–Samaria became a prime geographical, political and settlement subject, and all activities there were so intensive that it is doubtful whether they can be reversed. Yet the accelerated settlement suffered from lack of resources. It was obvious that the establishment of such a ramified complex of settlements would be at the expense of development within the 'Green Line', especially in Galilee and the Negev, but also on the Golan Heights. The settlement drive in Judea–Samaria started at a time when there was a considerable decrease in immigration, and, because of the difficulties involved, Israelis did not hasten to leave the coastal plain to settle in Judea–Samaria. Table 2 shows the settlement situation in Judea–Samaria at the time.

TABLE 2

JEWISH AND ARAB POPULATION IN JUDEA–SAMARIA, 1978

Place	Jews	Arabs	% Jews of Total
Etzion bloc	1,402	–	
Gush Emunim sites	1,878	–	
Others	530		
Total:	3,810	696,908	0.5
Jordan Valley	3,990	26,220	15.2
All Settlements:	7,800	723,128 ˙	1.0

Thus, a year after the Likud's accession to power, the Gush Emunim settlements accounted for most of the Jewish population in the Judea–Samaria hills and, together with the Etzion bloc, the vast majority. Yet all together they amounted to no more than 0.5 per cent of the Arab population. And as the figures show, the Jewish hill population was about equal in size to that of the Jordan Valley settled earlier in accordance with the Allon Plan. The entire Jewish population of Judea–Samaria was no more than 1 per cent of the existing Arab population.

In all their settlements together, Gush Emunim had 500 acres of land. Each site had few inhabitants, mainly young couples. In some places housing was in trailers or army installations. Employment was outside the area, with commuting to Jerusalem or the coastal plain. Most of the residents held on to their former dwellings as well. Thus, in the first two years of the Likud government, Gush Emunim succeeded in creating many faits accomplis which were superficially impressive, although the percentage of Jews to Arabs was practically nil. The government gradually acquiesced in the settlement aspirations of Gush Emunim. Its policy was, among others, to break up the continuity of the Arab population by means of the Jerusalem area settlements in the centre, those of the Allon Plan to the east, and of Gush Emunim in the heart of Samaria, in order to make sure that no autonomous Arab organization above the level of local council would develop.

COMMUNITY SETTLEMENTS

The accelerated activities of Gush Emunim led to the introduction of a new type of settlement, the community settlement, based on a few dozen families in each place, on private initiative, on partial cooperation, with no obligation to work in the settlement itself. The new form was most suited to the geographical conditions of the hills, characterized by too little land and water for agriculture, and only small sectors that could be prepared for settlement. The new form also suited many of the residents, who had no agricultural background and at times no profound ideological one either. It was possible to live in a community settlement of this kind and commute to work in the towns of the coastal plain. Eventually, the Gush Emunim settlements were accorded official recognition as a settlement movement and benefited from a proportional share of the allocations for settlement in Israel.

There is no denying the fact that the Gush Emunim settlements appeared on the Judea–Samaria map as a new form joining the Jordan Valley settlements, the new neighbourhoods around Jerusalem, and the Etzion bloc locales that preceded them. In July 1980 there were 18 Gush Emunim settlements in Judea–Samaria. Just before the 1981 elections some land was released for settlement, and another four settlements of the movement were established.

The settlement developments in the decade and a half following the Six Day War can be classified in three periods. The Alignment tradition, encouraging primarily Jordan Valley settlements in accordance with the Allon Plan, operated between 1967 and 1973. Little attention was paid to the hilly areas of Judea–Samaria, since the primary interest was in defensible borders along the Jordan river. The 1974–77 period was characterized by the emergence of the extremist Gush Emunim group which worked for the overall settlement of Judea–Samaria. The 1978–83 period saw more extensive settlement in the hill region, going beyond the Allon Plan, and even far beyond what the Gush Emunim people themselves had envisaged. The Gush Emunim settlement map in the early 1980s shows concentrations in the hills along an axis traversing Samaria, and concentrations also around Qadum, Ofra, Beth El, Giv'on and Kokhav Hashahar, as well as Yatir and Zif in the south. Most of these settlements are still dependent on government support both for infrastructure and for their daily existence.

The outstanding feature of the Gush Emunim settlement endeavour is the fact that it crossed the line of legitimacy, and acquired the establishment's recognition post factum. This is a well-known political phenomenon, as an organized group without parliamentary representation seeks to influence the policy of the government or public bodies. A pressure group of this kind generally manages to affect decisions. The extent of its influence of course depends on the qualitative and quantitative resources at its disposal and the effectiveness of its leadership. Its usual means of applying pressure is through garnering votes in the election campaign. In this case, the movement has succeeded in establishing settlements of geopolitical significance in Judea–Samaria, and both its actions and its ideology have been endorsed by the Likud government.

THE 'LAST BATTLE' OF GUSH EMUNIM

The coming into office of the Likud government, the enormous funds that poured into the settlements in Judea–Samaria, the splits and conflicts within Gush Emunim with the discovery of the Jewish terrorist organization in mid–1984 – all these actually led to the dissolution of the Gush. Their motivation weakened and a sense of helplessness beset the central leadership, which is now scattered among several groups and parties. The Gush Emunim institutions are in fact paralyzed; the only active element is the settlement body, the Amana movement. Political reactions, arrangements for protest demonstrations, contacts with the government – all these are now handled by a different group, the Council of Settlements in Judea, Samaria and Gaza. This body includes all types of settlers in the occupied territories, from Alignment members to supporters of Rabbi Kahana. But this body cannot serve as a true replacement for the revolutionary zeal that characterized the Gush Emunim people at the outset.

Within the Likud government the ministers competed with each other in favouring the settlers and settlement in general. In that government there was no opposition to settlement in the occupied territories. The Alignment opposition contented itself with condemnatory declarations of one kind or another in the Knesset or the press. Even the 'Peace Now' movement began to subside along with its rival, Gush Emunim. In the meantime, the Likud government proceeded to encourage settlement until there were only 20 to 30 more localities to establish in order to complete the master plan for the year 2000. What was left for the more extremist settlers were two places, Hebron and (Shekhem) Nablus. Despite their genuine cooperation, the Hebron settlers did not manage to implement their plan for islands of settlers within Hebron itself before the advent of the national unity government in 1984.

The settlers' plan is to scatter islands of Jewish settlers among the Arab population in the town, and in the second stage to unite these islands into a large Jewish bloc in the heart of Hebron, from Qiryat Arba to the Cave of Makhpela, and from there to the Arab vegetable market, the expropriated Arab bus station, the Hadassah building up to the new island now established on Tel Rumeida near the Jewish cemetery. The linking of those islands means the confiscation of hundreds and perhaps thousands of Arab houses within the city and the removal of their Arab residents to other locations outside it. The settlers are now trying to implement their plan speedily lest the political wheel turns. Settlement within Nablus has also recently shown early signs of growth. If the prime minister and minister of defence are able to act jointly and vigorously against these first signs of law-breaking on the part of the Hebron and Nablus settlers, they will have prevented open rebellion and an important victory of the extremists among the settlers. It is still possible to avert the transformation of these two Arab cities into sites of violent clashes between Arab and Jewish nationalists. If now too the response is hesitant and there is an inclination to compromise of the Sebastia type, the government will again be forced to adhere to the line of the remnants of Gush Emunim.

CHAPTER FIVE

Hebron – a Jewish–Arab Struggle in a Built-Up Area

The renewal of the Jewish quarter in Hebron at the present time has political implications that underline the conflict between Jews and Arabs on the municipal plane. What is happening is penetration and settlement in a Muslim urban area of a group of extremist Jews with the intention of co-existing. It is an unusual occurrence with respect to Jewish settlements in the occupied territories. Up to now we have seen separate Jewish settlements, distant from Arab localities, while Hebron is the site of an attempt to develop Jewish settlement within an Arab city, for religious, spiritual and ideological reasons.

THE JEWISH COMMUNITY IN HEBRON IN THE PAST

Ever since the Patriarch Abraham bought the Makhpela Cave at Hebron to serve him and his heirs as a burial place, Jews throughout all the generations have venerated Hebron. There was a Jewish community in the town continuous up to the riots of 1929, although it constituted no more than a small percentage of the total Arab Muslim population of the town and occupied less than one per cent of its land area.

Until the nineteenth century the Jewish population was concentrated in a quarter known as the Ghetto. There was a clear separation between the Jewish residential district and the rest of the town, and its effect on the economy and life of the city in general was minimal. Towards the end of the nineteenth century there were changes within the Jewish population of Hebron, which reached 1,400, or 10 per cent of the total population of 14,000. As the number of Jews grew, they began to settle beyond the ghetto, purchasing land and houses from Arabs. For easy access, these were mostly along the main roads, one leading to Jerusalem, and one to Beersheba. The community as a whole was concentrated in the southern part of the town where the topography was convenient.

There was an obvious geographical proximity between the Jewish buildings, a characteristic that can be explained by the desire of the members of the community to create a geographical continuity between the structures, so far as possible, and thus avoid complete assimilation and absorption within the Arab population. The Jewish-owned buildings served as dwellings, and other uses such as a hospital, religious institutions, bakeries, etc. One of the first areas to be built on outside the Jewish quarter was the site of the Romano Building, which provided for living quarters, a guest house, a synagogue and a study house. Another main building of the Jewish community was the Hadassah House, which became a clinic thanks to donations received from the Hadassah Organization abroad (Figure 12).

RENEWAL OF THE JEWISH QUARTER 1968–1979

The year 1967 was marked by a policy change and a change in the political map of the State of Israel. At that time various groups began to organize in order to return and settle in places where Jews had lived in the past, and one of them was Hebron. Their purpose was to return to the town from which Jews had been evicted after the bloody disturbances of 1929 and establish a Jewish settlement on the remnants of the one that had been destroyed.

A short time after the Six Day War, a group headed by Rabbi Levinger applied to the government to allow settlement in Hebron. The government refrained from any response which showed from the beginning the lack of a clear policy on the reestablishment of Jewish Hebron, and this remained true. Nevertheless, the would-be settlers decided to carry out their plans, sure that government approval would be given post factum. One of the heads of the movement for the 'Greater Land of Israel' said on the eve of their settlement: 'If the government does not bless us now, let us settle there and gain their blessing afterwards.' Thus at the outset their strategy forced the government to acquiesce in what was happening in the field, practical activity towing policy behind it.

The settlers reached Hebron in April 1968 and leased the Park Hotel there on the pretext that they wished to spend the Passover holiday in that city of the patriarchs. After the holiday they announced that they were the pioneers of settlers who had come to establish a Jewish community in Hebron, and declared that they would ignore any government decision to remove them.

There was considerable hesitation regarding any sort of decision on the subject, and the government solution was to transfer the

FIGURE 12

JEWISH SITES OF INTEREST AND JEWISH-OWNED PROPERTY IN HEBRON

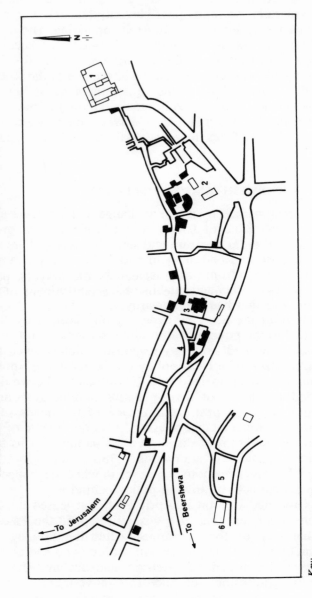

Key:
1. The Cave of Machpela
2. Centre of Jewish quarter
   ('The Ghetto')
3. Romano House
4. Hadassah House
5. Jewish cemetery
6. Tel Rumeida

settlers to the military government building. The settlers were thus 'under government protection' and viewed that step as official recognition of their right to remain in Hebron. Some time later, the government resolved (1) to allow the group of settlers to live in Hebron; (2) to assist in setting up a Yeshiva there; (3) that its decision did not constitute approval for the establishment of a Jewish city or industrial enterprise.

The settlers remained in the military government building, but caused disturbance when they set up a kiosk near the Machpela Cave. The military government removed it, but in compensation they obtained approval for holding prayer services in the Cave. The lesson learned was that obstinacy and systematic disregard of government decisions paid off.

The Jewish prayers at the Cave led to Arab preventive measures in the form of hand grenades tossed into the place. The government then decided on the erection of Qiryat Arba as a separate administrative unit from Hebron itself. The settlers, however, viewed Qiryat Arba as a unit integrated with Hebron from the spiritual standpoint, and thus as a further step towards their return to that city. The settlers' activity in the city, especially the prayers, put pressure on the government to decide on the establishment of a Jewish centre opposite Hebron. When its construction was completed, the settlers left Hebron proper, although for two years or so various attempts were made to settle within Hebron, which the IDF frustrated. The separation between the Arab city and the adjacent Jewish neighbourhood at Qiryat Arba was sustained until 1979, when a group of women took up residence in Hadassah House in the heart of the Arab city. That was the signal for the start of a renewed confrontation and a new campaign to allow Jews to settle within the Arab city.

NEW CONFRONTATION IN HEBRON AND THE COURSE OF EVENTS

From 1979 on, as noted above, there began a Jewish penetration into the heart of the Arab city of Hebron, initiating a new confrontation that is still continuing. Three forces are involved on the Jewish side: (1) the settlers, who are endeavouring to establish themselves in buildings and on sites owned by Jews in the past; (2) the government, which expresses no stand or clear opinion on what should take place; and (3) between them the security forces, that regulate the settlers' activity.

In April 1979 a group of women and children left Qiryat Arba and took up residence in Hadassah House. The Arab side voiced objections, but the group closed the building to prevent both entries and exits and arranged for guard duty. These steps aroused Arab ire, which culminated in the murder of Yeshiva student Yehoshua Salma in 1980.

The political response to the murder was a government announcement of its intention to Judaize the old city part of Hebron and set up a Jewish quarter within the city, although various individuals expressed their opposition. In practice, what happened was that the IDF took over the Romano Building which was being used as an Arab school, and a few weeks later returned it to the school, and gave permission for the Tel Rumeida cemetery to be used again.

The situation quietened for a time, but in May 1980 six Yeshiva students were killed at the entrance to Hadassah House. The government response was the destruction of the homes of suspects adjacent to Hadassah House, the dismissal of Mayor Kawasma, and the eviction of Arab residents from the Shenorson House and its transfer to the IDF. Later it sanctioned the occupation by the settlers of two buildings adjacent to Hadassah House, and the establishment of a Yeshiva in the Hadassah House.

An additional hostile act on the part of the Arabs was the attempted murder of a Jewish youth near the Romano Building, and the reaction of the authorities was to close the Arab school in that building and turn the premises into a military base.

In July 1983 a Jewish student was murdered in Hebron and the government responded by having the IDF close the central bus station in the city, a day later dismissing the Arab mayor and appointing a Jewish one.

The Jewish settlement picture of Hebron today features four separate points lacking territorial continuity. The locations were chosen for the ease with which they could be obtained, either because they were abandoned sites, places where monetary compensation could be paid for the evacuation of Arab residents, or places the army had seized in the wake of attempts against the Jewish population. Today there are 30 families, numbering some 200 people, living in the four locations within the city.

BALANCE SHEET OF THE CONFLICT

The settlement in Hebron is exceptional in that it involves a Jewish population making its way inside the municipal area of an Arab population. It represents a political ideological struggle against an urban background. It is a penetration and settlement process with no demographic motives, and a struggle in which the two opposing parties are of unequal strength. On the one hand there is the Jewish population which has strength and authority, and on the other the Arab population lacking any formal means of defence.

Because of the absence of a clear, consistent government policy, the settlers' actions force the authorities to go along with what occurs in practice. There is a force that pushes, a force that impedes, and the military manoeuvre between them. The violence perpetrated against the settlers provides legitimation on the part of the authorities for further settlement activities. The following sketch may perhaps clarify the process

Lack of clear policy
↓
Establishment of faits accomplis by the settlers
↓
Agitation within the Arab population
↓
← Government response →

To the Jews:
Legitimation of the
faits accomplis

To the Arabs:
Locating the people
responsible
Deporting notables
Destroying houses

The settlement map of Hebron does not show a city within a city, but rather homogeneous islands isolated both spatially and socially.

The main struggle is over the Central Business District of Hebron. That is where the city began to develop, so the return is to that place where formerly Jews lived. The Central Business District is the main livelihood of the residents, which makes for a hard struggle.

Decisions on the continuation of this sort of settlement depend on the respective political forces in key government positions. Even if the politicians decide to legitimize the continuation of settlement in the region, that will not necessarily lead to true national co-existence. There is no chance for national co-existence until each of the parties obtains reasonable satisfaction of its own national aspirations. Some would term this situation 'zero sum confrontation', when the benefit to one side is exactly counterbalanced by the degree of harm to the other, in contrast to confrontations in which both sides may gain something.

CHAPTER SIX

The Great Settlement Plan for Judea and Samaria

Of all the territories occupied by Israel, Judea and Samaria are the hardest nuts to crack, because of both the demographic complexity of the region and the political sensitivity prevailing there. The Israeli settlement policy in the region has exhibited a variety of paces, methods and strengths, some planned and most sporadic. They began with military conquest, continued with political decisions regarding selected areas, and ended with a massive settlement sweep for the purpose of establishing rapid and unequivocal faits accomplis in the territory. Although this latter phase is still in full progress, we shall attempt to analyse its main components against the background of the physical features and the possibility of establishing autonomy there in the future.

THE BACKGROUND TO THE DEVELOPMENT OF 'OCCUPIED TERRITORY'

After the War of Independence, some 77 per cent of the territory of western 'Land of Israel' remained in Israeli hands, the rest having been conquered by Jordan, except for the Gaza Strip which the Egyptians seized. The number of Arab refugees who left the areas conquered by Israel was then about 760,000. Of these some 180,000 fled to the West Bank region, 190,000 to the Gaza Strip, and 170,000 to Jordan, the remainder to other Arab countries. Before 1967 the Arab population of Judea and Samaria was about 840,000, of whom 760,000 lived on the hills and their western slopes, and 80,000 in the Jordan Rift Valley.

In the course of the Six Day War, Israel seized areas three times the size of its own territory, and one of these was Judea and Samaria with an area of 2,270 sq. miles. This conquest provided Israel with a fine opportunity to extend its frontiers and improve its security situation, and at the same time realize the nation's historic rights to the 'Greater Land of Israel'. During the conquest of Judea and

Samaria, some 250,000 Arabs fled the region – the largest population flight that had ever occurred in the region in such a short time. The Jordan Valley in particular lost much of its population. Before the Six Day War there were three refugee camps around Jericho with some 60,000 people, and 50,000 fled. Within a decade, about 10,000 returned, but they relocated mainly in Jericho and its environs. Jerusalem and Ramallah suffered a lesser loss of population as a result of flight, and Nablus a very small loss. Although Jerusalem and Nablus were the sites of heavy fighting during the war, relatively few Arabs fled from there, while considerably more fled from Hebron and Ramallah where there was almost no combat. The people with family connections across the Jordan took advantage of these in their hour of need. The differences in the proportion of residents who fled can be explained by the great fear the Mount Hebron people had, having experienced IDF raids in the past, and the fact that in Nablus the concentration of Palestinian nationalists prevented the population from leaving. Furthermore, for those with radical political views flight could have been very complicated. In the mountainous area, the fleeing residents hid in caves and ruins during the fighting. The people in the Jordan Valley crossed the river, and it was hard for them to return after the war. Israeli pressure for the evacuation of the Latrun enclave led to the flight of the villagers along the Latrun–Ramallah–Jericho axis. Relatively few Arabs fled from the mountain ridge, the Gaza Strip and Sinai. In general, Arab flight at the time of the Israeli conquest was marked by high percentages in certain places, but few demographic changes in most of the region.

The flight of the Arabs during the war led to the later entrance of Jews into many of the territories, and this facilitated subsequent Israeli settlement there. The mass flight from the Jordan Valley and Golan Heights was very important, for these were regions Israel sorely needed for security reasons. Also the fact that the rural population fled in greater numbers than the urban provided Israel with potential land for settlement.

The Six Day War has thus had a great influence on developments in the settlement geography of Israel. The changes varied from region to region, but the greatest were in areas where the Arab population abandoned their homes. The large, dense Arab concentrations in Judea and Samaria did not experience Israeli penetration, at least not till the mid-1970s. East Jerusalem, on the other hand, was a focus of rapid Jewish settlement, and the site of the most massive Jewish penetration into a dense Arab population, to the point that the Jewish population of East Jerusalem is bigger than the total Jewish population beyond the 'Green Line'. Apart from the Golan Heights, which is an almost totally Israeli region, the other 'occupied territories' have a mixture of Jews and Arabs.

In Judea–Samaria Israel seems to have got into the position of maintaining a colonial regime. A colonial situation is one in which one society rules another in the same territory, the first having a complete monopoly of political and military power and a disproportionate share of the economic resources. The social structure in such a situation is characterized by segregation, either by law or as a result of social dynamics. It takes the form of separate dwellings, preferential status, etc., and to these is generally added economic employment segregation – the less lucrative and prestigious jobs are reserved for the native population. This social system is maintained not only by force, but also by beliefs and opinions – a member of the inferior society is considered essentially inferior; he is naturally violent so there need be no hesitation about using force against him; he is cunning and unreliable so he should be restricted and watched.

Since 1967 Israeli society has been finding itself more and more in a colonial situation. About 3.6 million Jews have a complete military and political monopoly over a territory where 1.3 million Arabs with no political rights live. These Arabs are segregated in their neighbourhoods and employment, are at the bottom of the scale of prestige, are doubtfully defined as a people, and therefore lack the right to self-government beyond the municipal level, and even a considerable portion of the land and water, vital for any agricultural society, is not under their control.

More than a hundred thousand residents of the occupied territories are employed in Israel, mostly in work that Israelis began to abhor after the Six Day War: construction, factory work, sanitation and services. Gradually, the villagers began to leave the work in the fields for the Jewish population centres where more lucrative and less tiring work was available. After 20 years of Israeli occupation, Arabs alone are doing all the hard jobs in Israel.

As the Iran–Iraq war escalated, the economic situation worsened in the oil states to which tens of thousands of residents of the territories had annually repaired, seeking better paid jobs than are available in Judea–Samaria. The stream has now begun to change direction. Instead of large numbers leaving for those countries, now the number of those entering the territories through the Jordan bridges exceeds the number leaving.

In the economic crisis Israel is at present experiencing, the Arab workers have nowhere to go. In the early 1970s they could be advised to return to their earlier agricultural work. But a considerable proportion of them left immediately after elementary or high school to work in Tel Aviv, Jerusalem or Beersheba, or in the Jewish moshavim in the Lakhish region, or paving roads in Judea–Samaria. Some of the fields they had previously farmed have been abandoned, some taken over by the Israeli government either by expropriation or by declaring that particular land to be State land. Only a few thousand of the dismissed workers will perhaps find agricultural work, though with great difficulty. For 20 years a deliberate policy led to the unification of the economies of Israel and the occupied territories. Between 1948 and 1967 the Jordanian government had deliberately favoured the 'East Bank' over the 'West Bank' with the result that the economic infrastructure of the latter was meagre.

The various Israeli governments continued the Jordanian policy of non-development of the West Bank economic infrastructure. Just as under Jordanian rule almost no large plants and other local sources of employment were created, so too during the period of Israeli control. The Jordanians feared the development of a Palestinian centre independent of the East Bank authorities, and the Israelis persisted in this policy in fear of the rise of a Palestinian State, as well as for economic reasons. The Israelis operated in the belief that the economic boom would continue. Now, however, the inhabitants of the occupied territories are faced with a two-fold crisis; neither Judea–Samaria nor the Gaza Strip has an infrastructure capable of absorbing them. It turns out that political considerations do not necessarily coincide with economic ones.

Seeking to prevent the establishment of an independent economic infrastructure in the occupied territories that might serve as the infrastructure for a Palestinian State, Israel now has the burden of supporting thousands of families in those areas. If their economy is indeed integrated with that of Israel, and the creeping annexation becomes absolute, the Arab workers must be treated like Jewish workers. Otherwise, if they are treated differently and are the first to be dismissed from their jobs, a security risk is involved. It is, therefore, necessary to embark immediately upon the development of the economic infrastructure in the territories, even if that might risk the development of an infrastructure for an independent Palestinian State, or for an autonomous region.

Zionism, which endowed the Jews with means of coercion and rule even after the establishment of Israel, was able at first to elude the trap of a colonial situation. That does not mean that everything was perfect in the first two decades of the State. Until 1966 the Arabs were under a military government and were allotted few of the available economic resources, but they had the right to vote for members of the Knesset and some Knesset members defended their rights. They had free education and the possibility of higher learning. This was according to the model the State set itself in its Declaration of Independence which posited fully equal rights. However, from the outset Israeli democracy established patterns of control of the minorities living in the country, and also corrective measures for preventing arbitrary acts.

After the Six Day War Israel found itself in a position embodying all the basic features of a potentially colonialist situation. At first the presumed impermanence operated to block such a development, but as time passed, partly because of Arab unwillingness to reach a peace agreement, inertia tended to reinforce the colonial elements. This was aggravated by the acceleration of the military government, the pressure of messianistic and nationalistic elements in the community, and in 1977 a massive push on the part of the Likud government. Those who find it hard to ignore the contradiction between the value of Israeli democracy and of a colonial regime are living in the present colonialist situation with an unclean conscience.

The penetration into a territory for the purpose of settlement is generally quite a complicated process. In the modern world the general practice when settling a new area is to make all the basic surveys regarding the physical features, and then to formulate a policy on development and settlement which is then translated into a programme that is supposed to guide settlement and economic development. It is also the practice for the various bodies involved to decide together on the practical steps, and the priorities in the implementation, so that all components cooperate to realize the goal they all are aiming at. It is also usual for the existing circumstances – the settlements, roads, land use – to constitute basic data that must be carefully considered before any attempt is made to change or reverse them, for there are generally historical and good, justified objective reasons for them.

If we examine the settlement in Judea and Samaria during the past 20 years, we will find that the principles noted above are not its strong point. Jewish settlement, which began as soon as the war ended, was the result of historical and nationalist motives, of the considerations of those in charge of security policy, and of the pressure of people with extreme political views striving for 'the

Greater Land of Israel', and believing that agricultural settlement was a desirable means to the achievement of the aim. But there is as yet no agreement among the bodies in charge of settlement on the chances of survival of all that has been established, on the desirable size of the various types of settlement, on the expected population total, and on when the settlement is to take place. Nor is it yet clear how the new settlement system with all its components will operate, or how it will combine with the settlement system within the 'Green Line', if at all. No overall development plan for Judea and Samaria has been approved that would guide future physical and economic development and set the tone for the region. There has been some progress in defining the aspirations of the people interested in the region but there is no sign of coordination or formulation of the aims. On the other hand some settlements are set up before adequate land is prepared for them, homes are built when no work is available for the residents, and industrial plants are constructed without evidence of their profitability. The attachment of many Judea and Samaria residents to their former homes and their commuting to work within the 'Green Line' indicates that deep economic roots have not yet developed in the occupied territory.

Judea and Samaria is today a region whose political future has not yet been decided. Yet many unilateral settlement faits accompis have been carried out by the government of Israel and the Settlement Department of the Zionist Organization. The few Jews in the region, who constitute 1.5 per cent of the Israeli population and about 7.8 per cent of the Arab population, still take drastic actions which arouse both domestic and international political controversy. Consequently, there is reason to examine the directions that development and settlement have taken in recent years, and to consider their geographical and political meaning.

It was to be expected that the Likud government, which was in power between 1977 and 1984, would not be willing to rely exclusively on the settlement activity of Gush Emunim or on the Allon Plan. It needed a more comprehensive settlement plan that would radically change the settlement situation in the entire region. However, none such was ever formulated. A brief review of the approaches to populating Judea–Samaria of both Alignment and Likud governments reveals various ideas and proposals, characterized by the absence of a general overall plan adopted in advance, and by the search for reasonable solutions while simultaneously making and implementing short-term decisions.

SUCCESSIVE PLANS

The first plan was the Allon Plan, which emerged in the wake of pressures applied by settlement bodies to resume the settlement of the Jordan Valley. The first places established were Mehola, on land of absentee owners, Qalya, in the area of the Dead Sea concession, and Patza'el, on government land. When water was discovered in the neighbourhood of Patza'el it was decided to establish a chain of settlements in the Jordan Valley. Upon the discovery of additional water sources it was decided to set up a line of settlements at the foot of the Samarian hills as well.

The second plan was that of Moshe Dayan. Its aim was to reinforce Israeli control of the mountain crest, together with army camps, each stronghold to be connected with the area within the 'Green Line' through a network of roads, water pipes and electric cables. The sites chosen were Bezeq, Hawara, Beth El, the Etzion bloc and Adorayim. The idea behind the plan was implemented only in the Etzion bloc, as difficulties in land acquisition emerged in the other places.

The third plan involved the reinforcement of the environs of Jerusalem, and was handled mainly by the ministerial committee on Jerusalem and the ministerial committee on settlement. Its aim was to broaden the Jerusalem corridor northwards to the Bet Horon road and southwards to the Etzion bloc. Up to now the plan has only been partially implemented.

Another plan was connected with the erasure of the 'Green Line'. As the security border adopted by the government was along the Jordan river, it was decided to erase the previous border to the west of the Samarian hills by means of almost contiguous Jewish settlement. Beginning in 1976, therefore, one or two settlements were established beyond the 'Green Line' as an extension of the settlement complex within Israel proper.

In addition, the government recognized post factum the settlement initiatives of Gush Emunim in the midst of areas densely populated by Arabs.

Since the Likud's rise to power in 1977, there has been a clear, declared policy on settlement in Judea–Samaria aspiring to establish a strip of Jewish settlements along the main roads that would disrupt the continuity of the existing Arab sites. Here there are two basic views. One favours the establishment of dozens of small units even without an economic base in situ, while the other would prefer to concentrate settlements in urban and semi-urban developments, with a solid employment base, that would attract residents from all over Israel.

PRESENT-DAY SETTLEMENT AND POPULATION IN JUDEA–
SAMARIA

The Central Bureau of Statistics estimates that at the end of 1986 there were some 65,000 Jews living in Judea–Samaria. The region has some 120 sites either completed or in various stages of construction. In all, about 13,500 homes in the region are occupied, while another 4,000 are ready. Government bodies are making great efforts to complete longitudinal and lateral roads in the region by-passing Arab villages, to facilitate rapid movement between Judea–Samaria and the centre of the country. The infrastructure now being built will permit the future establishment of dozens of additional settlements and of industrial plants. In the wake of this government policy, numerous private, government and Histadrut construction companies embarked upon intensive building in the region. Not far beyond the 'Green Line' they have built suburban settlements such as Nofim, Alfe Menashe and Sha'are Tiqva – on a purely commercial basis. At the end of 1987 there were about 50 settlements in Samaria, 20 in Judea, 22 in the Jordan Valley–Judean Desert region and 26 in the Jerusalem Mountains (Figure 13).

Such a large number of settlements, in addition to the infrastructure for development plants, require a great deal of land, and the Israeli government has adopted various means of obtaining land in Judea–Samaria. Until 1979 the procedures were consistent with Jordanian law, which allows the government to make use of lands of absentee and government ownership for public purposes. Other land was taken over for military purposes by confiscation or enclosure. The total acquired by these means was 437,500 acres, in all about 30 per cent of the area of Judea–Samaria.

Following a High Court decision of October 1979 forbidding the confiscation of privately-owned land for settlements, the government adopted a new policy that enabled it to seize land for its own needs, based on a government decree and the Ottoman land law stipulating that the local proprietors, not the government, must prove ownership. The Ottoman law provides that land between villages for which there is no deed belongs to the Sultan. As only a third of the land in Judea–Samaria was ever registered, the owner-

FIGURE 13
JEWISH SETTLEMENTS IN JUDEA AND SAMARIA

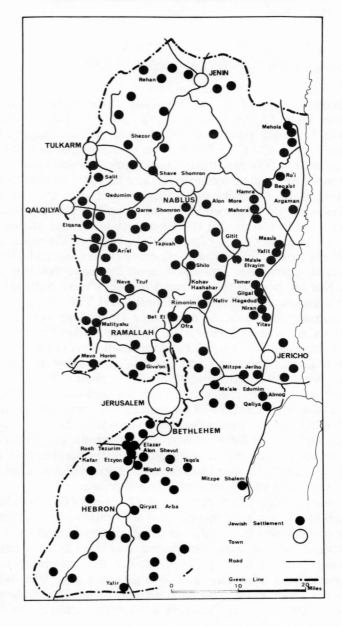

ship of two-thirds cannot be proven. The upshot is that 64 per cent of the land in Judea–Samaria became potentially confiscatable for the purpose of establishing new Jewish settlements.

The expropriation of land for military purposes was accomplished by its requisition for security reasons, the establishment of Nahal (military settlement unit) strongholds or the demilitarization of strongholds and their transformation into civilian settlements. Another way of acquiring land was by purchasing it from local Arabs prepared to sell. At present various private companies are engaged in the hasty acquisition of such land. Land acquired in this way totals 7,500 acres. Such methods of acquiring control of land enable the government to build in Judea–Samaria almost without restriction. If it can pour large sums of money into the various construction projects, there is no doubt that it will be able to establish dozens of additional settlements and totally transform the map of Judea–Samaria.

THE HUNDRED THOUSAND PLAN

A more comprehensive plan for the settlement of Judea–Samaria was formulated by the Settlement Department of the Zionist Organization, with the collaboration of the government and the IDF. That plan had two targets: a short-term target – the settlement of 100,000 Jews there between 1982 and 1987; and a long-term target – the settlement of half a million Jews there by 2010.

The Alignment party prefers to establish more settlements in the Jordan valley, according to the Allon Plan, around Jerusalem or at peripheral areas in Judea and Samaria, while the Likud party prefers to settle Jews mainly on the hill country, between existing Arab villages, near Arab towns and even inside them, as in the case of Hebron. The annual population increase there is estimated at 20,000. About 20 sites are today in preliminary stages of planning and the intention is to establish settlements there within a few years. Some thousands of dwellings are in the process of being approved for construction.

The settlement plan provides for the establishment in the main of urban settlements, not based on residents with ideological motivations. These being established on the west of the Samarian hills and in Judea are actually residential suburbs of the Tel Aviv agglomeration and Jerusalem, which offer Israelis high level housing at relatively low cost. The fact that the aim of populating Judea–Samaria with Jews accords with the economic and social interests of Israelis has in recent years led to a dramatic change in the scope of settlement in that region.

A survey conducted in mid-1983 shows that 10 per cent of families in the Tel Aviv area, representing a potential of 25,000 families, intend to move to Judea–Samaria, or at least purchase a one-family house, apartment or lot there. The survey also shows that the influence of ideological considerations upon their planned move is marginal. The main motives are improved quality of life, fine housing conditions, and the relatively low cost of apartments and lots.

The Settlement Department of the Zionist Organization has recently prepared an expansion of the Hundred Thousand Plan, in view of further data gathered. It points chiefly to a rate of construction and preparation of land for 165 settlements in 30 years to provide for 1,300,000 Jews in Judea–Samaria. Of these settlements five would be large urban ones (two towns and three urban boroughs with 10,000–30,000 families each), 36 suburbs (with 3,000 families each), 65 communities (with 400 families each) and 59 kibbutzim and moshavim. The plan considers that the construction of 5,000–6,000 dwellings per annum would ensure the completion of the plan by the target date. The plan also proposes concentrating in the coming years on the paving of 250 miles of roads at the rate of 60–100 a year; the expansion of the 80 existing rural settlements and the 18 urban ones already established; the demilitarization of 15 strongholds; the early establishment and rapid development of 52 proposed settlements; the development of industrial zones at the rate of 100–125 acres per annum to provide 3,000 jobs in industry each year; continued allocation of government-owned land, and acquisition of land by both government bodies, and private individuals; the preservation of 5,000 acres of government land by afforestation and the development of grazing areas; and the promotion of recreational and tourist sites. The areas the plan indicates as requiring immediate implementation are Greater Jerusalem, the strip along the roads of the eastern slopes of the hills, the eastern part of Mount Gilboa, east of Tulkarm to Qedumim, and the south of Mount Hebron.

The goal of this great settlement plan for the next 30 years is the greatest possible spread of Jewish population in important regions, with little government input, in the shortest possible time. This requires the functional exploitation of the various types of settlements and their location in various areas according to importance. There are natural processes arising from demand, and these are directed to regions with a high demand potential. There are artificial, directed processes based on ideologically motivated settlement, and these take the form of small settlements with high social quality, supported, subsidized and directed to regions where the demand is low (Figure 14).

In order to select the appropriate settlement type, the plan defined 'demand zones'. For that purpose the Tel Aviv area and Jerusalem area were treated as a centre, the population in each of the relevant 'demand zones' around them likely to move to Judea—

FIGURE 14
DEMAND ZONES FOR HOUSING IN JUDEA AND SAMARIA

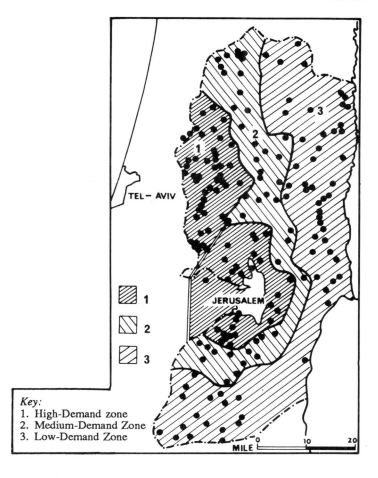

Key:
1. High-Demand zone
2. Medium-Demand Zone
3. Low-Demand Zone

Samaria being estimated, and the zones of settlement importance indicated.

The plan divided Judea–Samaria into three 'demand zones' for residence and employment, according to criteria of the time required to travel there from the centres (Tel Aviv and Jerusalem areas) via the roads planned, and of various attractive local factors. The zone of high demand was defined as within a 30-minute commuting distance from the outer ring of Tel Aviv, and a 20-minute distance from Jerusalem or other towns in the coastal plain. This demand zone extends geographically for six to ten miles east of the 'Green Line', from Tulkarm in the north through the Jerusalem area to the Etzion bloc in the south. As settlement in this strip is subject to great demand, the plan suggests that settlement types there should be adapted to public and private enterprise with a low subsidy content. An essential condition for ensuring demand in this strip is adequate roads connecting it with the large cities and bringing it physically and psychologically closer to the population of the coastal plain. The plan envisages in 30 years a Jewish population in this strip of 250,000 to 450,000, constituting 65–75 per cent of the total Jewish population of Judea–Samaria. The Jerusalem area is apparently not expected to contribute to much settlement beyond the limited zone of influence of the city, whose Jewish population in 30 years is estimated at 700,000.

The area of medium demand is defined as being a 50-minute commuting distance from Tel Aviv and a 35-minute distance from Jerusalem or from other towns in the central coastal plain. It is set east of the high demand zone and includes the eastern slopes of the Samarian hills, the Rehan bloc (Dotan), the Rimonim bloc (Kokhav Hashahar), Ofra, and the strip from Ma'ale Amos to Ofra and the Etzion bloc. The requirements for populating this region would be adequate roads, settlement with a high degree of subsidy, the provision of services of a proper level, and the maintenance of a low proportion of commuting. The Jewish population in the area in another 30 years would be expected to reach 100,000 or 150,000, constituting 20–25 per cent of the Jewish population of all of Judea–Samaria in 2010.

The low demand zone is east of the previous one, east of the mountain slopes of Judea–Samaria, and on the southwestern slopes of Mount Hebron. The zone is characterized by great commuting distances and the settlement planned for it is based on an ideologically motivated population in small settlements with a high level of subsidy. The plan proposes locating these settlements in clusters or blocs, and constructing regional and local roads to connect them with the other settlement regions. The Jewish population there in 30 years is expected to number from 40,000 to 70,000, or 10–15 per cent of the Jewish population of Judea–Samaria in 2010.

The implementation in Judea–Samaria is subject to an order of priorities as well. The potential land for planning settlement is not of equal availability, as it includes State land and rocky land in a poor state of cultivation. The potential is expressed in 'islands' of various sizes. The importance of the settlement or any other activity in each of the 'islands' is determined by different criteria.

The criteria for determining the importance of any measure taken may be termed interconnection, interpolation, and insufficiency. Interconnection refers to the necessity of settling the region so as to connect with existing settlement regions both in order to establish a geographical continuity and in order to improve services in the region. Interpolation refers to the prevention of uncontrolled Arab expansion and the development of predominantly Arab blocs of villages. Insufficiency refers to the paucity or absence of Jewish residents in a region. These three criteria combine professional planning elements with political ones, and the relative importance of each is the prerogative of the decision-makers. The establishment of an order of priority taking the three criteria into account has developed a basis for determining the type and pace of settlement in each and every region.

Regions that are vital for interconnection on the regional or local level are the strip along the water divide on the east of the mountain, which joins the Jezreel Valley to Jerusalem, and Jerusalem through the Etzion bloc and Mount Hebron to Beersheba; the settlement region west of Mount Gilboa which links the Bet She'an valley with northern Samaria; the regions along existing and planned roads crossing Judea–Samaria from west to east and north to south, including the northern Samaria lateral connecting Hadera with Rehan; the central Samaria lateral connecting the Netanya area to the Jordan Valley through Enav; the main Samaria lateral connecting the central bloc to Ma'ale Efrayim through Ari'el; the Binyamin lateral connecting Ashdod and Ashqelon with the Dead Sea through the Etzion bloc and Efrat; and the southern Judea lateral connecting Qiryat Gat with Telem, Qiryat Arba and the Judean desert. To these must also be added settlements north and south of Jerusalem connecting Neve Ya'aqov with the city and Neve Ya'aqov with Beth El, and those connecting south Talpiyot to the settlements near Herodion; and the Qiryat Arba region connecting the Teqo'a bloc and Ma'ale Amos with Qiryat Arba and the area southeast of Mount Hebron.

Regions that would urgently need to be settled for purposes of interpolation are the neighbourhood of the Jerusalem municipal boundary, where the Arab population is increasing rapidly and spreading out untrammelled; the strip along the eastern part of the hills, from northern Samaria to southern Judea, where most of the Arab population is concentrated in both urban and rural settlements; the strip along the 'Green Line' from Rehan through Tulkarm and Elqana, expected to become a district of Arab settlement; and the area south of Mount Hebron between Yata and Eshtemo'a, where Arab expansion is extensive and uncontrolled.

Areas that would need to be settled because of lack of Jewish population include the Hermesh–Enav–Qedumim strip in northern Samaria; western Gilboa; east of Ari'el; west and south of the Binyamin region.

Areas where all three criteria apply include Jerusalem, inside and outside the municipal boundary; the strip along the eastern slope of the hills; western Gilboa; east of Tulkarm–Eshtemo'a–Maoz–Carmel–Ma'ale Amos.

Areas with a low priority are the strip east of the 'Green Line' along the Elqana–Modi'im–Latrun axis and west Jerusalem. There it would be important to limit various types of Jewish settlement; because they are desirable areas, settlement there is likely to be detrimental to Jewish settlement in Jerusalem and in places where it would contribute to interconnection and interpolation, and remedy insufficiency.

TABLE 3
LONG-TERM TARGETS IN MAIN URBAN SETTLEMENTS

Town	Planned Area (in acres)	Planned Number of Housing Units	Planned Population
Ma'ale Edumim	3,430	10,000	40,000
Ari'el	7,375	25,000	150,000
Emanuel	1,000	5,000	20,000
Qarne Shomron	550	5,365	30,000
Qiryat Arba	130	6,000	25,000
Giv'on	325	1,900	30,000
Efrat	60	6,000	25,000
Elqana	100	–	–
Total:	12,970	59,265	320,000

Table 3 shows the planned population in the main cities of Judea–

Samaria according to this long-range plan. This great plan expresses the position of the Likud government, which believes that settlement in the entire country means security and right. The plan also assumes that Israel will hold on to Judea–Samaria indefinitely, and that in order to make that clear to the Arabs rapid settlement should be carried out wherever possible. The plan favours the occupation of all territory vital to Israel, even if it is necessary to learn to live there with and among Arabs. The intention is to encircle the Arab villages with belts of Jewish settlements which in the future would form homogeneous blocs on State-owned land or land of absentee owners. These would be clusters of settlements in Judea–Samaria, some of which would spread over both sides of what was the 'Green Line'.

IMPLICATIONS OF THE GREAT SETTLEMENT PLAN

In order to settle 100,000 Jews in Judea-Samaria, the government would have to invest about three billion dollars. Presumably such an investment would come at the expense of Galilee, the Negev and the development towns. As Israel's resources are in any case limited, any priority granted one area would necessarily result in stagnation and regression in others. Signs of this process are already evident today. It should also be borne in mind that settling Jews in Judea–Samaria is contrary to the central Zionist goal, which is the establishment of a State in the Land of Israel that would maintain a Jewish character and at the same time be democratic and just. The creation of a Jewish minority in Judea–Samaria is likely to produce another instance resembling the situation in the mountainous areas of Galilee.

The Hundred Thousand Plan settlement did not concern itself with the empty areas east of the water divide but aimed mainly at the spaces between the Arab villages on the eastern slopes. The existing settlements, roads and land use were not the basis of the proposed plan at all. The model proposed is one line of settlements to the east loosely strung from north to south, and blocs of settlements to the west. The link between the blocs would be maintained by a new system of local and national roads. The urban complex and the Jewish rural complex would be connected mainly with areas within the 'Green Line'. Thus the plan proposes a separate system that is not integrated into the existing Arab one. Rather, what is produced is a forced settlement segregation, for the new model disregards the existing settlements and establishes no economic ties with them. A considerable proportion of the Jewish settlements would be no more than dormitory towns whose inhabitants would commute daily to areas within the 'Green Line'. Only an extensive infrastructure of science-based industries which by nature do not require large populations would be able to establish the Jewish population in Judea–Samaria on an economic footing.

The plan is concerned primarily with reinforcing the existing settlement blocs and does not offer an orderly settlement model. The present pattern seems to be a conglomeration of local solutions which do not coalesce into a rational regional alignment.

THE NEW SETTLEMENT – A MIXTURE OF TYPES

A geographical analysis of the settlement process in Judea–Samaria clearly reveals a disregard of outstanding features of the area which should be the point of departure for any planning, development and settlement, and especially a disregard for the Arab population there and its villages and towns. There is no denying that rural Arab settlement in Judea–Samaria is an age-old geographical and demographic fact which evolved against the background of the physical features of the region in conditions of technological underdevelopment and an autarkic farm economy. In that settlement we find a pattern of natural spread on the hills and slopes, and the exploitation of the physical conditions in order to live and maintain a rural and semi-urban way of life suited to the physical and ecological balance of the region. In this traditional Arab way of life we find the hills and their fertile plateau inhabited, intensive cultivation on the hillsides by means of terracing, agriculture on the desert border, the town located on the eastern slopes of the hills along the ancient 'mountain raod', large border villages south of Mount Hebron, cultivation in patches in the valleys between the mountains – all in all a natural settlement according to the conditions established by nature, with no artificial tissue disturbing the regional geographical balance.

The Jewish settlement endeavour from 1967 on was faced with these clear, unequivocal facts when coveting Judea–Samaria for settlement – especially with the population of 835,000 which in the course of time had occupied most of the sites suited to settlement and was not prepared to leave them of its own free will.

How did Israel approach settlement in the light of these facts? At first the method adopted was trial and error, which did not lead to a comprehensive approach but rather to a mixture of old types of settlement taken from the recent past and applied to the new situation.

In the mountainous region, which was already densely populated, settlements were placed at various points that were important to the settlement authorities for security, political or ideological reasons. These points were necessarily on unoccupied State-owned land, inferior for agriculture, and sometimes far from the main roads. These settlements were individual 'footholds', with no all-embracing system. In the western and southern part of the region, the bloc system was adopted, as in the settlements in the Bet Horon bloc, the Salit bloc, and the revived Etzion bloc. In the Jordan Valley, which was almost empty of local residents and abounded in unoccupied areas, the settlement system involved an urban centre in the hills, like Ma'ale Efrayim, and rural settlements along the Jordan Valley from Mehola in the north to Yativ in the south. Near Jerusalem and Hebron the closely linked urban model was adopted, requiring the construction of additional residential neighbourhoods near existing towns in order to occupy large municipal areas. In Qiryat Arba near Hebron this model also reflected religious and ideological interests, while around Jerusalem the aim was simply to enlarge the metropolitan expanse. In other places in Judea–Samaria unsuited to the agricultural or city-linked model because they were located on stony soil or far from a large town, the model adopted was the townlet, which had been frequently utilized within Israel, and on that basis Elqana, Qarne Shomron, Ari'el, Giv'on, Ma'ale Edumim and Efrat were established, to serve various functions, not always crystal clear. An intermediate type between village and townlet was also tried, the industrial village; it became rather fashionable and was the model for Bet Horon, Ba'al Hatzor, Kokhav Hashahar and others. Recently another model has been introduced, the dormitory suburb near large urban concentrations.

The fact that so many types of settlement are being considered provides a clue to their history: the 'footholds' had their source in the pioneer settlements of the 'tower and stockade' type; the bloc pattern revives the regional idea applied in the past at Tel Mond, the Hefer valley and the Zebulun valley, and was repeated in the Besor region, the Lakhish region and the Jerusalem corridor; the town-linked model is inspired by the experience of Upper Nazareth, near Nazareth; the townlet model is based on the experience acquired settling new immigrants in the development towns; and to these is added the industrial village which attempts to adopt industry and services as its basis instead of agriculture.

GPI—G

While each model originally fulfilled a crucial function adapted to its time, and then gave way to a successor model better suited to the new situation, what is being established in Judea–Samaria is a mixture of models with no system or comprehensive approach, with the result that today, after close to two decades of settlement, it is still difficult to envisage what the region will look like in the future. The 'foothold' type is the most widespread, and perhaps the most effective politically, but its economic and social weakness is so blatant that its chances of survival seem doubtful. The bloc model is no more than a transition between 'foothold' and region, but has in the course of time lost any independent function. The town-linked model is perhaps the most convenient and efficient for attracting population, but it is extremely expensive, requires tremendous capital for its infrastructure, and must have a large population potential available. The townlet model has advantages so far as occupying territory is concerned, but it has great economic weaknesses, as was proved in many development towns within Israel proper. The industrial village model is so new that it cannot as yet be evaluated.

The mixture of settlement types in Judea–Samaria seems a reflection of the conceptual confusion prevailing in regard to the settlement of that region. In the absence of a comprehensive approach and system to development, the region has become a kind of laboratory for settlement experiments that are extremely costly for the Israeli economy, especially since the mixture is no guarantee of a rational settlement development.

CHAPTER SEVEN

The Struggle for the Land in Judea–Samaria

What is happening today regarding land in Judea–Samaria is a reflection of the political struggles between two peoples with a long history of open hostility each of whom aspires to gain control of the area – for sovereign territory provides a spirit of security and economic reinforcement.

One of the basic channels of the struggle is the land both as territory and as a source of livelihood. As the land potential is absolute, each party wishes to take possession of as much as possible. The Arabs hold on to their land because it is ancestral, and for them land means a living, happiness and honour. The Jews on the other hand hope to detach the Arabs from their land as a practical means of settling in the area, for reasons of religious tradition, ideology, security, and the quality of life.

In this struggle each party has had achievements and failures, but statistics show that more than 52 per cent of the land has passed from Arabs to Jews, and the many different means employed reflect the nature of the struggle.

LAND ARRANGEMENTS IN THE PAST

When the IDF entered Judea–Samaria in 1967, an area of 1,445,000 acres came under its jurisdiction. This occurred in the midst of a process, begun in the British mandatory period and continued by the Jordanians, of establishing order in land registration by determining and recording the various landowners in the registry. It was the first attempt ever made in the area to organize land registration in a thorough and modern way. This formal process, which would have required a great many years to complete, was interrupted at a time when only 30 per cent of the land in Judea–Samaria had been registered. This was mainly the area north of the Jerusalem–Jericho line, including Jerusalem, Nablus, Jenin, the Jordan Valley, Tulkarm and Qalqilya. The registration stopped with the conquest of the area, as the Geneva Convention forbade changes to be instituted under a military government.

In the areas where the registration was completed, there are accurate records of ownership, and the Israelis can operate easily only in connection with State land. The term actually covers all categories of land, except the land owned by local residents; these categories all now have the legal status of 'land in direct Israeli ownership'. In other areas, the major part of Judea–Samaria, no registration took place, and the ownership is not recorded. In the face of this anarchic situation, the Israeli government adopted a land policy based on the Ottoman land law which states:

> Empty land, such as mountains, rocky areas, rough terrain, pastures, which are not owned by anyone on the basis of a deed, and are not designated for the use of any city or village-dwellers, and are such a distance from cities or villages that a person's voice cannot be heard in the closest settlement [those areas] are known as dead land ... any person who needs such land can with the consent of the official, cultivate it, except that the absolute owner will be the Sultan.

The meaning of this law is that any land that is uncultivated or uncultivable, and is not recognized private land, is State land. In view of the fact that 60 per cent of the land of Judea–Samaria is not cultivable, a large proportion of it in the unregistered areas can be considered State land (Figure 15).

The Ottoman law allows the exception of a person who cultivated such land by permission, and indeed the Israelis allow certain rights on the land to residents who have cultivated a piece of land for at least ten years. Consequently, under conditions of non-registration, in most of Judea–Samaria it was possible, around the time of the conquest, to consider as potential State land all land except: (a) land registered as private property and which can be proved to be such, (b) land cultivated for at least ten years, giving the farmer certain rights over it, and (c) land belonging to 1967 absentees managed under the abandoned property decree, and returnable in the condition it was in at the time of seizure, when the owners return. At the same time, there is a military government with extensive powers regarding land which, in the absence of registration, operates on the basis of national and security needs and considerations. This often leads to legal confrontations between local residents and the Israeli authorities and against the background of the confusion prevailing many difficulties arise. Certainly, if land registration were completed

FIGURE 15
AREAS WITH LAND SETTLEMENTS

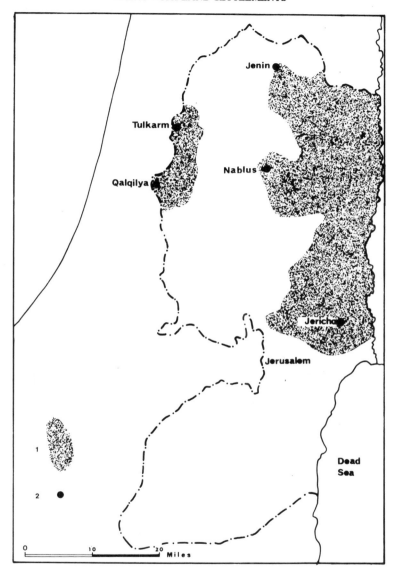

Key:
1. Land Settlement up to 1967
2. Town

for all of Judea–Samaria, it would be useful to both parties, and many unpleasant episodes related to competition for land would be avoided.

THE ALIGNMENT LAND POLICY 1967–1977

In the ten years between the occupation of Judea–Samaria and 1977, the Alignment was the party in power in Israel. This fact is important for understanding actions taken regarding land during those years, the ideology justifying what was done, and the methods that were employed. The Alignment was the instrument implementing the old ideology of the Labour movement, which since pre-State days had posited settlement on an agricultural basis through kibbutzim and moshavim. That ideology was also applied to Judea–Samaria, and it was necessary to find fertile land to cultivate, a difficult task in the physical conditions of the region, for much of the land is rocky, and the little cultivable land was already exploited by the locals. Consequently it was a problem to obtain agricultural land for the settlements that were planned. It was solved by the Alignment government through the military government, which either declared the land as belonging to absentees and leased it to the settlers, or carried out 'seizure for security purposes'. Thus in addition to the little agricultural land registered in the name of the Jordanian government or the king, the Israeli government managed to put together areas of agricultural land in certain places.

During that ten-year period, ten settlements totalling 3,000 people were set up in Judea–Samaria, mainly for mountain cultivation in the prevailing climatic conditions – fruit trees, hothouses for house plants, grapes, etc., chicken coops, cow-sheds and bee-hives. The most outstanding settlement during this period was in the Jordan Valley, in the spirit of the Allon Plan, where 13 agricultural settlements were founded, for purely security reasons, and based on the natural advantages of the region for early ripening winter crops and tropical fruits.

THE LIKUD LAND POLICY 1977–1984

The rise to power of the Likud in 1977 brought with it a change in the concept of settlement across the 'Green Line'. That government favoured settlement in all parts of the historical 'Land of Israel' and began locating settlements in Judea–Samaria. In some cases the government was faced with a lack of State land in areas it was interested in and sought, like its predecessor the Alignment government, to confiscate land for supposedly military reasons and then establish settlements on it. In 1979 the Supreme Court issued a decision stipulating that confiscation for military purposes could not be the pretext for the establishment of a permanent civilian settlement, and that method was not utilized thereafter.

Following the court's decision, the land required for Jewish settlement was obtained by declaring it 'State land', based on Ottoman law. A protracted process was undertaken to put together 'stony land and rocky places' not recorded in the land registry. As some two-thirds of the land of Judea–Samaria was not registered, it is hard for the local people to prove ownership, and the government can take over large areas because of the sad fact that the local people cannot prove their claims to land legally, or even in any other convincing manner. Rocky areas and unused land throughout Judea–Samaria were pinpointed through aerial photography, and soon declared to be State land, especially in places that had been selected by the planning and settlement authorities.

The urban character of settlement under the Likud aegis does not make agricultural land a requirement, and makes it possible to use stony fields which are supposedly all State land. The situation resulting from the fact that two-thirds of the land is unregistered, and 60 per cent is defined as uncultivable, is that all restrictions have been lifted as regards occupying land for Jewish settlement! This approach made a great deal of land available, for urban settlements on a relatively small area, with no need for an agricultural hinterland.

An examination of the Likud settlement achievements from a historical viewpoint shows that there was intense activity, and that all the settlements, some 70 in all, are located on State land, without impinging on privately owned Arab land, without confiscation, and without expropriation for military needs. Consequently, the settlements of the Likud period do not earn their living from agriculture, as most are located on uncultivable land and a few even in the desert.

The Likud period was also characterized by variety in the means of acquiring land, beginning with a continuation of Alignment methods, through putting together State land and declaring other tracts to be such, and even by outright purchase.

PRESENT OWNERSHIP OF LAND

All the land in Judea–Samaria can be classified in three main categories of ownership: land privately owned by Arabs, land privately owned by Jews, and State land.

Private Arab land is land that can be proved to be private property. For land that was registered, the registration is unequivocal proof. For unregistered land, however, it is up to the claimant to prove his ownership. There is a catch here, because the only proof recognized by law is the 'registration extract' which is issued upon completion of the registration procedure, and the land in the area was never registered. Account may therefore be taken of other evidence, such as entry in tax lists and recording in the mukhtar's ledgers. It was found, however, that most of the tax entries refer to ownership of land that is not taxable, or for which tax was paid on only a small part, and if the entry shows that no tax was levied, that casts doubt upon the claim to the land. If it belonged to the claimant and he cultivated it and lived off it, or held on to it as material property, he would have had to pay taxes on it. Thus the tax lists can at most serve as partial circumstantial evidence submitted along with the other more telling evidence, if it exists.

Private Jewish land is Jewish-owned land in Judea–Samaria that was legally acquired before 1948. The best known are the tracts in Hebron and the Etzion bloc. At that time land was also acquired there by various bodies, the largest being the Jewish National Fund (JNF). The total is estimated at 8,000 acres. From 1967 permission to purchase land in Judea–Samaria has been given to Jews, at first to public institutions like the JNF, and since 1979 to private individuals.

All the land acquired by Jews is intended to provide for the infrastructure for private settlement of a new pattern, known as the 'exurb'. Unlike the policy within Israel, in Judea–Samaria the rest of the land the settlers need in order to develop the infrastructure, pave roads, and evolve commercial, public and industrial land uses, is not private land, but rather State land or private Arab land legally appropriated for public purposes – the public being the Jewish population which since 1972 has been legally recognized as part of the West Bank population. It appears today that the amount of private Jewish land in Judea–Samaria is very small, for there is both a financial and a political risk in such purchases; they seem in any case quite superfluous in view of the enormous land reserve at the disposition of the government. The estimated total of all Jewish-owned land there, acquired before 1948 and after 1967, is about 17,500 acres.

State land includes most of the territory of Judea–Samaria under direct Israeli control and is classified in the following formal categories:

a. *Absentee land* – land or other property belonging to citizens of Judea–Samaria who left after 1967. This land is managed under the Abandoned Property Order by the Official in Charge of Absentee Property in the Israel Land Authority. In many cases this land is left unutilized and no changes are instituted in it (retaining the status quo in case the owner returns), and in others the Official has leased it to private individuals to cultivate, but the absentee can recover it upon his return. A large proportion of the land in the Jordan Valley is absentee land leased to the settlements there, and the rental fee is credited to the original proprietor. About 107,500 acres in Judea–Samaria is land in this category.

b. *Registered State land* – this is land registered in the name of the King of Jordan or the British High Commissioner who preceded him. The Military Government acts as a temporary authority, but in practice deals with it as it does with Israeli State land and leases it to Jewish settlers. A considerable proportion of the Jewish settlements are located on land of this category, with leases issued for 49 or 99 years and options to extend. This was possible only due to the official interpretation of Israel's status in Judea–Samaria as the original ruler that had returned. On the other hand if Israel annexed the region and became the legal heir of the Jordanian authorities, the land would become its absolute property. Registered State land amounts to 175,000 acres, about one-eighth of all the land in Judea–Samaria.

c. *Land expropriated for public needs* – land laws in all progressive countries allow the authorities to expropriate land for the needs of the local citizenry. The intention is primarily for roads and infrastructure. In fact, land in Judea–Samaria has been expropriated from the local people for blazing roads, and paving arterial roads and access roads to Jewish settlements. The amount of land expropriated for roads is estimated at about 25,000 acres.

d. *Areas closed for military purposes* – these are areas closed by the Military Government, on the basis of an 'Occupation Order', which are intended for manoeuvres, training, shooting ranges, security zones, etc. This land remains the property of the local owners, who in many cases are permitted to cultivate it. In some cases these areas may be occupied for long periods.

e. *Land confiscated for military purposes* – this is land, privately owned by Arab residents, which is taken over by the Military Government on the ground that it is vital for military purposes. There is no real dispossession, for the registered ownership is preserved and the Military Government pays the landowner a fee in compensation for the crop.

f. *Land without owners* – this is land to which the local people cannot prove legal ownership. It becomes State land, on which new settlements can be established.

OCCUPATION OF STATE LAND BY ARABS

Paralleling the Jewish aspirations to control the land in Judea–Samaria, there is action on the part of the Arab population which takes the following forms: (a) unsupervised extension of village areas by scattered buildings; (b) construction in isolated spots unconnected with villages; (c) resumption of cultivation of abandoned fields. This activity has political encouragement and outside financing, as a reaction to the policy of the military government and to Jewish interest in land in Judea–Samaria. Actually, the Arabs occupy State land, and land that may potentially become State land, and entrench themselves on it by establishing faits accomplis, hoping thus to expand their future subsistence area, which is being reduced with every new Jewish settlement founded. They do so by building around existing villages in a wide circle aimed at physically extending the village area, and also outside the villages on State land where they put up provisional structures and undertake some cultivation that will enable them to live there and later demonstrate their connection with that tract of land. This is especially obvious around Jerusalem and along arterial roads, and also along Israeli territory west of the 'Green Line'.

It is technically difficult for the Military Government to control such measures by applying the law, and in view of the creeping 'invasion' that has now attained disquieting dimensions, the following methods have been adopted: (a) physical occupation of State land by the Jewish National Fund; (b) division of Judea–Samaria into regional councils, and insistence on the villages' abiding by expansion programmes prepared for them; (c) establishment of Jewish settlements in regions especially subject to such manifestations, and involvement of the Jewish settlers in monitoring them and warning off the perpetrators.

OCCUPATION OF STATE LAND BY THE JEWISH NATIONAL FUND

In view of the increasing penetration of the Arab population into State land, in 1981 action was taken to prevent or reduce such operations, by seizing State land in order to establish or consolidate State ownership. The aims were: (a) to safeguard the boundaries of the Jewish settlements and adjacent State lands; (b) to secure land reserves for future settlement, or for developing industrial areas; (c) to ensure physical continuity between the Jewish settlements, in the long term and at small cost; (d) to create sources of employment and livelihood for residents of the adjacent Jewish settlements; (e) to safeguard land for which no physical development had been planned for the near future. The means employed by the JNF to carry out these aims were the creation of land uses for agriculture: preparation, development of pastures, afforestation to occupy territory as well as for the benefit of the residents, parks for residents and tourists, and archeological excavations. These activities involved more than physical occupation of the land; because they entail investment in the short term as an incentive for the development of physical presence in these areas, they contribute to the expansion and variety of employment opportunities there. Thanks to these JNF activities the areas are protected from 'infiltration'. Up to now 8,000 acres have been afforested, pasture land has been prepared up to the 8 inch average annual rainfall line in the east, and fenced in an area of some 17,500 acres, parks have been planned for 3,500 acres and altogether the plan is to ocupy 52,500 acres (Figure 16).

FIGURE 16

AREAS SEIZED BY THE JEWISH NATIONAL FUND (J.N.F.)

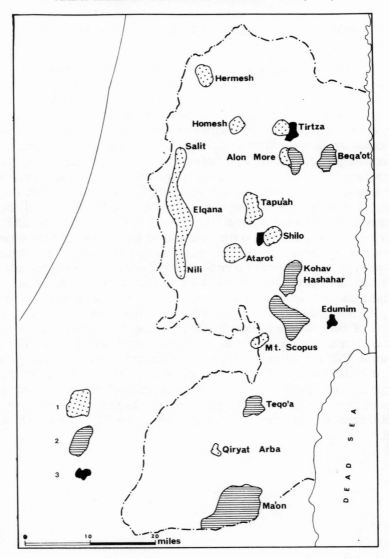

Key:
1. Afforestation
2. Grazing
3. Parks

CHAPTER EIGHT

Territorial Autonomy in
Judea–Samaria

As we have seen, since the Six Day War numerous development and settlement activities have been carried out in Judea–Samaria that have changed the structure of the region considerably. Many settlements have been established in the Jordan valley, and in the Judean and Samarian hills, the Etzion bloc has been enlarged, new roads paved, the municipal area of Jerusalem expanded, and residential neighbourhoods have proliferated. Many of these development activities have been accomplished through separate planning and administrative bodies with no reciprocal relations between them, to the point where the region seems to lack the overall regional planning approach that would make it possible to take advantage of the situation already obtaining in the field for the benefit of the two peoples living there.

The attitude of the settlement authorities is likely to prove most important in the future when the question of autonomy in Judea–Samaria is discussed, not only personal autonomy which the Likud government favoured, but also territorial – which will entail determining unequivocally how the various parts of the region will be allocated.

We shall attempt, against the geographical background of the region, to analyse a series of possible models of territorial autonomy giving varied degrees of importance for Jews and Arabs, from the political as well as the planning and functional viewpoint.

NATURAL GEOGRAPHICAL AREAS IN JUDEA–SAMARIA

In order to consider possible ways in which autonomy might be firmly established in the region, it is worth noting the natural divisions likely to form the basis for the boundaries of various areas. Judea–Samaria is divisible into discrete geographical sub-units for purposes of physical planning and development, or separate autonomous districts. These geographical sub-units do not in all cases have clear boundaries, which are sometimes difficult to fix, as for example between the Samarian hills and northern Samaria, or between Mount Hebron and the area south of it. Furthermore, it should be borne in mind that most of the geographical units in Judea–Samaria are not in themselves complete, their physical continuation being within the 'Green Line'.

The following is a topographical and lithological classification of obvious sub-regions (Dan, 1968)(Figure 17):

Northern Samaria: An area with mountains as high as 2,100 ft. and hills separated by relatively broad valleys such as the Sanur valley and Zababide valley. The valleys are 600–1,200 ft. above sea level. The mountains are of hard rock, mainly hard Eocene chalk and dolomite. The valley slopes are steep and stony, and the area is topographically distinct from its surroundings, while roads and settlements encircle it.

Southern Samaria: A mountainous area between the mountains of Beth El and Nablus. In the north it reaches an elevation of 2,400 ft. and in the southeast 3,000 ft. To the west the area becomes gradually lower. It is crossed in its length and breadth by valleys, the broader valleys being in the northeastern part, including the Mikhmetat valley, the Shechem valley and the Ein Soher valley. It is characterized by chalky rock, dolomite and marl, and escarpments facing west and east.

The Gerizim–Ebal Bloc: This is a bloc of mountains made of hard chalk. The mountains are very steep and stand out against their surroundings. Mount Ebal is 2,820 ft. high and Mount Gerizim is 2,643 ft. The centre of the bloc features flat plateaus. The Shechem valley bisects the bloc of mountains. In this valley there are deep strata of Senonian, and here flow springs that supply water for Nablus and its environs. Most of the mountain consists of Eocene rock more than 900 ft. thick.

The Southern Jezreel Valley and the Dotan Valley: A flat to hilly area which extends from Mount Gilboa on the east to the Amir ridge on the west. The valleys are 400–900 ft. above sea level. The valleys are alluvial plains distinguished from their surroundings by the cultivated fields and the rural settlements along the edges.

The Samarian and Beth El Hills: The border between these two hilly regions is not clear because there is no conspicuous mountain-fold line or pass to a high plain. West of the Beth El hills there is terracing

FIGURE 17
NATURAL GEOGRAPHIC REGIONS IN JUDEA AND SAMARIA

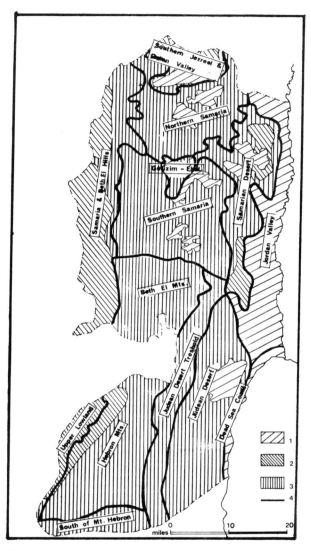

Key:
1. Valleys
2. Lowland

3. Mountains
4. Natural Geographic Region

in the Beit Sira–Na'alin–Deir Balut section, but this disappears further north. The upper boundary of the hills goes along the 900 ft. contour line in the southern part of the area and gradually descends to the 600 ft. line in the northern part. The area is characterized by relatively hilly plateaux and mountain ranges broken up by narrow wadis that widen towards the coastal plain. Escarpments and fault lines mark the eastern part of these hills.

The Samarian Desert: An area extending east of northern and southern Samaria, which makes a steep descent into an area of mountains and valleys whose heights range from 900 ft. in the west to sea level in the east. The area is crisscrossed by many streams, the largest of which is the Fari'a, and by a series of canyons in the zone between the mountains and the Jordan Valley. The Samarian desert is narrower than the Judean, and also less well defined topographically. Steep escarpments mark its eastern boundaries and it also has parallel fault lines between the mountains and the Jordan Valley. The rock is mainly from the upper Cenomanian period, but there are strata of lower Cenomanian rock in its northern part.

The Jordan Valley: A long, narrow alluvial area that is part of the Syrian–African rift that crosses the country from north to south. West of the Jordan the area is narrowest opposite the Buqe'a, but extends northwest to the Samarian hills as the Fari'a valley, while toward the Dead Sea the area widens. The Jordan Valley as a whole is below sea level and broken up by shallow wadis. In cross-section it is possible to identify its upper part, the 'Ghor', and its lower part, the 'Zor', where the river winds into its channel.

The Beth El mountains: A broad mountain plateau north of the Judean hills, reaching 3,048 ft. at Mount Ba'al Hatzor. In general it ranges in height between 2,100 and 3,000 ft. It is broken up only on its western and eastern edges by streams. Suitable for extensive development of settlements and roads. Escarpments and fault lines mark the boundaries of the area on the west and east, with large canyons between the plateau and the Judean desert.

The Hebron mountains: This area includes the plateau from the Hebron area to the southern part of Jerusalem. The elevation ranges from 2,400 to 3,000 ft. and the area is not much cut up, but characterized by low hills alternating with flat valleys. On the east and west the area is broken up by streams. On the west it has a mountainous fold-line which separates it from the lowland, and on the east it is bounded by a steep mountain terrace.

The South of Mount Hebron: An area extending southwards from Hebron to the mountains of Yatir, Anim and Ira. It has an elevation of 1,800 ft. in the southwest, rising to 2,400 ft. and more in its northern and eastern parts. It is characterized by steepness on the slopes of the anticlines and in the neighbourhood of the streams. The profile of the area is relatively moderate despite its considerable elevation.

The Upper Lowland: A section of a broader area extending westward to the Judean lowland. Located at an elevation of 1,200–1,800 ft., it has gentle slopes and broad valleys, and consequently the settlements are too densely positioned. It is bounded on the east by the fold-line of Mount Hebron which is the main morphological feature in the area.

The Threshold of the Judean desert: A strip 3.7–5 miles wide separating the mountain plateau from the Judean desert. It is 1,800–2,400 ft. in elevation and contains heights with relatively deep soil.

The Judean Desert: An area with a special morphological structure along the east of the Judean hills, which stretches from the northeastern Negev to the east of the Beth El hills. It is marked by a set of terraces with escarpments between them, and ends in a steep escarpment which falls to the Dead Sea and the Jordan Valley. Many wadis cross it from northwest to southeast, creating deep canyons in the passage from the mountains to the coast. Its elevation ranges from 1,200 ft. in the west to 600 ft. in the east before the descent to the Dead Sea and the Jordan Valley.

The Dead Sea Coast: A narrow coastal strip extending from cliffs of the Judean desert on the west to the Dead Sea coast on the east, made of fans of alluvial silt. North of the Dead Sea the strip widens and also includes salt deposits.

This geographical area division leads to the following conclusions:

a. The topographical structure of the region results in a desert all along its eastern part, which reduces development options, restricting them to the central and western sections and certain sectors in the Jordan Valley.
b. The structure of the region results in favourable climatic conditions (rain and temperature) in the central and western parts; however, more difficult conditions in the east would limit agriculture and settlement, making an artificial water supply necessary for intensive development.

GPI—H

c. There is a link between the location of settlements in the region and the topography expressed in the selective choice of sites on the plateau or mountain ridges.

d. The corridor between the mountains and the desert generally encourages the location of large settlements on the edge of the Judean and Samarian deserts, while in the centre and western part of the mountains a continuous series of small and medium-sized rural settlements develops.

e. There is a distinct separation between mountain and desert which must be borne in mind in planning the distribution of population, the type of population in the two zones, the employment provided, and the development projects needed in each zone.

f. The minerals in the northern part of the Dead Sea constitute a great potential for economic development, in the vicinity and in general.

g. Agricultural development is possible in the valleys and in relatively non-steep mountain areas, after preparation and terracing of the land. Agricultural areas can be extended in areas that are topographically and lithologically suitable, such as the Dotan Valley, the Samarian hills, the Beth El mountains, and the Mount Hebron plateau.

h. This mountainous region limits urban development both in area and population, due to the escarpments, the difficult construction conditions in the mountains and the absence of the necessary economic base.

i. The terrain does allow for the construction of longitudinal roads, on the mountain plateau and the Jordan Valley. However, the escarpments on the east and west make development of lateral axes only minimally possible.

j. Possible lines of transport must be linked to the dominant topographic structure, with little possibility of manoeuvre eastwards or westwards of the mountain ridge.

k. The landscape of the region is a natural tourist attraction, because of the great variety in scenery and climate within a short distance.

l. The mountain is suitable for extensive afforestation and the fostering of natural flora.

SPATIAL PATTERNS OF JEWISH–ARAB INTERRELATIONSHIPS

Dominant geographical features in Judea and Samaria, which could be the basis for Jewish–Arab interrelationships, could also be used as a foundation for the development of various autonomy arrangements. These features are:

- the concentration of Arab settlement in the mountainous parts of Judea and Samaria
- the absence of Arab settlement in the Jordan Valley and the Judean Desert
- the concentration of Jewish settlement in the Jordan Valley
- the haphazard distribution of Israeli settlement in the hill country
- the existence of the Etzion bloc between Jerusalem and Hebron
- the network of medium-sized Arab towns spread all over the region
- the prominence of Arab urban settlement on the ridge of the Judea and Samaria mountains
- the state of 'rivalry' between the traditional Arab and the new Jewish patterns of settlement
- the continuous and fairly intensive growth of building activity in most Arab towns
- the rapid development and construction of Jewish semiurban centres, and the means taken to encourage people to settle in them
- an improved road network and communications between the various parts of the region.

With these features as a background, it is possible to develop spatial patterns for a number of interrelationship or autonomy arrangements, with each pattern representing a combination of dominant elements, Israeli or Arab, both physical and demographic, while stressing their interrelationship. Such patterns can be presented on a rising scale, from a spatial minimum to a spatial maximum, or vice versa.

The various plausible spatial situations are presented below as six patterns of autonomy, with particulars of the geographic and demographic elements of each pattern. The six suggested patterns are (Efrat, 1982);

1. Return to the pre-1967 spatial pattern.
2. Return to the pre-1967 spatial pattern, excluding East Jerusalem.
3. Return to the pre-1967 spatial pattern, excluding East Jerusalem, with minimal border revisions.
4. Return to the pre-1967 spatial pattern, excluding East Jeru-

salem and the Jordan Valley, with minimal border revisions.
5. Division of the region between Jews and Arabs, excluding East Jerusalem and the Jordan Valley, with minimal border revisions.
6. Enforcement of Israeli sovereignty over the entire region of Judea and Samaria.

These are basic patterns whose political implications have to be considered carefully. There are of course also other possible variants, which incorporate elements from one or another of the above patterns.

Pattern 1: Return to the Pre-1967 Spatial Pattern.

In view of the many physical changes that have taken place in Judea and Samaria since the Six Day War, a return to the 1949 armistice line boundary would bring about a situation in which many elements would be cut off from their ties with Israel and from their continuity with the State (Figure 18).

The new Jewish quarters surrounding Jerusalem, such as Gilo, Ramot, Shapiro Quarter, Neve Ya'aqov, East Talpiyot, and Greater Sanhedriya, would be left outside the municipal boundaries of Jerusalem. These quarters house today about 100,000 inhabitants, and this number will eventually rise to 150,000. The large public building complex recently built on Mount Scopus (which was an Israeli enclave between 1948 and 1967) would also be cut off from the Israeli part of the city.

Qiryat Arba would be cut off from its surroundings and remain as an isolated quarter next to Arab Hebron. Its distance from Jerusalem, 22 miles, would, in the absence of a continuous connection, lead to a falling off in population and development.

The semiurban settlements, some of which are already being built, while others are yet in the planning stage, would remain without a regional centre in their vicinity. Severance of their link with Jerusalem and the State of Israel would render their existence pointless. There are at present eight such settlements, among them Ma'ale Edumim, Giv'on, Ari'el, and Elqana. Others are in an advanced planning stage.

The Jerusalem–Tel Aviv motorway might again be cut between Sha'ar Ha–Gai and Latrun. Jerusalem would cease to be linked by road to Nablus, the Jordan Valley, the Dead Sea, and Beersheba by way of Hebron. The connection between Gaza and Hebron through Beersheba would probably also be affected.

The Atarot airfield, with its improved landing strip, would no

FIGURE 18
IMPLEMENTATION OF AUTONOMY IN JUDEA AND SAMARIA, PATTERN 1

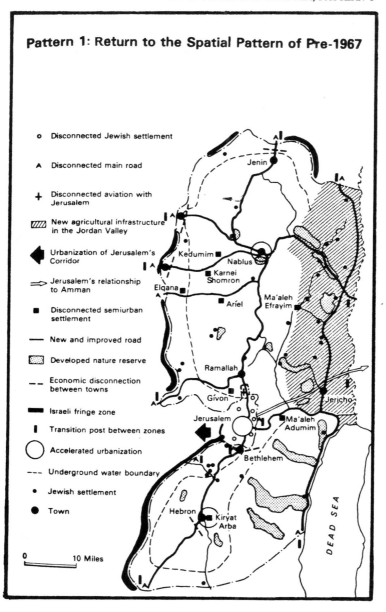

Pattern 1: Return to the Spatial Pattern of Pre-1967

o   Disconnected Jewish settlement

▲   Disconnected main road

+   Disconnected aviation with Jerusalem

▨   New agricultural infrastructure in the Jordan Valley

◀   Urbanization of Jerusalem's Corridor

⇒   Jerusalem's relationship to Amman

■   Disconnected semiurban settlement

—   New and improved road

▨   Developed nature reserve

--   Economic disconnection between towns

▬   Israeli fringe zone

❙   Transition post between zones

◯   Accelerated urbanization

---   Underground water boundary

•   Jewish settlement

●   Town

0   10 Miles

longer be able to serve Israeli aviation, which would be unable to operate the air routes between Atarot and other parts of the country. A considerable portion of the present airspace would be lost to Israeli civil and military aviation.

Israel would leave in Judea and Samaria a greatly improved infrastructure of traffic arteries, such as the Jerusalem–Ramallah road, the Bet Horon road, the Jerusalem–Dead Sea road, the road from Jericho to En Gedi, and the Jordan Valley road, in addition to the widening and improvement of many other roads carried out in the course of the last few years.

At Ma'ale Edumim the infrastructure of a large industrial zone would remain, and it is doubtful whether the Arabs would be able to utilize it efficiently.

In the Jordan Valley there would remain an extremely advanced agricultural infrastructure, with newly prepared soil, a new network of irrigation pipes, and fields of crops hitherto unknown in the region.

As in the past, Jerusalem would have to turn in the only direction left to her, namely to the west, to prepare the corridor for the urban development that would be required in the capital. The lack of a sufficiently wide infrastructure would necessarily bring about the curtailment of building activity in the city.

The partition between the two sections of Jerusalem would strengthen the ties between the Old City and Amman. East and West Jerusalem would develop in opposite directions, with a consequent waste of planned land uses.

The interruption of the economic links which have developed between pairs of towns on both sides of the armistice line, such as Kefar Sava–Qalqilya, Netanya–Tulkarm, Afula–Jenin, Jerusalem–Bethlehem, Beersheba–Hebron, etc., would be a loss to the Jewish population as far as the employment of 100,000 Arab workers who commute daily from the occupied territories and mutual relations are concerned.

There would be a renewal of frontier settlement along the armistice line, together with the attendant security installations. This would lead to an increase in population of areas and settlements on both sides of the frontier, with a consequent rise in tension, both in security and agricultural matters.

If links were to be established between both sides of the armistice line, new entrance and exit points or frontier checkpoints would be required opposite Bet She'an, Tulkarm, Qalqilya, Jerusalem, Latrun, and east of Nablus.

There would be an accelerated growth of Nablus and Hebron, the urban centres of influence in Samaria and Judea, respectively.

Israel would lose control over the groundwater resources of Judea and Samaria, which are an undivided part of the country's groundwater system. Such control is necessary in order to regulate pumping and to utilize the water in the coastal plain.

If the present Jewish population of Judea and Samaria should be forced to vacate their homes, the problem would arise of settling about 65,000 persons in towns and villages within the armistice line.

Pattern 2: Return to the Pre-1967 Spatial Pattern, Excluding East Jerusalem.

It is possible that East and West Jerusalem would continue to be united and form, as is the case today, a single municipal, economic, and administrative unit, while the remaining parts of Judea and Samaria would return to the situation existing before 1967 (Figure 19).

In this event, development of both sections of Jerusalem, Jewish and Arab, which has been held up in recent years owing to the political uncertainty, would be accelerated. In particular, there would be more Jewish building in the areas that were annexed to Jerusalem after 1967.

Jerusalem would gradually strive to achieve a metropolitan structure, by strengthening the Jerusalem–Shu'fat–Ramallah axis, by completing the building up of the hills to the south, by extending in the direction of Bethlehem, Beit Jala, and Beit Sahur, and by filling up the as yet unbuilt areas in the city itself.

The physical and economic growth of Jerusalem might cause changes in the settlement pattern over a wide area surrounding the city, such as the rapid urbanization of villages and the building of new Arab satellite towns. There would also be changes in the uses of agricultural land near Jerusalem, and an accelerated creeping urbanization.

There would be a growth in size and population of the Arab villages between Ramallah in the north and the Etzion bloc in the south because of the increased economic strength of Jerusalem, with the risk of upsetting the balance between the Jewish population of Jerusalem and the Arab population of the surroundings.

Increased investment in Greater Jerusalem would arrest the urban flow to the Jerusalem Corridor. The possibility of allocating more area in the city proper for building purposes would prevent the

FIGURE 19
IMPLEMENTATION OF AUTONOMY IN JUDEA AND SAMARIA, PATTERN 2

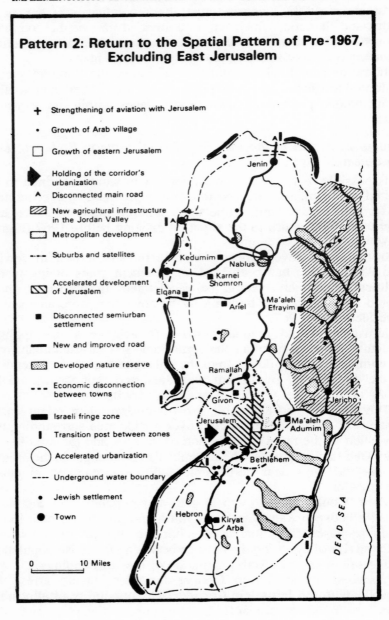

Pattern 2: Return to the Spatial Pattern of Pre-1967, Excluding East Jerusalem

+ Strengthening of aviation with Jerusalem

• Growth of Arab village

☐ Growth of eastern Jerusalem

◗ Holding of the corridor's urbanization

ᴧ Disconnected main road

▨ New agricultural infrastructure in the Jordan Valley

▭ Metropolitan development

‒·‒ Suburbs and satellites

▧ Accelerated development of Jerusalem

■ Disconnected semiurban settlement

▬ New and improved road

▒ Developed nature reserve

‒ ‒ Economic disconnection between towns

▰ Israeli fringe zone

❙ Transition post between zones

◯ Accelerated urbanization

‒‒‒ Underground water boundary

• Jewish settlement

● Town

0   10 Miles

conversion of the villages in the corridor into semiurban settlements. The growing importance of East Jerusalem as part of Greater Jerusalem would reduce the importance of Hebron and Nablus as district centres. Economic and social activity would naturally be concentrated in the largest and most populous centre, which is Jerusalem. Its economic growth, and the consequent rise in the standard of living, would lead, if unchecked, to a rapid rise in the Arab population of East Jerusalem.

The more stable conditions in Greater Jerusalem and the granting of special status to Christian and Muslim holy sites would increase the flow of tourists from overseas and from the neighbouring countries, and widen the scope of reconstruction, restoration and conservation work in the city.

Pattern 3: Return to the Pre-1967 Spatial Pattern, Excluding East Jerusalem with Minimal Border Revisions.

Adding minimal border revisions along the armistice line to pattern 2 would maintain the operational unity of road transport and agriculture, and prevent the displacement of a number of settlements and sites which are important from a security point of view. The following are recommended revisions (Figure 20):

a. The required border revisions would affect the Latrun enclave, the area west of Tulkarm, Battir village, the area near Ramot, and East Atarot. What used to be a no-man's-land between double armistice lines would have to be abolished.

b. The border revision at the Latrun enclave would be necessary for maintaining normal road services between Jerusalem and the coastal plain, and in order not to interfere with the Jerusalem–Tel Aviv motorway.

c. West of Tulkarm it would be necessary to annex a medium-sized area of land in order to permit the undisturbed operation of freight trains using the Lod–Haifa railroad.

d. West of Battir in the Jerusalem Corridor the railroad right-of-way would have to be widened in order to secure the regular rail service to the capital.

e. The northwestern part of the Jerusalem municipal boundary would have to be modified so as to include the almost completed Ramot quarter within the municipal area of the city.

f. The municipal boundary would also have to be changed east of Atarot in order to allow for enlargement of the airfield and its conversion into an international airport.

FIGURE 20
IMPLEMENTATION OF AUTONOMY IN JUDEA AND SAMARIA, PATTERN 3

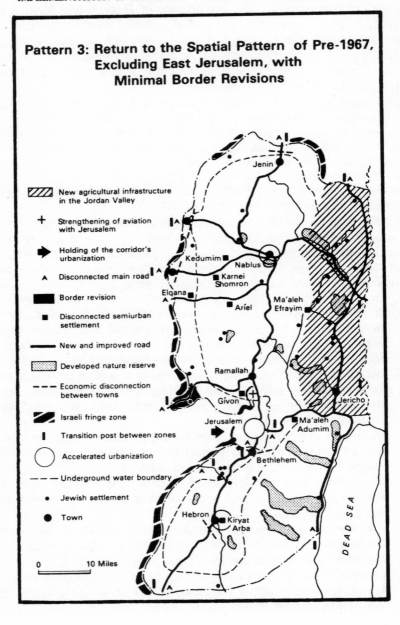

**Pattern 3: Return to the Spatial Pattern of Pre-1967,
Excluding East Jerusalem, with
Minimal Border Revisions**

Pattern 4: Return to the Pre-1967 Spatial Pattern, Excluding East Jerusalem and the Jordan Valley, with Minimal Border Revisions.

It is very possible that the Jordan Valley, which has only been sparsely settled in the past but since 1967 has undergone intensive development, both as regards population and agriculture, would constitute a special and important element within an autonomy framework. This is the part of Judea and Samaria which has had the greatest influx of Jewish settlers (Figure 21) and where there have been the largest investments. The inclusion of the Jordan Valley in the area of Israeli sovereignty would have the following consequences:

a. A continuous physical link between the Jordan Valley and the rest of the State of Israel would have to be provided, if not by territorial additions, then at least by special traffic arteries in the direction of Bet She'an in the north and Jerusalem in the southwest, in addition to one or two latitudinal axes crossing Samaria and connecting the Jordan Valley with the coastal plain.
b. Traffic corridors to and from the valley would be needed, as well as entrance and exit points for the Jewish and Arab inhabitants. It would also be necessary to ensure the interregional traffic between the Transjordan and Judea and Samaria, using the Jordan bridges and the corridors leading to them.
c. Increasingly intensive Jewish settlement in the valley would necessitate massive investment, both for securing the Jordanian border and for achieving the greatest possible productivity in this area, once all territorial disputes are settled.
d. It is to be expected that Jericho would grow in size and population, as a result of its new role as a transit town between the Jordan Valley and Jerusalem and the State of Israel, in addition to its position on the main route between both sides of the Jordan. It is therefore possible that, in addition to tourism, Jericho would also attract industries and services connected with agriculture.
e. There would probably be some thickening of border settlement, mainly to the east, south and west, and consisting of defence installations, military camps, and various types of military agricultural settlement.
f. Israeli sovereignty over the Jordan Valley would make possible the establishment of a number of urban settlements between

FIGURE 21

IMPLEMENTATION OF AUTONOMY IN JUDEA AND SAMARIA, PATTERN 4

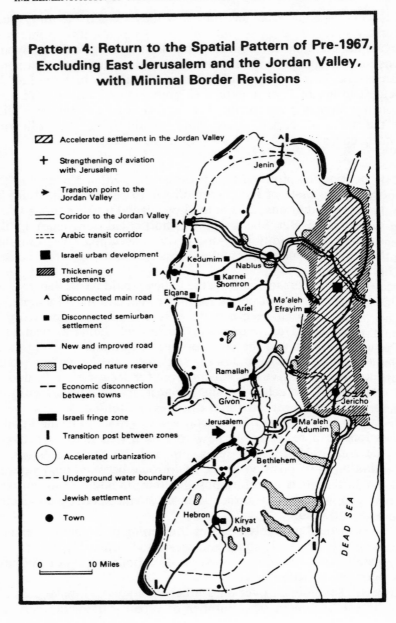

Pattern 4: Return to the Spatial Pattern of Pre-1967, Excluding East Jerusalem and the Jordan Valley, with Minimal Border Revisions

Jericho and Bet She'an, thus creating an urban continuity from north to south.

g. It may be assumed that the Jordan Valley would be intensively exploited, for agricultural, engineering, and other kinds of installation especially suited to this region.

Pattern 5: Division of the Region between Jews and Arabs, Excluding East Jerusalem and the Jordan Valley, with Minimal Border Revisions.

There exists the possibility that, with the exclusion of East Jerusalem and after minimal changes along the armistice line, the whole of Judea and Samaria could be partitioned between Jews and Arabs, with each party exercising sovereign rights over the territory and the population of its area (Figure 22). In this event it would be necessary to define the areas with predominantly Jewish or Arab population, the transit points between the two areas, the relationship between them, and the axes of interrelation necessary for safeguarding the territorial interests of each side. Plausible solutions would be as follows:

The whole area north of Beth El up to the armistice line to be allocated to the Arabs, with the exclusion of the Rehan and Salit enclaves and the whole of the Jordan Valley.

The greater part of the Hebron Mountains and the Judean Desert to be allocated to the Arabs.

The whole of the Etzion bloc, including all existing and proposed settlements between Hafurit in the west and Teqo'a in the east, would form part of the Jewish area.

The whole of the Jordan Valley, within the boundaries of the agricultural and regional settlement plans, from the Bet She'an valley in the north to Jericho in the south, would be one continuous Jewish area.

Existing Jewish settlements within areas that for the purposes of autonomy had been defined as Arab, would be independent enclaves or a part of axes of a certain defined width.

There would be an axis of Jewish settlements in the Samaria Mountains, in the general direction of Jerusalem–Shiloh–Nablus.

A western longitudinal axis would be required, in the direction of Jerusalem–Ari'el–Nablus–Dotan Valley.

There would have to be a number of transverse Jewish settlement axes from Baq'a el Garbiya to the Jordan Valley, from Kafr Qasem to Ma'ale Efrayim, from the Modi'im region to Giv'on, from Hafurit to Teqo'a, and from Lakhish to Qiryat Arba.

FIGURE 22
IMPLEMENTATION OF AUTONOMY IN JUDEA AND SAMARIA, PATTERN 5

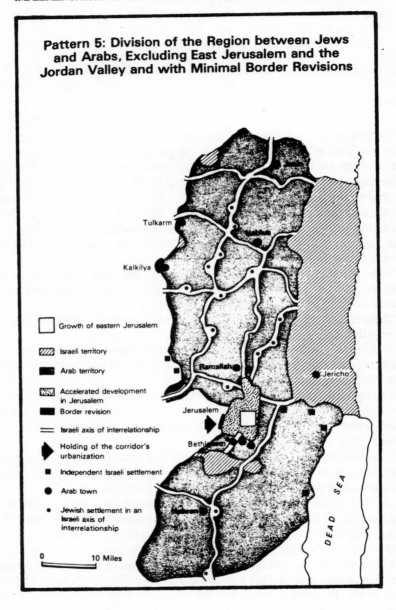

Pattern 5: Division of the Region between Jews and Arabs, Excluding East Jerusalem and the Jordan Valley and with Minimal Border Revisions

There would also have to be a Jewish longitudinal axis from Jerusalem to Qiryat Arba, and from there to Arad, in order to ensure the link between existing Jewish towns without having to cross the mountain ridge.

Axes of communication would also be required between Jerusalem and Ma'ale Edumim, between Jerusalem and Giv'on in the north, and between Jerusalem and the Etzion bloc in the south.

Pattern 6: Enforcement of Israeli Sovereignty over the Entire Region of Judea and Samaria.

If we accept the premise that the whole of Judea and Samaria remains under Israeli sovereignty, that the armistice line ceases to have any significance, and that the Jordan River is the only national boundary to the east (Figure 23), we can expect the following main phyiscal consequences in the area:

There would be intensive building of installations and of settlements along the Jordan Valley near the Jordanian frontier, and on the eastern slopes of the Samaria Mountains, in order to secure the area against the Arab states to the east.

The metropolitan area of Jerusalem would spread beyond the ring of rural settlements which encircle the city at a radius of 3–6 miles.

Arab building in Jerusalem would lessen, while Israeli building would increase, both in the city itself and in the outskirts.

Settlement in the Jerusalem Corridor would expand north- and southward. There would be a development of agricultural settlement between the former armistice line and the Bet Horon road to the north, and the Bet Govrin–Hebron road to the south.

New north–south and east–west traffic arteries would improve communications between Judea and Samaria and the State of Israel.

There would be an increase in the number of settlements in all parts of the region. New settlements would be established in the southern part of the Jordan Valley, the Etzion bloc on the Hafurit–Teqo'a axis would be extended, more settlements would be built in the Samaria Mountains, and the periphery of Jerusalem would be developed.

The Dead Sea littoral would benefit from greater investment in tourism and bathing-beach improvements. The nature reserves on the slopes of the Judean Mountains would be expanded and form part of the Dead Sea shore development.

Selected localities in the region would be the subject of intensive

FIGURE 23
IMPLEMENTATION OF AUTONOMY IN JUDEA AND SAMARIA, PATTERN 6

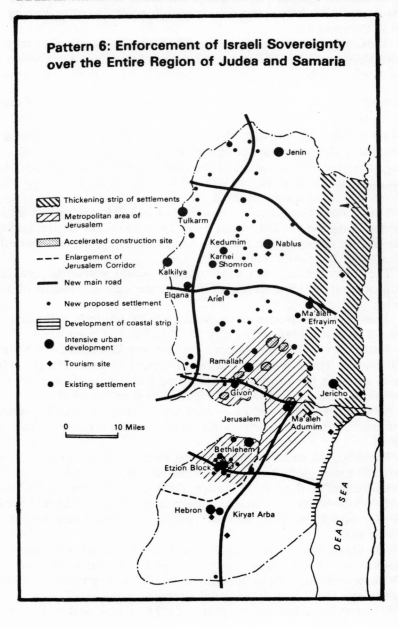

Pattern 6: Enforcement of Israeli Sovereignty over the Entire Region of Judea and Samaria

urban development, the most important among these being the Etzion bloc, Ma'ale Edumim, Giv'on, Ari'el, Qarne Shomron, and west Samaria opposite the Tel Aviv conurbation.

It is to be assumed that the new urban and rural settlements in the region would form a hierarchy distinct from that of the Arab sector. It would be based on Jerusalem as the primary town, on a system of medium-sized satellite towns, and on an additional system of medium-sized towns over all of Judea and Samaria.

There would be intensive development of tourist sites in Judea and Samaria, including archaeological and historical sites, parks, and nature reserves.

CONCLUSIONS: ADVANTAGES AND DISADVANTAGES IN THE CHOICE OF SPATIAL PATTERNS

The six patterns presented here offer political leaders various alternatives for the future of Judea and Samaria and exhibit four basic elements:

– the extent of Israeli spatial autonomy;
– the extent to which facts established in the past will be accepted;
– the possibility of increasing the Jewish population of the region;
– the status of Jerusalem.

It is clear that patterns 1 and 6 represent extreme and opposing situations, namely, either a return to the pre-1967 situation, in which Israel's spatial autonomy would be almost nonexistent, or full spatial control, in which Israel's autonomy would approach a maximum.

A more detailed examination of patterns 2–5 may, however, lead to other solutions which highlight other elements in various combinations within the spatial framework of autonomy. Readiness to accept moderate status for Jerusalem and to forgo all other options leads to pattern 2. Such a status for Jerusalem, combined with the possibility of a moderate population increase in the region, leads to pattern 3. A demand for limited spatial control over the Judea and Samaria region, combined with at least some measure of preserving the status quo and a moderate status and population increase in Jerusalem, leads to pattern 4. Finally, a large degree of spatial autonomy, maximizing population increase and strengthening Jerusalem, with less weight given to keeping the status quo, leads to pattern 5.

Due regard would in all cases need to be paid to the physical features such as agricultural areas, roads, settlements, interrelationship axes, water resources, and industrial areas.

Such an overall perspective of Judea and Samaria from a spatial point of view, examining the various alternatives, can aid decisionmaking regarding the implementation of autonomy and the establishment of a satisfactory mutual relationship between Jews and Arabs in this region.

CHAPTER NINE

The Golan Heights – From Conquest to Annexation

Israel was always sensitive in regard to the Golan Heights because Syria posed a threat to the settlements of the Hula Valley and Galilee below, and also because of the danger that the Syrians might divert the water of the Banias and prevent the flow of water to the Jordan, which is Israel's principal water source. The conquest of the Golan Heights in the Six Day War removed the Syrian threat and for the first time created a substantial distance between Israel's northern settlements and Syria. The strategic advantage gained through the conquest of the Golan Heights may explain the speed with which Israel took steps to settle the conquered region.

FIRST PLANS

After the Six Day War the various settlement institutions and bodies got together to work out a plan for the settlement of the Golan Heights. Kibbutzim of the HaKibbutz HaMeuchad movement, wishing to put their political views into practice, applied the 'faits accomplis' method in the region in order to force the hand of the government and the public, by accelerating settlement at Israel's northeastern border, thus obviating any possibility of withdrawal. Initial surveys were then conducted in regard to land, water, climate and infrastructure and a programme was prepared for populating, developing and founding a regional settlement complex to be integrated into the national settlement picture. The settlement was to be based on agriculture, as a means of occupying the land, a device which had proved effective in the past. In order to avoid creating an additional development area whose crops might compete with those raised in Israel, a study was made to discover profitable crops suited to the region. The northern part of the Golan Heights was found to be suitable for walnut trees, potatoes, sheep and cattle, the southern for field crops, subtropical and other fruits, and olives.

Because of the urgent necessity to settle people on the Golan Heights, not all the economic possibilities were examined. The priority was to settle population there even if the infrastructure was not yet ready for it. The proposal was to establish 17–22 settlements in the first ten years, among them a large urban centre. Some 20–25,000 people were expected to live in the rural settlements, and about 10,000 in the urban centre. The few Druze villages left in the region were to account for a further 10,000 people. The region was subdivided geographically, and it was decided that the rocky centre of the Golan Heights, which was hard to develop, would in the meantime remain vacant and constitute a reserve for industrial development. As the northern Golan Heights had most of the water sources but too little land, while the south had most of the land but few water sources, it was possible to base the economy of the northern part on intensive cultivation under irrigation, and in the south develop agriculture based on water from the north. In the end it was decided to work in the south, which had 15,000 acres of the 17,500 of cultivable land on the Golan Heights. In the south it was possible also to settle population quite rapidly without investing too much in the infrastructure. The townlet of Quneitra was considered the urban centre of the subregion. Tourism was proposed as a profitable supplement for the settlements, since the relatively small area was rich in extreme geographical contrasts, ranging from snow-covered Mount Hermon in the north to the shores of Lake Kinneret and the springs of Hamat Gader in the south.

A later plan, made in January 1969, was based on 50,000 people living there within ten years – 20,000 people in the rural villages and 30,000 in the town, which would be both a tourist and an industrial centre. The alignment of settlements according to this plan was along the main Golan Heights north–south axis with no more than three to six miles between settlements. The plan favoured the kibbutz and moshav form, with the outermost line three to six miles from the Syrian border.

STRUCTURE OF THE SETTLEMENT

Until 1973, priority was given to settlement in two subregions, the southern Golan Heights and the Quneitra area. Planning the settlement was quite difficult because on the one hand the area had strategic importance and had to be settled, and on the other it could add very little to the Israeli economy in view of the needed investment in infrastructure. The inability to populate the centre of the region was likewise a disadvantage; not much could be done with uncultivable land.

During the first years after the Six Day War, 11 agricultural settlements were established on the Golan Heights, some of them by 'Nahal' units; the settlers were young people from kibbutzim and moshavim who were given new tracts of land to cultivate. To begin with the settlement had a rather temporary character because there was litle confidence regarding the future of the region. The government was being politically cautious, hesitant in regard to chances of success, and had only minimal impact on happenings on the Golan Heights. However, by 1973 the population had gradually consolidated, and later it became more varied, as newcomers from different countries settled there, and some of the 'Nahal' settlements were demilitarized. In the course of the settlement endeavour the principle of location along the border came to be adopted. It was then that a start was made in establishing blocs of three or four settlements with six to 12 miles between the blocs. Most were in the south, fewer in the north, with a gap in the centre.

The population of the Golan Heights is located in five main blocs. The southern kibbutz bloc consists of Mevo Hama, Kefar Haruv, Afiq and Geshur. The Bene Yehuda bloc comprises five settlements: the three moshavim Ramot, Givat Yo'av and Eli'ad, the cooperative moshav Ne'ot Golan, and the regional centre Bene Yehuda. The Hispin bloc includes three cooperative moshavim: Ramat Magshimim, Nov and Hispin. The bloc in the Quneitra area includes three kibbutzim: Merom Golan, En Zivan and El Rom, all in the HaKibbutz HaMeuchad federation. The Druze bloc is composed of four villages – Majdal Shams, Buqa'ta, Masada and Ein Qinya – and the cooperative moshav of Neve Ativ. A new bloc of two moshavim has been planned for the vicinity of Mount Odem (Figure 24).

In regard to the geographical distribution of settlement types on the Golan Heights, those moshavim which are based on family labour require a lot of land near the homes, and consequently most of them are located in the south. Kibbutzim and cooperative moshavim, which are more flexible regarding distance from their fields, and can cultivate scattered areas, were established mainly in the north. After most of the areas suitable for agriculture had been used, the cost of land preparation and irrigation increased, and this has left the centre of the Golan Heights relatively empty.

FIGURE 24
SETTLEMENT IN THE GOLAN HEIGHTS

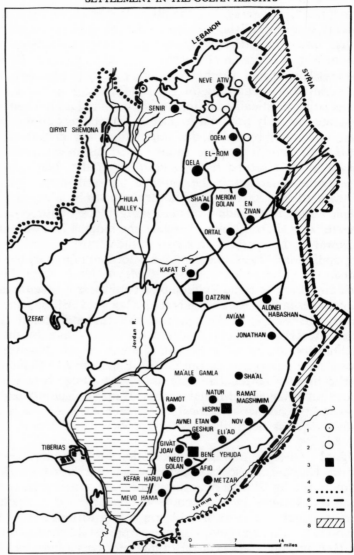

Key:
1. Ilawy Village
2. Druze villages
3. Post-1967 urban settlements
4. Post-1967 Israeli settlements
5. Boundary
6. Israeli frontier since 1974
7. Syrian frontier since 1974
8. Demilitarized Zone

THE ECONOMY OF THE GOLAN HEIGHTS

In the first phase of settlement the aim was to occupy the agricultural land. The 15,000 acres suitable for cultivation quickly passed into Jewish hands. At that time considerable funds were invested in experimental orchards. There were also investments in unquestionably profitable agricultural branches such as apple orchards and poultry, so as not to endanger the economy of the settlements. By 1974 13,250 acres in the north and south were under cultivation, providing for the livelihood of 13 settlements. About two-thirds of this total was not irrigated. The areas of natural pasturage of 75,000 acres were reserved for raising cattle and sheep. In the south the stress was on field crops, pasturage, and subtropical fruit, particularly on the relatively warm slopes facing Lake Kinneret. While the northern Golan Heights have more rainfall, the sources of water for irrigation are more limited, which restricted the agricultural development there. The south, which had always been recognized as the granary, now acquired an agricultural character similar to the other parts of Galilee.

The agricultural base of the Golan Heights did not allow for more than 2,500 residents. In order to achieve the quota of 50,000, it was necessary to develop other branches, in particular tourism and industry. The establishment of Neve Ativ based on winter tourism, and an industrial plant at Bene Yehuda, are examples of the attempt to diversify the employment possibilities of the inhabitants. Then two settlement blocs, each with residents having similar backgrounds, began to develop the location of each bloc determined by strategic and regional considerations.

EFFECT OF THE YOM KIPPUR WAR ON SETTLEMENT

The Yom Kippur War caused great destruction on the Golan and cast doubt on the economic development capacity of the region. Some of the settlements were abandoned, and the defence status of the Golan Heights as a border region was considerably reduced. The Israeli government's conclusion from the war was that the Golan Heights needed to be better fortified. It believed that despite what had happened civilian settlement was the best solution for security problems, and revealed great sensitivity regarding the centre of the Heights, which remained vulnerable, bare. When the Likud rose to power in 1977, the settlement of the Golan Heights centre became an urgent priority, the goal being to close the 17-mile gap between Ramat Magshimim in the south and En Zivan in the north. Despite pressure by the US and Arab countries, the settlement of the Golan Heights advanced considerably. Between 1973 and 1975 priorities changed and the main effort was moved from the south to the Quneitra area. During the war the Syrians had pushed through to the heart of the Heights where there were no settlements. Consequently the Golan Heights centre was now settled in three sectors: a forward line of semi-rural settlements opposite Quneitra, two additional settlements in the south, and one more in the north between Quneitra and Mount Hermon. In 1974–7 it was decided that in the empty spaces of the central Golan Heights, amounting to 160 sq. miles, industrial villages and an urban centre should be established. The villages organized like cooperative moshavim, were to have touristic, service and industrial functions, and plants employing between 30 and 100 people were planned for them. It is quite possible that had it not been for the unfavourable outcome of the Yom Kippur War, this settlement endeavour in the central Golan Heights would never have been initiated; the planning was done under the pressure of the geopolitical situation of the Golan Heights.

In 1975 a broader settlement endeavour was decided on comprising four settlements combining agriculture and industry, four industrial villages each of 4,500 inhabitants, and a town. Since at the time doubts arose as to the effectiveness of civilian agricultural settlements in regional defence, it was decided to fortify the settlements opposite enemy lines and turn them into buffers if necessary. When the Golan Heights settlement began to be designed as a security and strategic buffer, resources started streaming into the region, and the population developed an increasingly adamant objection to any territorial compromise there. Accordingly the settlements opposite the Syrian border were strengthened, and the kibbutzim and cooperative moshavim were seen as the most important elements in a line of defence. It is hard to judge whether increased population will facilitate freer manoeuvring by the army in case of an attack, and hard to estimate the optimum population size for the maintenance of security on the Golan Heights. The Yom Kippur War was certainly a critical turning point with regard to the development of the region, particularly of its centre.

THE GEOPOLITICAL BACKGROUND FOR THE SETTLEMENT OF THE CENTRAL GOLAN HEIGHTS

The debate that developed after the Yom Kippur War in the international and domestic arena regarding the settlement of the Golan Heights contributed to a certain delay in the settlement process. The United States wanted long-term security arrangements between Israel and Syria even at the cost of a partial Israeli withdrawal from the Golan Heights. Its main interest was the stabilization of its position in the Middle East in the wake of the oil crisis. Opposing it were forces in Israel demanding immediate, accelerated settlement. Even among Alignment leaders there was serious concern about Syria, which led them to reinforce the security settlement on the Golan Heights as a buffer between Israel and Syria, while the Likud, then the parliamentary opposition, took a more extreme position, objecting to giving up any territory at all. As the Alignment weakened, groups in the country began to be critical of US intervention and of the government's timidity. The Golan Settlements Association, together with the Gush Emunim group, grew stronger through publicity and propaganda, and tipped the scale in favour of an uncompromising stand on the Golan Heights, compelling the government to expand the settlements and establish the Golan Heights town. They were also given permission to cultivate lands beyond the border recognized till 1973.

Heavy pressure exerted by the United States, European countries and others influenced by the OPEC countries somewhat restrained Israel's expansionist aspirations. Israel's policy was to remain within the pre-1973 borders with a slight rearrangement near Quneitra, but withdrawal or the destruction of settlements would have aroused strong opposition and led to the fall of the government. Meanwhile Syria had not emerged from the war strengthened enough to demand Israel's withdrawal from the Golan Heights. In that geopolitical situation, the settlements in the eastern part of the Heights constituted a reasonable borderline. Demonstrations in support of the Golan Heights persuaded the government to make no concessions. This was one of the first times that the government used public opinion, including demonstrations in support of the Golan Heights, as a support of their political stance. The Settlement Committee was given a great deal of encouragement by religious and nationalistic groups, so that for the first time a link was established between the Golan Heights and the territorial problems involving Judea–Samaria. Centres of political activity which developed in Merom HaGolan on the one hand and the Etzion bloc on the other gained public support and prevented, among other things, a partial withdrawal from the Golan Heights. Responding to the threat of the possible evacuation of Quneitra, the Merom HaGolan people seized land in the vicinity and even prepared houses in Quneitra for habitation. In the bargaining on Quneitra, Merom HaGolan and En Zivan, the existence of agricultural settlements and cultivated land was an important element. A group called Qeshet attempted to settle in Quneitra, believing they would be included in the HaKibbutz HaMeuchad settlement endeavour along with El Rom, Merom HaGolan and En Zivan, but were not supported by that kibbutz federation's secretariat. The temporary settlement of Qeshet then became a symbol of the opposition to negotiations on withdrawal from the Golan Heights. The eventual agreement between Israel and Syria turned Quneitra over to the Syrians but left its western suburbs and the surrounding hills in Israeli hands. Later the Qeshet group obtained permission to settle in the Hushaniya camp in the central Golan Heights. The settlement of that area did not arouse much enthusiasm in the Alignment ministers, some of whom felt that the establishment of a town on the Golan Heights was dangerous; setting up small settlements as bargaining points in the future was, they felt, easier than founding a town likely to have 20,000–30,000 inhabitants. The commitment in establishing and defending a city is very great (this was before the sad experience of the town of Yamit). Abraham Ofer, then minister of housing, made little haste in advancing the construction of the town; he conducted exhaustive negotiations with the Golan Heights Settlement Committee, postponing as long as possible the establishment of the town – it was hard to get him to implement a project he opposed. A town on the Golan Heights was also objected to by Israeli groups who were interested rather in the advancement of development towns or older towns like Safed and Tiberias. It was obvious that if investments were to be transferred to the Golan Heights town, the share of the Galilee towns would be reduced. The government was extremely cautious regarding any decision on the matter, especially in view of Washington's sensitivity on the subject. However, a terrorist operation in the southern Golan Heights at the end of 1975, and Syrian support of PLO policy as presented at the UN, led to stronger public pressure on the government and the adoption of a hard line on the Golan Heights town. In 1976 the minister of housing could no longer hold out, and more energetic activity in establishing the town was begun. It was to be called Qatzrin, and to have an area of 625 acres and 5,000 housing units to accommodate a population of about 30,000.

Qatzrin was just the first stage in filling the empty space in the centre of the Golan Heights. The Golan Settlements Committee demanded the establishment of five more settlements. In order to hasten a decision on the matter, Gush Emunim set up the village of Yonatan near the Syrian border. The government was reluctant to clash with Gush Emunim and took no steps to remove the settlement which had the backing of the ministry of defence. The non-removal of that settlement operated as pressure on the government, and it was decided to set up four settlements in the Golan Heights central zone. Qeshet and Yonatan were legitimized as were, early in 1976, the moshav Ma'ale Gamla and the cooperative moshav Sha'al. As US pressure on Israel lessened due to the election campaign, and objections from within Israel diminished, early in 1976 settlement on the Golan Heights swung into higher gear.

NEW DEVELOPMENT DIRECTIONS AFTER 1977

As development accelerated on the Golan Heights roads, water pipelines, electricity and sewage facilities were added. The Syrian facilities that remained were quite superficial and mainly positioned north to south, with only one lateral axis linking the Benot Ya'aqov Bridge with Quneitra. Now four east–west roads were added and a more secure longitudinal road farther away from the cease-fire line. Also, the road to Mount Hermon was paved.

Water consumption on the Golan Heights was planned at 16 million cu. m. a year, 1 per cent of Israel's total consumption. The Golan sources provide only 7 million cu. m., and the rest had to come from Israel, that is, from Lake Kinneret. Two systems were constructed, one to the south of the Heights, and the other to the north. As the number of settlements and cultivated areas increased, so did dependence on Israel's water. When development was undertaken in the central part, it was necessary to take water from both the northern and southern facilities.

Between 1977 and 1987 the population of the Golan Heights rose from 2,200 to 6,500, and the number of settlements reached 31: the settlement of Senir, in the centre, the three community-type settlements of Qela, Ani'am, and Kafat B, the kibbutz Ortal and the moshav Odem; and in the south the two kibbutzim Natur and Metzar and the moshav Avne Eitan. The goal was to establish five industrial villages in the central Golan Heights plus four villages combining agriculture and industry. Qatzrin was developed and populated rapidly and soon became the largest concentration of population on the Heights, with an economy based on light industry. It is still questionable whether Qatzrin will be able to attract more people and reach the 50,000 quota planned, since at present it has only 1,500 inhabitants. In 1981 the government decided to extend Israeli law to the Golan Heights, a unilateral step in respect of Syria and other countries, and a step implying territorial annexation which makes any likelihood of negotiations regarding its future status doubtful.

The residents of the Golan Heights placed great hopes on the extension of Israeli law to their region, believing that such a step would provide the impetus for its accelerated development. But they proved to be mistaken. An absurd situation ensued, in which after confirmation in December 1981 of the law, which aroused dissatisfaction and anger throughout the world, the pace of development slowed. In 20 years 31 settlements have been established – 11 kibbutzim, ten moshavim, five cooperative moshavim, two urban centres, two Nahal establishments, and one town, Qatzrin. Only 6,500 Jews live in the settlements – about half the number of Druze in the area – and another 1,500 in the town.

Obviously, Jewish settlement on the Golan Heights is still very sparse. Between 1982 and 1984 the accelerated development ceased, and the establishment of new localities has almost stopped. There is also a growing tendency among the settlers to abandon agriculture and seek other channels for investment, particularly in recreation and tourism, in hopes that they will be more profitable. It was decided to give priority to industry and recreation and forgo further agricultural development. In February 1982 the Settlement Department of the Jewish Agency together with the Golan Settlements Committee published a plan for the accelerated development of the Golan Heights. The plan envisages an additional 20,000 people within five years through the expansion of industry, tourism, agriculture, regional enterprises and housing. This addition would presumably result in a more balanced distribution of population in the northern part of the country and make possible the provision of services of a high standard meeting the expectations of the Golan Heights residents.

However, the town of Qatzrin, for instance, which was most carefully planned, is having difficulty meeting the great demand of families that wish to settle there, for it has a serious employment problem. The fine plans for industrial enterprises and increased population in Qatzrin have remained in the realm of dreams, as have many other plans relating to the rural settlements in the region.

From the geopolitical viewpoint the Golan Heights is an arena in which events are characterizable as follows: conquest for the purpose of accelerated security settlement and defence; pressure for land for settlements with political motives and for cultivation; regional planning in order to integrate into the existing settlement complex in Galilee; development of agricultural branches that do not compete with those within the 'Green Line'; gradual settlement while learning the physical properties of the region; taking the relatively easy path and giving the southern part of the Heights priority; setting quite exaggerated population goals in a region of strategic importance; organizing settlement along lines paralleling the Syrian border, and in blocs; intensification in developing and populating the region as a result of the shock of the Yom Kippur War; initial hesitation about continued settlement and later succumbing to public pressure to the point of extending Israeli law to the Golan Heights. All in all, the Golan Heights is far from the goals set by the planners, and it appears that natural conditions on the one hand, and the development priority accorded Judea–Samaria on the other, have blocked its further progress.

CHAPTER TEN

The Sinai Peninsula – From Conquest to Withdrawal

One of the more unusual political developments in Israel was the Israeli military deployment and civilian settlement in Sinai, the establishment of the Yamit region, its enforced abandonment, the scattering of its settlers throughout the entire country, and the establishment of the Shalom region. What seems to have been involved here was a combination of political steps against a desert geographical background, with little basis in reality even at the outset. It produced one of the most serious settlement traumas ever experienced in Israel, in which an entire development region was removed, and utterly destroyed, so that the inhabitants were obliged to decide on their future, either in resettlement in the substitute Shalom region, or in urban or rural settlements within the 'Green Line'.

Let us analyse the settlement geography of the site where events in 1981 shocked the entire country.

THE SINAI PENINSULA

The tragedy of the forced evacuation of the Sinai peninsula acquired extraordinarily large dimensions at the time, and was reported continuously in the communications media. Descriptions of incidents in the Yamit region and Ofira abounded in terms such as 'irreparable blow', 'ruin', 'trauma', and even 'holocaust'. Despite the sorrow and pain of those uprooted, the events should be considered in proper proportion and viewed against the background of Israel's settlements situation.

The Sinai peninsula is a desert triangle with an area of 23,622 sq. miles, an extension of the great Sahara Desert. Accordingly, its climate is difficult, its mineral deposits scanty, its summer temperatures extremely high, its water resources meagre, its cultivable land almost non-existent, its traversability onerous; human habitation is possible mainly on narrow coastal strips on the north and west, and at a number of oases. The peninsula was never densely populated, and for many years its population amounted to only a few thousand residents of villages and townlets, plus nomads. In 1967 there were 33,000 people in the peninsula, most of them in the town of el-Arish, and the rest scattered through the desert. Aside from that town, not a single large settlement or concentration of population developed in Sinai. The continuous settlement along the southern coastal plain of the Land of Israel stopped at Rafah, and that in the Arava region at the north end of the Gulf of Elat, never actually penetrating the peninsula. The desert blocked settlement from all directions, and made it difficult for anyone coveting the area for settlement.

It is thus evident that the geographical conditions of a desert are quite dominant, and to the extent that they do not offer level topography, water sources, arable land and economic natural resources are not hospitable to man. Wild landscapes, marvellous natural sights, rolling sands, hidden inlets with mangroves and tropical animals will attract the hiker, the naturalist, the tourist, but not the permanent settler, especially not one from the developed and sophisticated civilization of the West, which requires a complex system of services that no desert can provide.

Anyone settling in such a desert must be aware that he will be in a border area with the following geographical characteristics: settlements at separate points with no guarantee of settlement continuity, difficult climatic conditions, remoteness from the centre of the country, isolation, sparsity of population, and political and security instability. He must also bear in mind that border settlement is no guarantee of continued presence, is subject to regional changes, requires mobility, and is likely to be faced with surprises generated by nature and man. A person deciding to settle in a border region beyond the sovereign territory of his country must realize that his risks are multiplied and the factor of uncertainty in his deeds is so great that it is tantamount to gambling. That is not the case, of course, when an army carries out political and security actions, for its characteristics are ability to control, rapid mobility, the creation of a holding depth with minimum manpower, and its logic in advancing or retreating does not derive from sentiment or love of country, but from orders. Civilian settlers undertaking political and security tasks through extra-sovereign border settlement are likely to be subject to changing political forces, while lacking the ability to overcome the new situation physically, technically or psychologically, especially since their 'possessions' – which include families, property, investment, and sources of livelihood – may totally determine the course of their life.

Most of the desert border regions of the world are not marked by large permanent populations. There is no prosperous border settlement along the edges of the deserts of western and southern Australia, nor the desert of Patagonia in southern Argentina, nor the deserts in Nevada and Arizona in the United States, and certainly not near the Atlas mountains or the Kalahari desert in Africa. Some success can be found in border regions based on permanent, promising natural resources, within the territory of the countries hoping to exploit them. Fairbanks in central Alaska, Arica north of the Atacama desert in Chile, the oil and gas towns in the Canadian province of Alberta, and even the towns along the trans-Siberian railway to Vladivostok on the Pacific are perhaps examples of settlements and areas playing economic and political roles in defined, sovereign territories. But there is no instance in the world in which a country has developed civilian border settlement outside its sovereign borders, on an area more than triple its own, as Israel did in Sinai. In such a case, in order to consolidate its hold on the peninsula, Israel should have settled there at least 600,000 people, in an average density of 25 per sq. mile, the norm for such arid deserts. To settle a few thousand people, with an average population density of 0.4 per sq. mile, in a non-sovereign desert region, scattered in no geographical continuity, as was done, was an act of delusion, devoid of spatial sense both geographically and economically.

UNNECESSARY INVESTMENT AND VAIN ENDEAVOURS

The construction and development experiments at Yamit, Ofira, Nevi'ot and Di-Zahav were extremely interesting and there is no belittling the development accomplishments there. Despite the absence of any political and sovereign basis for the settlement, a great deal of capital and knowledge was invested. While in border regions elsewhere in the world constructions were light and could quickly be dismantled at minimal cost, in the Sinai settlements the planning and construction was far more modern, superior even to those in the development towns within the 'Green Line', both in architecture and in the service infrastructure. There is no doubt that the enormous investment in such a style enhanced the delusion of stability felt by the settlers on the edge of the desert.

Civilian settlement in Sinai did not make the slightest change in

Israel's settlement picture and had no connection with it. The Sinai settlement did not extend any existing continuum and did not in fact complete anything. Its only effect on Israeli settlement was to deprive it of billions of dollars which could have completed and strengthened it. It should be kept in mind that for the previous 30 years the settlement of the Negev, in the south of Israel, had been neglected. Since 1964, only four new kibbutzim had been established there, and since 1961 only six moshavim. Constituting half of the country's territory, the Negev holds only a tenth of its population, more than half of whom live in Beersheba and the surrounding townlets. While the Negev townlets were suffering from a negative emigration balance, the Besor district opposite the Gaza Strip was static, the central Negev height remained desolate, the Arava region was eager for additional settlements, and Elat became a transfer point for travellers to Sinai, enormous sums were being invested in the limited agricultural and urban sector of Sinai, the Negev expanses were disregarded, and the dream of developing them abandoned.

In the wake of the peace agreement with Egypt and the removal of the territorial military threat, the Israel Defence Forces withdrew in a gradual, planned, efficient manner, in almost total silence, adopting new strategic positions, while the civilian sector continued to be a problem, preoccupying the country and forcing it to assume a heavy financial burden. It was suddenly realized that the geographical anomaly which had been created was extremely costly.

For a small population in the great expanse of Sinai to attempt to create a new security, political, and geographical reality was unreasonable to begin with and devoid of any possibility of survival for any length of time. It is, therefore, no wonder that that settlement complex was compelled to disappear in the course of one political change in the region.

THE EVACUATION OF THE YAMIT REGION

The abandonment of a settlement area in circumstances other than war was then a new phenomenon in Israel. The decision of the government, in the wake of the peace agreement with Egypt, to evacuate the Yamit region was the first instance of the return of a settled area, which included 15 rural settlements and one large town in which tremendous sums had been invested, and the evacuation of several thousand people from it.

The settlement of the Yamit region after the Six Day War was viewed as a political necessity deriving from the principle that territory is acquired by settling it, which ensures control of strategic places and at a later stage also sovereignty. This approach led in 1969 to the establishment of Diqla, in 1970 of Nahal Sinai and in 1971 of Sadot, all before a comprehensive plan for the settlement of northern Sinai had been evolved. Later, following further investigation of the geographical conditions of the region and its potential, and in view of the capacity to apply advanced agro-technical methods in desert territory, an ideological programme called 'The Southern Endeavour' was formulated, and the Yamit region was part of it.

The settlement of the Yamit district embodied two themes, the geographical political one and the economic agricultural. The geopolitical aim was to spread settlement as densely as possible as a continuation of the Eshkol district, in order to establish a separation between the Gaza Strip and the Sinai desert, which under peaceful conditions would make possible supervision of the movement of Arab inhabitants between the Gaza Strip and Egypt. The economic agricultural goal was to raise quality crops by sophisticated methods, exploiting the fine climatic advantages of the region (Figure 25).

The plan envisages a settlement with an extensive spread for the Yamit district, from the Eshkol region on the east to Nahal Sinai on the west, some 12.5 miles. About 50 to 60 agricultural settlements were planned, to be based on the raising of vegetables and flowers for export in greenhouses, a method possible due to the strong sunlight in northern Sinai most days of the year, the temperate climate, the absence of frost, and the availability of sandy soil suitable for the purpose. The type of pioneers who chose to settle in the region also favoured sophisticated agricultural experiments of that kind.

The region was designed as a hierarchical model around the central town of Yamit, where educational and cultural institutions, services and commercial facilities of a high threshold sales level were concentrated. While the purpose of the district was geopolitical, it was intended to ensure a high quality of life for its population. The town of Yamit was set on the seashore with the potential of developing as a port and as a resort.

Two blocs of settlements were established in the region. The one east of the town of Yamit included Pri'el, Talme Yosef, Netiv Ha-Asara, Ugda, Nir Avraham, Prigan, Sadot, Diqla, and the bloc centre Avshalom, while the bloc south of the town included Atzmona, Tarsag, and Ne'ot Sinai.

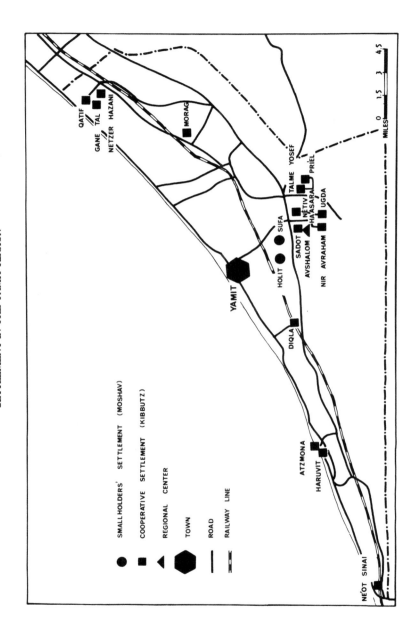

FIGURE 25
SETTLEMENT IN THE YAMIT REGION

By the time of the 1982 evacuation, the town of Yamit had 3,000 residents and the rural sector of the region a further 2,000. The decision to evacuate the Yamit region led to a hitherto unknown manifestation, the geography of withdrawal, characterized by the need for people and settlements to relocate, either in the neighbourhood or in other parts of the country. Numerous problems arose. What was the new dispersion of settlements to be? Was there a clear policy in regard to the nature of the dispersion? Was the district as a whole relocated to a new place? How would the withdrawal from the Yamit region affect nearby urban and agricultural settlements?

THE NEW LOCATION OF THE YAMIT REGION POPULATION

An investigation of 708 (70 per cent) of the 1,023 families in the Yamit region – 334 out of 437 agricultural families and 374 out of 586 urban families – resulted in some quite interesting findings.

The dispersion of the Yamit region population was found to be in concentric circles, whose absorption of the evacuated residents diminished with their distance from the Yamit region. A large proportion of the evacuees settled in the southern district, especially in the first three dispersion circles, which account for 423 out of the 708 families (60 per cent)(Figure 26). Most relocated in new villages or in the existing development towns. The surprising thing is that the fourth circle, which includes the greater Tel Aviv metropolitan area, reabsorbed most of its residents – 221 families – as evidently most came from there and returned to their original places. The circles of the northern part of the country did not reabsorb all the people who had left them to go south. Thus most of the population gain of the southern district came from the north and centre. An examination of the areas in the south according to the percentage of Yamit evacuees they absorbed shows that Beersheba received 9 per cent (65 families), Ashdod, Ashqelon and Mizpe Ramon together 6.6 per cent (49 families), making 15.6 per cent (114 families) in all for the southern cities. Jerusalem welcomed 5 per cent (36 families). A considerable number of the evacuees ended up in the substitute settlements of Netiv Ha-Asara, En Ha-Besor, Sufa, Deqel and Prigan.

The urban population from Yamit is more widely dispersed than the agricultural population. It settled mainly in the fourth circle between Tel Aviv and Jerusalem, where 50 per cent of the evacuees were absorbed. The southern district in the first three circles received 41.4 per cent of the families (155 out of 374); the northern district, in circles six and seven, received only 2.6 per cent (10 out of 374) (Figure 27).

FIGURE 26

NEW RELOCATION CIRCLES OF THE YAMIT REGION RESIDENTS
(IN FAMILIES) (BY NUMBER OF FAMILIES)

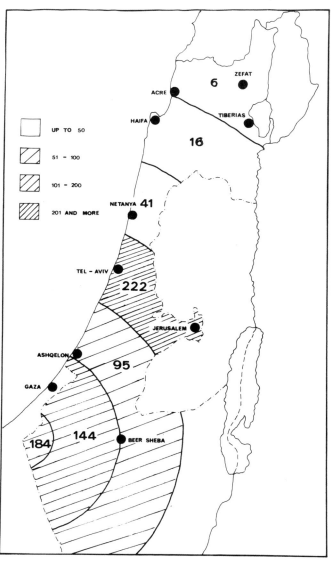

FIGURE 27
NEW RELOCATION CIRCLES OF THE YAMIT TOWNSPEOPLE
(BY NUMBER OF FAMILIES)

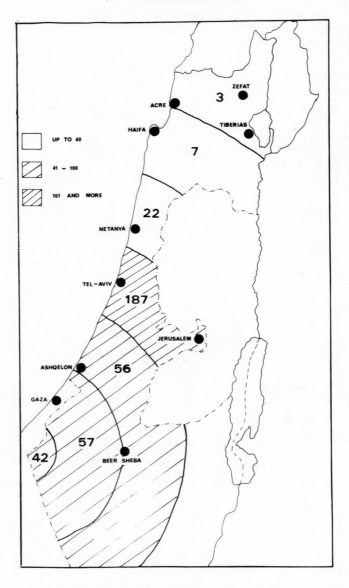

PROVENANCE AND RETURN OF EVACUEES FROM THE
TOWN OF YAMIT

A comparison of the original residential area of the Yamit townspeople with the places they settled in after evacuation is shown in
Table 4. It can be seen that the north lost more population than the
centre, and the south gained population from both. Table 5
compares the provenance and relocation of Yamit evacuees
according to type of settlement. The findings show that the rural
sector gained 14 per cent at the expense of the urban, while
development towns maintained a balance. The moshavim established to replace the Yamit region villages absorbed the larger
proportion of the evacuees.

TABLE 4

PROVENANCE AND RESETTLEMENT OF YAMIT TOWNSPEOPLE
ACCORDING TO DISPERSION CIRCLES (in %)

Circle	Provenance	Resettlement	Population Gain or Loss
1	0.36	11.28	
2	17.64	15.24	
3	10.66	15.00	
Total South	28.66	41.52	12.9% gain
4	57.35	50.00	
5	1.10	5.90	
Total Centre	58.45	55.90	2.5% loss
6	11.40	1.87	
7	1.47	0.80	
Total North	12.87	2.67	10.2% loss

TABLE 5

PROVENANCE AND RELOCATION OF YAMIT RESIDENTS
ACCORDING TO SETTLEMENT TYPE (in %)

	Urban Settlements	Development Towns	Moshavim	Kibbutzim
Provenance	88	8	2	
Relocation	74	8.8	16.6	0.9

TABLE 6
PROVENANCE AND RELOCATION OF YAMIT TOWNSPEOPLE
ACCORDING TO URBAN SETTLEMENTS (in %)

Town	Provenance	Relocation	Town	Provenance	Relocation
Beersheba	15.8	13.6	Rehovot	4.4	1.1
Jerusalem	8.8	7.7	Ramat Gan	2.6	0.5
Rishon Le Ziyyon	7.3	8.2	Haifa	2.6	0.5
Petah Tiqva	6.6	1.3	Ashdod	1.8	2.7
Qerayot	7.0	0.8	Kefar Sava	1.1	5.0
Holon	6.2	2.1	Ra'anana	1.1	2.1
Tel Aviv	5.9	3.5	Hod Hasharon	0.3	2.1
Ashqelon	4.0	5.6			

A comparison of provenance and relocation according to urban settlements appears in Table 6, whose findings show a tendency to return to the original town. It should be noted that the addresses the evacuees returned to were in better neighbourhoods than those they left, an improvement made possible by the compensation they received upon evacuation. In Rehovot there was a preference for the Havatzelet quarter, in Beersheba for Omer, in Ashqelon for Barne'a and Afridar; others went to detached home zones in Kefar Sava, Ra'anana, Hod Hasharon and Caesarea. Another feature is that many families decided to relocate in the vicinity of others, apparently the result of good neighbourly relations in Yamit.

The more scattered relocation of the evacuated Yamit towns-people was caused, among other things, by the fact that no urban replacement was established. While agricultural settlement could be organized quickly and efficiently if land was available, the founding of a town is a more complicated matter requiring a long time. Furthermore, the establishment of an additional town not far from those already existing in the western Negev would have reduced its chances of development. Nor was it possible to find a coastal location for a town that would provide space for a port, for resort facilities, and tourism. It must however be noted that most Yamit residents had urban mentalities, and would perhaps have been prepared to adjust to a new town on the sands of Halutza, for instance, as the fact of their social integration in a moshav such as Deqel seems to indicate.

SUBSTITUTE AGRICULTURAL SETTLEMENT IN THE SHALOM
REGION

The establishment of the Shalom region is on the one hand a
substitute for the Yamit region and on the other a continuation of
the settlement endeavour in the western Negev initiated in the
1940s. The borders of the Shalom region are the Gaza Strip, the
international border with Egypt and the sands of Halutza. Its
geographical features are very similar to those of the Yamit region.
The soil is sandy, and arable after irrigation. Its conditions allow for
intensive cultivation almost uninterrupted. As the rainfall in the
region is small, agriculture requires continual irrigation throughout
the year, so that it will be necessary to seek innovative sources of
water, such as desalinated water or drainage water.

By government decision, in June 1980 eight moshavim and two
kibbutzim, one near the Magen intersection and the other near the
Ziqim intersection, were started in the Shalom region. To date, the
two kibbutzim, Sufa and Holit, have been built, and six moshavim:
Prigan, Deqel and Talme Yosef for the Yamit region evacuees, and
Yated, Yesod Ha-Darom and Yevul for settlers who had intended
to make their homes in the Yamit region and had not managed to. In
addition En Ha-Besor, near the Magen intersection, was set up for
the evacuees, and Netiv Ha-Asara on the Ziqim sands for evacuees
from Netiv Ha-Asara at Yamit. In the first stage 40 houses were built
at each moshav, and in the region as a whole 250 acres of orchards,
vineyards and mango were planted. By the mid-1980s the Shalom
region was expected to include 20 settlements comprising 1,200
farm units.

Attempts were made in the region to raise vegetables under glass
so as to supply the market during the winter. The 'Southern
Endeavour' project has been operating since 1975, aiming at the
establishment of a large number of settlements raising luxury
agricultural products for export. In 1976 it was decided to develop
the region on a combined agro-technical basis supported by
research and physical planning. In 1978 the development of the
Shalom region as a substitute for the Yamit region was first mooted.
Settlement throughout the region was to be based on farm units of 5
acres under irrigation, half an acre in greenhouses, and 2.5 of
orchard with a quota of 10,000 cub.m. of water per annum. In 1979 a
team organized to implement the removal of the Yamit region to the
Shalom region, should such a political decision be taken (Figure 28).

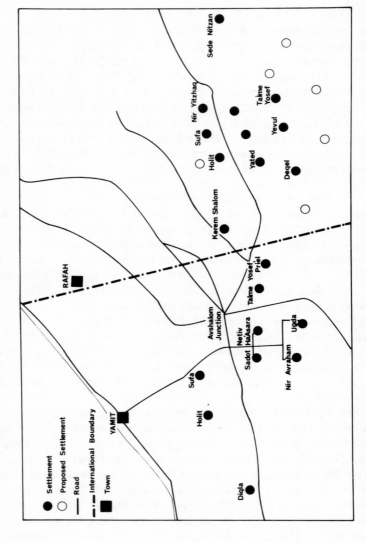

FIGURE 28
SETTLEMENT OF SHALOM REGION COMPARED WITH YAMIT REGION SETTLEMENT

When the evacuation was decided on, the agricultural settlements were offered a substitute in a region very similar to the Yamit area; the new settlements built in the Shalom region were based on the same sources of livelihood and are a kind of copy of what existed on the other side of the border. The Shalom region absorbed 231 of the 437 agricultural families from Yamit, and this can be viewed as some success.

TABLE 7
PROVENANCE IN YAMIT REGION AND RELOCATION IN SHALOM
REGION OF AGRICULTURAL FAMILIES

Yamit Settlement	No. of Families in 1979	No. of Families Followed Up	Relocated in Shalom Region	Remarks
Neot Sinai	21	–	–	Broke up before evacuation
Diqla	39	39	9	Before settlement, failed socially
Sadot	67	64	31	Social and economic success
Netiv Ha-Asara	58	55	38	
Ugda	52	46	20	
Nir Avraham	41	40	4	
Sufa	30	30	30	
Holit	26	12	12	Some left before the evacuation
Tarsag	28	–	–	
Talme Yosef	27	27	19	
Pri'el	28	28	8	
Prigan	20	20	20	
Total:	437	361	191 + 40 at Deqel = 231	

Table 7 shows the provenance in the Yamit region and relocation in the Shalom region of the 231 families. It can be seen that the substitute settlements quite successfully absorbed 231 families, amounting to 53 per cent of the agricultural families in the evacuated region, or 44 per cent if we subtract Deqel, which absorbed families from the town of Yamit. It should also be kept in mind that half of them, 123 families, joined two moshavim outside the Shalom region, En Ha-Besor and Netiv Ha-Asara. The success of the substitution project, now including two kibbutzim and three moshavim, and accounting for 108 families (about a quarter of the evacuees), must be viewed with a measure of scepticism. The region also contains three moshavim settled by groups who had planned to move to the Yamit region (240 families). If we compare the number of Yamit region evacuees in the Shalom region in 1981 (about 240 families) with the number of agricultural families in the Yamit region in 1979 (437) together with the number designed to be settled in the Shalom region by 1983 (990 families in 20 settlements), the success is even less impressive. The Shalom region has attained only half the agricultural population the Yamit region had in 1979. It enjoyed a great spurt after the Yamit evacuation, but there has been little progress since then. It should be borne in mind as well that some Yamit region residents relocated in agricultural settlements in the southern part of the country: 15 families in the Mivtahim bloc, ten in Ofaqim, four in Sadot, and 27 in the Ashdod–Qiryat Gat–Ashqelon triangle. The total number of agricultural families relocated in southern agricultural settlements is 287, including those in Deqel, and they amount to 86 per cent of all the agricultural families evacuated from the Yamit region. It may therefore be concluded that the evacuation of the Yamit region accelerated the settlement of the south, particularly the western edges of the Negev, a region whose development was arrested 25 years ago. It thus appears that the settlement of the Yamit region was quite artificial and arbitrary with geopolitical purposes, and that was why it became necessary to move it. The Shalom region, on the other hand, profited from the political process of the withdrawal from Sinai. The Eshkol region opposite the Gaza Strip also revived surprisingly under the new circumstances that developed. It appears that agricultural settlements adjust more quickly than urban settlements to political changes. While the urban base is destroyed irremediably, the agricultural fabric slowly returns to its previous state.

Another manifestation was that residents once 'burned' in the political sense, tended to avoid relocating once more beyond the 'Green Line'. Only four families settled in Judea and Samaria, and only 14 in the Qatif bloc in the Gaza Strip.

The lesson to be learned perhaps is that any political settlement endeavour must be accompanied by a possible plan for withdrawal. The patterns of withdrawal from the Yamit region were characterized by settlement shrinkage, considerable movement over short distances, a tendency to settle areas close to the evacuated one in repeated settlement in a similar geographical area, and by the tendency of the urban population to return to its city of provenance. On the other hand, the settlement staying power of the rural population is greater than that of the city-dwellers.

CHAPTER ELEVEN

The Gaza Strip – From Conquest to Taking Root

The Qatif bloc is an Israeli settlement zone in the southern part of the Gaza Strip, designed to be a wedge between the Egyptian border at Sinai and the dense Arab population of the Strip, to maintain an Israeli presence in that sector of the occupied territories, and to establish a focus of Jewish settlement in a region whose political destiny has not yet been determined. It is a settlement bloc surrounded by a dense Arab population, grappling with problems of insufficient land and water, which due to its physical and geographical conditions does not allow for extensive Jewish settlement on its territory. However, since the settlement was undertaken for security and political reasons, and a great deal of money was invested in it, there is justification for an analysis of it from the geographical, political and economic viewpoints against the background of the physical, economic and demographic features of the Gaza Strip.

THE GAZA STRIP – A DENSELY POPULATED REGION

The area of the Gaza Strip is 140 sq. miles. It is 29 miles long and for the most part 3–5 miles wide. Its widest point in the south near the Egyptian border is 10.6 miles. It is long and narrow and mostly covered by sand dunes. It has two linear transport arteries, a coastal road and a railway. Three areas are discernible in the Strip: the western belt characterized by dunes 3 miles wide, among which are small cultivated sectors using underground water which is close to the surface there; the folded valley in the centre, 1.2–1.8 miles wide, where most of the cultivable land is to be found, with alluvial soil that was deposited by Wadi Gaza; and a sandstone ridge 240–300 ft. high cut in several places by riverbeds.

Most of the Gaza Strip population is Arab, and totals about 542,000, composed of local people, refugees and Bedouin who came from the Negev and Sinai. The population is concentrated in the bigger cities: Gaza, Han Yunis, Deir el-Balah and Rafah, and in the refugee camps of esh-Shati, Jebaliah, and the large villages of Lahiya, Beit Hanun and Nuzeirat. The population density is 3,872 per sq. mile, one of the highest in the world. Table 8 shows the age distribution of the Gaza Strip population. The outstanding finding is that the 0–14 age group makes up about half the Strip population.

TABLE 8

ARAB POPULATION IN THE GAZA STRIP 1980, IN AGE GROUPS

Age Group	Population in Thousands	Percentage
0 – 14	214.3	47.4
15 – 29	126.1	27.9
30 – 44	51.6	11.4
45 – 64	44.7	9.9
65 +	15.3	3.4

The original Gaza population accounts for more than a third of the total. In 1948 the population numbered 60,000–70,000. Table 9 shows the growth of the population in recent years. Today 54 per

TABLE 9

GAZA STRIP POPULATION (IN THOUSANDS) 1975–1980

	1975	1976	1977	1978	1979	1980
Total	395	405	416	424	440	452
Refugees	224	229	235	240	250	257
Locals	161	166	170	173	178	182
Nomads	10	10	11	11	12	13

cent of the population are defined as refugees and 13 per cent are Bedouin. The refugees are residents who came to the Gaza Strip from the villages of the southern lowland during the War of Independence. They are physically and socially isolated from the other people, and the UN refugee organization was assigned responsibility for them. Camps were set up for them without a proper service infrastructure, with the result that the camps turned into slums with a population density of more than 12,000 people per sq. mile. Since 1967 their situation has improved, as Israeli policy has been to treat the refugees like the other inhabitants. In 1971 a beginning was made, infrastructure was built and the residents built their own houses on it. Of the 260,000 refugees in the Strip,

170,000 are still in the camps, and the rest in the towns and villages of the Strip.

Between 1947 and 1967 various political elements affected the settlement structure in the Strip. The mass movement of population to the Strip in the wake of the War of Independence, the declaration that the Strip was a separate political–administrative unit under Egyptian rule, the constant population increase, all these shaped its course up to 1967. Its economy was based on agriculture, handicrafts, and trade in traditional products. Of the total area of 140 sq. miles, 100 are under cultivation, the main product being citrus fruit. Only minor changes have taken place in the settlement structure of the Strip since 1967. There has been some growth in the cities, which are characterized today by high natural increase, ever greater overcrowding, unemployment, and a weak economic base. These features increased the social pressures of the population in the 1960s and 1970s and contributed to the emergence of extremist nationalist feelings. The housing provided by the Israeli authorities reduced the pressure, but the available land did not meet all needs. It must be borne in mind that in 1980 49 per cent of the population was in the cities, 38 per cent in the refugee camps and 13 per cent in the villages, that is, 87 per cent of the inhabitants were concentrated in the towns and camps where the demand for housing solutions was greatest.

The Six Day War and Israeli conquest of the Gaza Strip led to a considerable economic change. Opening the borders to the residents of the Strip and allowing freedom of movement and working in Israel bettered the situation of the population. Since then the standard of living has risen, agriculture has been improved, industrial plants have been established in the northern part of the Strip, and several roads have been repaired. Despite these ameliorations, it is very doubtful whether the basic geographical, physical and human conditions in the Strip make possible the addition of Jewish agricultural settlements requiring the same means of production – land and water – that the Arab community there lacks.

THE JEWISH POPULATION IN THE GAZA STRIP

The Jewish population of the Gaza Strip, today numbering 2,700 is concentrated in three settlement blocs – Lahiya, Netzarim and Qatif. The Lahiya bloc is north of the town of Gaza, and has sandy territory that has potential for the establishment of two further agricultural settlements in addition to Netiv Ha-Asara which is already there. Near this bloc is the industrial Zone of Erez, the main source of employment for the neighbourhood. Recently a new group of Sinai evacuees was established as Elei Sinai to operate as a community-type settlement. Some 400 families or 1,000 people are intended to live in this bloc (Figure 29).

The Netzarim bloc occupies 875 acres of State land from south of the town of Gaza to north of the settlement of Nuzeirat. The plan posits three moshavim or one community-type settlement and two agricultural ones consisting of 7.5 acre units using 20,000 cu.m. of water. Each settlement is to have 80 units and the entire bloc about 2,400 inhabitants.

The Qatif bloc is the largest of the three and half its planned settlements have already been established. It extends from north of the town of Rafah to south of Deir el-Balah. The plan calls for 2,500–2,800 families there, a total of 10,000–12,000 people. Thus a Jewish population of about 15,000 is planned for the three blocs together, facing an Arab population of 542,000 with a natural increase of 3 per cent per annum.

The existing and planned Jewish settlement is located on State land where there were no Arabs living, land which was vacant or temporarily cultivated; the total area taken over for Jewish settlement amounts to 14,000 acres. The three settlement blocs were established on the western sand stone ridge, mostly covered with sand, in places lacking any local or strategic advantage.

THE QATIF BLOC

The largest of the blocs, Qatif, includes eight settlements, separable into two groups. The northern part is the oldest, and contains Netzer Hazani, Qatif and Gane Tal, while the relatively more recently settled southern part includes Neve Deqalim, Gedid, Gan Or, Bedolah and Atzmona. Settlement in the bloc began in 1970 when a 'Nahal' unit resettled Kefar Darom, which had been in existence before the War of Independence. In 1972 'Nahal' units settled Netzarim and Morag. In 1975 interest was reawakened in the settlement of the Strip, and land in the Qatif bloc was handed over to the Hapo'el Hamizrahi moshav federation. In 1977 Netzer Hazani was established, and later Qatif and Gane Tal.

The Qatif bloc occupies 5,000 acres in the southwestern part of the Gaza Strip. On the west it is bounded by the sea, and on the east, north and south by Arab settlements. It is located on State land which before 1967 was controlled by the Egyptian army. The Qatif

FIGURE 29
JEWISH SETTLEMENTS IN THE GAZA STRIP

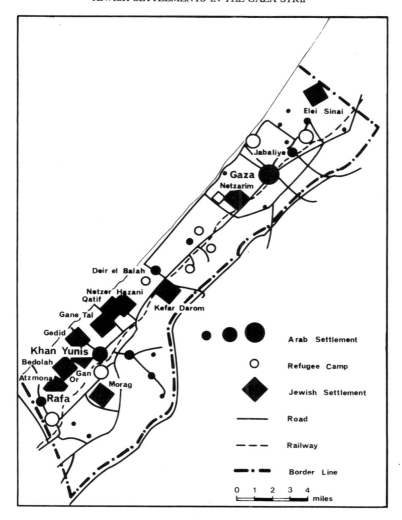

bloc has no particular locational advantages. It was placed where there was unoccupied land that could be settled after basic preparation. The only advantages it has are a fine seashore suitable for the development of tourism, a pleasant climate and local water sources. From the security viewpoint its virtue is that it creates a separation between the Arab settlements, restricting their urban and agricultural expansion, and establishes a settlement continuity from the coast through the Eshkol region to the Shalom region.

The usual settlement form in the Qatif bloc is the moshav, since the land was allocated to the 'Hapo'el Hamizrahi' moshavim who were faced with the problem of housing for the younger generation in their older moshavim. There are also cooperative moshavim in the bloc.

As to the Qatif population, several features are discernible. It is a young population, 20 to 30 years old, with lots of children; the 364 families living there have more than 800 children. The people came from all parts of the country, most from moshavim of 'Hapo'el Hamizrahi', some from 'Nahal' units of their Moshav federation, and the rest from the cities or development towns. There is a high proportion of university graduates. The ideology of the settlers is based on Torah and work, which involves compliance with the religious precepts together with agricultural work, the settlement of the 'Greater Land of Israel', of which the Gaza Strip is a separate part, and settlement in religious blocs in order to facilitate the provision of religious and cultural services.

Except from Atzmona, the settlements in the Qatif bloc belong to the moshav federation of 'Hapo'el Hamizrahi' which considers that bloc its chief settlement area. The movement organizes initial settlement groups and undertakes to provide them with social and agricultural guidance when they occupy a new site, represents the settlers in contacts with outsiders, and helps them financially if they should run into difficulties.

Atzmona, the exception in the bloc, was established following the evacuation of the Yamit region.

Table 10 summarizes the population structure in the Qatif bloc.

DEVELOPMENT PLANS

Until recently the Qatif bloc was developed on a local scale only. It was settled by the Settlement Department of the Zionist Organization together with Hapo'el Hamizrahi's moshav federation. Most of the planning was directed to the infrastructure

TABLE 10
THE QATIF BLOC POPULATION ACCORDING TO SETTLEMENT, NUMBER OF FAMILIES, SETTLEMENT TYPE, YEAR FOUNDED AND PROVENANCE

Settlement	Number of Families	Type of Settlement	Year Founded	Provenance of Settlers	No. of Families Planned
Netzer Hazani	44	moshav	1977	moshav born	100
Gane Tal	45	moshav	1979	moshav and kibbutz born	100
Qatif	16	coop. moshav	1978	western immigrants	100
Neve Deqalim	40	regional center	1982	whole country and Yamit	450
Gedid	28	moshav	1982	city and moshav born	120
Gan Or	20	moshav	1982	whole country	120
Bedolah	20	moshav	1984	successor generation	120
Atzmona	26	coop. moshav or community	1983	Yamit evacuees	120
Moraf	45	kibbutz	1982	kibbutz born	100
Kefar Darom	20	kibbutz	1982	kibbutz born	50
Mitzpe Atzmona	60	kibbutz	1984	kibbutz born	100
Total	364				1,480

of the settlements. As the final plan for establishing ten settlements and populating six of them took shape, simultaneously with the withdrawal from Sinai, planning was begun in regard to additional areas in the Gaza Strip held by the State; these were the Lahiya bloc, the Netzarim bloc, and areas in the Nahal Morag vicinity. There is as yet no regional plan for all settlement in the Gaza Strip, only ideas. These include the development of one or two urban centres, a southern port near one of the settlements on the coast, to be integrated with the once-planned Med–Dead Canal, urban development in the Netzarim bloc, a new longitudinal road to link the Jewish settlements that are separated from each other by Arab populations, and the linking of the Qatif bloc with the Eshkol via a road going east from the Morag intersection.

The impression left by the various development plans is that there is no consensus on the development patterns; what seems to be the primary concern of the authorities involved is safeguarding State-owned land and its speedy settlement by Jews.

The Qatif bloc is an example of the establishment of an independent religious settlement region beyond the 'Green Line' to serve nine religious settlements — eight of them agricultural and one to serve as an urban centre for the neighbourhood. The bloc faces a large number of problems, such as an insufficiency of the chief means of production, land and water. Even if the water problem can be solved from the national water carrier, there is no solution to the land problem because there is a dense Arab population in the region that is multiplying rapidly and needs land itself. The dependence of the bloc on means of production from outside naturally reduces its ability to exist independently. The Qatif bloc might find itself isolated from its surroundings in a changing political situation, and its ties with the Eshkol region are still weak. The economic basis of the bloc is not very stable either. Agriculture is the main economic sector employing 165 families, about two-thirds of those in the bloc. The typical farm in the bloc consists of half an acre of tomatoes in greenhouses, a $\frac{1}{4}$ of an acre of flowers, $2\frac{1}{2}$ acres of orchard in the Eshkol region, and $\frac{1}{4}$ of an acre of field crops. The crops the bloc is specializing in for export can easily lead to bankruptcy in depression years. The bloc is not favourably placed for industrial plants either. It appears that the establishment of a settlement bloc for geo-political and security reasons does not always mean economic success. Moreover, all the planning and development not-withstanding, the total Jewish population in the Strip has not surpassed 3,000. Consequently the effectiveness of a project of this sort must be considered doubtful, and although it is excellently organized, might recall the trauma of the Yamit region.

From all that has been said regarding the 'occupied territories', it appears that Israel's territorial expansion was exaggerated to begin with, and that in the light of internal and external political pressures it adopted other forms in the course of time. After the withdrawal from Sinai Israel's territorial picture was vastly improved and approached reasonable dimensions. The Golan Heights added a bit of territory and a security belt, but the Qatif bloc in the Gaza Strip hardly made any changes at all.

Thus the geography of Israel is in constant flux under the influence of prominent individuals, political attitudes within the country, and the actual external situation. At first the settlements were considered bargaining points for the future, then they became a permanent feature demonstrating power, and today they have a definitely nationalist and religious tinge. Obviously, this development did not soften Arab objections to a political solution, and only exacerbated the problem.

Israel's continued occupation will certainly increase Arab insistence that their land be returned. At present the two large political coalitions in Israel do not favour wholesale withdrawal from the territories. However, in the light of the above analysis of the geographical situation in the territories, it is possible that a partial selective withdrawal might lead to a legitimate solution and to a state of peace. Jewish settlement in parts of the Jordan Valley, the Golan Heights, and some urban concentration in Judea–Samaria is perhaps the necessary minimum.

Israel's settlement ability in the occupied territories is quite limited both economically and demographically. The investments lately made in the territories exhausted the development resources for the area within the 'Green Line'. After 20 years of continuous settlement, there are in the occupied territories, including east Jerusalem, only some 165,000 Jews as compared with 1,377,000 Arabs, no more than 12 per cent. If the Jews in east Jerusalem are discounted, the percentage of Jews in the territories is practically nil. The natural increase of the Arabs and their absolute growth far surpass those of the Jews, so that there is no possibility of a demographic victory. In the total area, Israel accounts for only 69 per cent, a proportion too small for effective, constructive control and development. Thus the gap between the political and territorial aspirations and the actual situation is extremely large, and it is doubtful whether it can be reduced.

CHAPTER TWELVE

The Jewish–Arab Political Struggle in the Galilee

Israel's geopolitical problems are not confined to the 'occupied territories'. Within Israel there are many regional-settlement situations with political, demographic and spatial significance which have not yet been solved. The relations between Jews and Israeli Arabs are a major problem, whose complexity leaves no doubt as to the need to find territorial and settlement solutions to the conflicts arising within the domain of Israeli sovereignty.

Galilee in the north exemplifies the struggle of two peoples for land, for settlement and livelihood, in the differing geographical conditions of mountain and valley.

In the wake of the geopolitical changes that have occurred in Lebanon, it behooves us today to turn our attention to Galilee for whose sake a long and extensive military campaign has been conducted. Presumably, in the new security conditions that will prevail in southern Lebanon, Galilee will be given priority in development and the investment of resources, as usually happens in regions suitable for population increase and settlement once they are free of tension and the danger of war.

The development and construction projects in Galilee in the past three decades have not made it attractive for mass settlement. Through the inspiration of David Ben-Gurion, priority in development was accorded the Negev, in both resources and population, and Galilee was left in an inferior position, although its objective geographical features – its proximity to the centre of the country and its infrastructure – were better than those of the Negev. The development towns established in Galilee resembled all the others, and had nothing that suited the character of Galilee. Except perhaps for Upper Nazareth, most of them never achieved a large population, never acquired a dominant regional status, nor even economic independence or self-sufficient urban functioning.

No regional conception that might have guided its development was formulated for Galilee. The well established agricultural sector proved its efficiency, as did certain industrial and tourist enterprises, but apart from these there were no discernible changes in the region. In recent years there has been an initiative establishing four new development areas – Segev, Tefen, Tzalmon and Nahal Zipori – containing several dozen settlements of a special type called 'top-sites', for the purpose of safeguarding State land and providing a base for the future population of Galilee by Jews.

The chief geopolitical problem in the north today is that of populating mountainous sectors of Galilee with Jews, despite the difficult geographical conditions, the large Arab population, and the conflicts between Arabs and Jews regarding land.

CENTRAL GALILEE AS THE ARENA FOR POLITICAL
CLASHES

Central Galilee is one of Israel's important development regions. The pre-State settlement history is characterized by a long-established dominant Arab community compared with quite a limited Jewish community. Both were at the time controlled by the mandatory government which was concerned to avert conflicts of interest between them. After the establishment of the State, a new set of relations evolved between Jews and Arabs. The Arab population, a minority in the country, is a demographic and settlement majority in central Galilee, with a large natural increase, so that central Galilee may in the future become the centre of the Arab population as a whole. Against this background the government initiated a policy of development for the purpose of 'Judaizing' Galilee. We shall therefore attempt to examine the characteristics of Galilee as a development area – the goals which were set based on its geographical features, and the possible solutions for its settlement by Jews, as proposed by government institutions.

The distribution of Jewish settlements in Galilee was dictated primarily by the location of the Arab settlements already there. In the late 1940s there were 190 Arab villages in Galilee. The geographical features of this complex were: the location of few villages on rocky soil; the spread of concentrations of villages along the margins of the rocky land close to valleys and land convenient for cultivation such as the Sakhnin Valley, the Bet Hakerem Valley, and on the margins of the coastal strip; careful use of agricultural land; location of villages so as to control roads and near water sources such as springs and brooks; concentrations of villages near Nazareth, a town which in 1945 had a population of 14,200; and absence of continuity in settlement due to topographic conditions.

Thus the Arab villages were not concentrated in one part of the region but were located near the means of agricultural production – land and water – and were based on an autarkic economy.

In contrast, the distribution of Jewish settlements developed in the following way. The first settlements were on the margins of the Hula Valley and Lake Kinneret, with penetration of mountainous Galilee at Rosh Pinna and En Zetim. The Jewish Colonization Association company purchased land on the margins of the valleys, where Arab owners were willing to sell, and Yavne'el, Ilaniyya, Yesud Hama'ala and other villages were founded. Settling the mountain was difficult because land could not be bought there except in small, separate plots, and also because there was little knowledge about how to cultivate rocky mountain land. By the end of World War I there were only ten Jewish settlements in all of Galilee (Figure 30).

Between 1919 and the start of the 1936 disturbances only one settlement, Kefar Hahoresh, was established in the mountainous part of Galilee. Of course in those days of the British Mandate, it became increasingly difficult for Jews to purchase land. When funds were available they were earmarked for flat agricultural land in continuous blocs, so that a number of settlements could be set up at one time. There was also a tendency to acquire land near existing concentrations of settlements or close to roads. All these considerations led to a preference for the valleys.

The disturbances of 1936–39 and the conclusions of the Peel Commission on the division of the country set new political goals for Jewish settlement and emphasized the importance of the distribution of the land purchases between the Jezreel Valley in the south and the Lebanese border on the north. The events led to a political-territorial view of settlement as a means of maintaining a presence in every possible place, not just in a settlement continuum as in the past. Because of difficulties in land arrangements, there was only limited settlement in the mountainous area. Hanita and Elon were established within the 'Stockade and Tower' framework and were unusual in their location. At that time, 21 new settlements were founded, most of them in the area between the Jezreel and Kinnarot Valleys.

Upon the establishment of the State, central Galilee became sovereign Israeli territory. In the wake of the War of Independence, many Arab villages were abandoned, and of the 190, only 66 remained. The Arab villagers in Galilee settled mainly around Nazareth, in the vicinity of the Bet Hakerem valley, and the

FIGURE 30
DISTRIBUTION OF SETTLEMENTS IN GALILEE

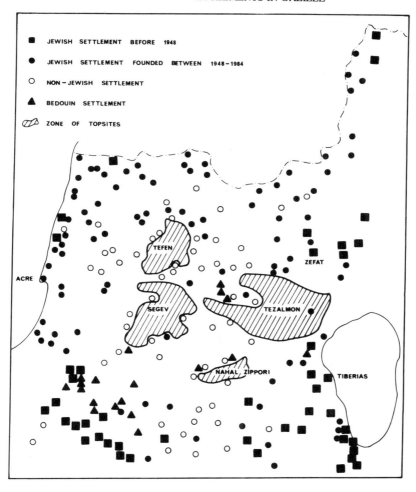

Sakhnin–Shefaram valley, and on the western edges of Upper Galilee. The contraction of the Arab settlement distribution opened the way for a great scattering of Jewish settlements and the utilization of mountain land with modern methods. It also became necessary to establish new border settlements along the Syrian and Lebanese borders. The government also decided to rapidly populate central Galilee as part of the policy of scattering population and settling areas with few inhabitants. During this period abandoned villages were resettled and newcomers with no agricultural training were directed to mountain settlements. At that time places like Meron, Sasa, Elqosh, Yir'on, Dishon and Shomera were settled, although their inhabitants suffered from remoteness from the centre of the country, poor communications, problems of water and problems of an economic base; the development towns of Upper Nazareth, Ma'alot and Shelomi were also established. In all, during that period, 38 new settlements were set up, making a first significant step forward in Judaizing and populating central Galilee.

Since the 1960s there have been repeated calls for populating Galilee with Jews, since the natural increase among the Arabs has reduced the proportion of Jews there. In the early 1960s the moshavim of Avivim and Dovev were founded, the development region of Segev was organized, and the new town of Karmi'el was established in Lower Galilee. The Six Day War and the new borders drawn on the Golan Heights, in Judea–Samaria and the Jordan Valley slowed down the pace of development in central Galilee. In 1969 only two new moshavim – Shetula and Hazon – were located there. The settlement policy for Galilee since the 1970s has amounted to the delineation of four settlement blocs: the Tefen bloc, stretching from south of Ma'alot to the Bet Hakerem valley; the Segev bloc, stretching from Haifa Bay to central Galilee; the Tzalmon bloc, between Lake Kinneret on the east and the series of central Galilee valleys on the west; and the Nahal Zipori bloc south of them. In addition it was decided to set up 30 topsites as footholds in important places where it was necessary to ensure control of State land. Since then another purpose has emerged – the development of industry in the settlements because of the limitation of the agricultural means of production, and the establishment of industrial zones as in Goren, Mahanayim and the Ahihud Crossroads. It was also resolved to reinforce the existing development towns by setting up industrial plants in them and improving their urban infrastructure. All in all, while the goals of Jewish settlement in Galilee changed from period to period, the actual process throughout was quite slow in relation to their needs on the one hand and the growth of the Arab sector on the other.

THE STRUGGLE OVER LAND

The struggle over land in Galilee has long existed. It evolved for historical reasons, namely the inefficient agrarian system in Ottoman times, the registration and mapping of land under the British Mandate, and the new land regulations since the establishment of the State. During the Ottoman period a great deal of land was registered under the effendi's name, because the owners did not wish to pay taxes on it. Of the 15 per cent of land that was then cultivated in the country, only 5 per cent was registered. Unregistered land reverted to the effendis, so that the concentration of land in their possession was very great.

During the British Mandate, the authorities allowed the occupation of 'dead' land for cultivation. In 1928 they began to reregister and map land, which enabled many villagers to enlarge their holdings with land they had previously worked. In 1943 the authorities also decided to turn over to the Arab villagers land that was registered with the High Commissioner. This land was earmarked for general use, so it could not be bought by Jews. Both the Turks and the British distinguished between State land and private land, to the latter of which rights could be acquired.

With the establishment of the State of Israel, a new category of land emerged – land owned by absentees, that is, the land of Arabs who had abandoned their villages and left their possessions. That land was transferred to the State and registered as the property of the Trustee of Abandoned Property. On the basis of an Ottoman law stipulating that land that was not cultivated for three consecutive years reverted to the State, additional land was acquired by the authorities.

As a result, a constant battle developed between the authorities who are interested in retaining and concentrating State land and the villages who wish to enlarge their holdings and prove that it is 'Miri' land, that is, State land given to the residents for temporary use, for either agricultural or construction purposes. In 1970 a law was passed providing that land that was frozen and registered could no longer be taken possession of or have rights acquired in it.

As a result of the long history of struggle for the ownership of land, under different regimes, a great rift has developed between State land of various sorts and privately owned land. It should be borne in mind as well that in addition to its economic value, land for the Arabs is linked to political power, influence and control. Confiscation of land from private owners means reducing their influence, status, and even leadership. Even when the Israeli authorities confiscate private Arab land for purposes of development for the Arab population, the act is met with suspicion and mistrust.

The distribution of land ownership in Galilee may explain the political problem and the reasons for the struggle. Table 11 shows that the area of jurisdiction of the Arab settlements is three times as large as that of the Jewish ones.

TABLE 11

JURISDICTIONAL AREA OF SETTLEMENTS AND LAND OWNERSHIP
IN GALILEE

	In thousands of acres	In percentage of the area of the region
Jurisdictional area of Jewish settlements	28.25	11.9%
Jurisdictional area of non-Jewish settlements	89	31.8%
State land (including nature reserves and parks)	157.75	56.3%
State land in area of influence of non-Jewish population (estimate)	76.25	2.2%

Source: R. Weitz, 'Preserving Galilee Land', Jewish Agency, Settlement Department, Proposal for Implementation (Jerusalem, 1978), p. 1.

It is also estimated that about half the State land in Galilee is within the area of influence of Arab settlements, that is, it is taken over from time to time by Arab residents who make illegal use of it for their own needs. The land is taken over quickly where state ownership is clear, but even more promptly where ownership is mixed or unclear. Since on much of the land there is no constant Jewish presence and it is not used for economic purposes, it is gradually being taken out of Jewish hands. The Arab land is of high quality for agricultural purposes, much better than the Jewish land. Given the occupation of land and the creation of faits accomplis, the geographical inferiority of the Jewish settlement in Galilee is understandable.

Land was requisitioned many times by the Jews for developing Galilee. In 1948 land was requisitioned in Iqrit and Baram for security reasons, in 1955 land was taken to build Upper Nazareth, in 1962 to build Karmi'el, in 1965 for the national water carrier, and in

1978 for further developing the Jewish settlement in Galilee. The land expropriated from private owners was greater in area than the State land earmarked for development purposes. It is reasonable to assume that most of the land turned over to Jewish local authorities since 1970 was State land that was uncultivated and unused.

The conflict between Jews and Arabs in mountainous Galilee sharpened recently with the establishment of a regional council for Misgav, covering an area of 45,000 acres, in order to provide a jurisdictional framework for the topsites. The Arabs claim that about 25,000 acres of the area is Arab-owned, belonging to 18 villages. While it is not all owned by Arabs, geographically speaking the land can be connected with the villages. As the Arabs are citizens of Israel claiming equal rights, they demand that the land be added to their villages to be used for expansion and development. The government on the other hand claims that the transfer of territory from Arabs to the Jewish regional council had already taken place and resulted in advantages for the Arabs because their infrastructure was improved by the development activities. The Arabs however fear that the inclusion of private land within a defined regional authority will, under the terms of the planning and building law, make it possible to expropriate 40 per cent for public needs, so that their land potential will be diminished. They also fear the taxes that the new council may levy on their land in order to develop the infrastructure. While the boundary of the Misgav council is very winding, indicating an attempt to exclude the land of Arab villages, there was no avoiding splitting it in some places. This fragmentation, and the lack of clarity regarding ownership, led to nationalistic feeling among the Arabs. Recently, the boundary has been corrected and the tension has somewhat diminished.

THE DEMOGRAPHIC PROBLEM – JEWS VERSUS ARABS

One of the main problems in Galilee arises from the demographic ratio between Jews and Arabs, which has no counterpart in any other region in Israel. The policy of scattering population from the 1960s on did not succeed in substantially increasing the Jewish population of Galilee, nor was a proper economic and social infrastructure prepared there that would attract Jewish population from the centre of the country. Since 1961, only 10 per cent of the newcomers who have arrived in Israel have been directed to Galilee, and the percentage of Jews in the region has continually diminished. In 1961 they constituted 57.6 per cent of the population in the region, in 1972, 54 per cent, and today only 51 per cent. There was a spurt in the late 1960s, but since the 1970s a steady decline in the proportion of Jewish population.

It must be borne in mind that the rate of natural increase is 17 per thousand for Jews, and 39 for Arabs, which gives the latter a potential population advantage. The emigration balance too is negative for the Jews, with about 2 per cent leaving the region annually, while almost no Arabs move away from Galilee. Thus the demographic force of the Arab population of Galilee is greater than that of the Jews, and in the absence of migration to the region, the percentage of Jews will decrease year after year. The lack of demographic parity between the two populations will have geo-political significance in the future as central Galilee is eliminated as a Jewish settlement region in Israel.

The Arab sector in Galilee is subject to great demographic pressure as a result of natural increase and no migration away from the region. The outcome is the growth of the villages and towns, their expansion on State land, and unlicensed construction. The concentrations of Arab population in Galilee are located in the Shefaram–Sakhnin area, the Nazareth area, the Bet Hakerem valley area and the Makher–Kefar Yasif area. It is reasonable to assume that by the end of the century the Arab population will have doubled, so that in the year 2000 there will be half a million Arabs in the region. More than 90 per cent of the villagers were born in the villages and continue to live there, so that natural increase will always be the main factor in population growth. In view of this demographic situation, settlement solutions must be found for the Galilee Arabs in their villages and close vicinity, and that is the reason for their objection to the Misgav regional council, for instance, which reduces their land potential for expansion and livelihood. In addition, the employment trend in the villages is to replace agriculture with industry and craft. Villagers quite often work outside the villages. Their income is not invested in industry, economic enterprises or even stocks and bonds, but in local con-struction and land. This leads to the urbanization of the villages, and an improvement in the quality of building and services. The commuting reaches all the Galilee development towns and Haifa as well. The outstanding settlement development in view of the improved condition of the Galilee Arabs is urban inter-village association, in particular in the Shefaram–Sakhnin area, the Bet Hakerem valley area and the Kafr Makher–Kefar Yasif area.

THE PLAN TO DEVELOP GALILEE FOR THE JEWS

Government policy on the development of Galilee is expressed in a series of plans and sets of priorities for carrying out projects there. Interest in planning Galilee was great, and some quite extensive projects were proposed. Quite conspicuous throughout the years however was the lack of coordination among the many plans, so that housing matters were not dealt with simultaneously with industrialization, for instance. The development policy on Galilee was not consistent through the years, and not always declared to have the highest priority, and Galilee did not have priority in the development of particular branches of agriculture or industry either.

The approach of the Israel Land Authority is to divide Galilee into three subregions, a western development sector, a central one and an eastern one, each with particular planning lines. The eastern sector would be linked developmentally with the others in three lateral axes – Haifa–Nazareth–Tiberias; Acre–Karmi'el–Safed–Tiberias; and Nahariya–Ma'alot. A link would also be developed between Safed–Hatzor–Qiryat Shemona and from there to the Golan Heights. (In development a link means Jewish linear settlement, roads, establishment of settlements and the preparation of land for settlement.) The central sector is capable of providing plenty of employment, because of its geographical advantages; it should also attract industry. Haifa and its environs would be an economic centre in the service industries, commerce and welfare services. The central sector has an advantage for residence, tourism and recreation and is therefore likely to attract suburban settlement or semi-urban settlement. Cities and towns in this sector, such as Karmi'el, Ma'alot and Safed, are likely to reach a population of 40,000 each. Greater Nazareth, covering Nazareth, Upper Nazareth and Migdal HaEmeq, would be a regional focal point and counterweight to Haifa, and according to this plan would reach 200,000 inhabitants. The eastern sector would be developed in line with its advantages in resorts and recreation, and with industry near Mahanayim.

This plan tries to exploit the geographical advantages of each sector and proposes solutions for it. Central Galilee, which is the most problematical for development, is scheduled for residence only in this plan.

The Ministry of Housing's approach to the development of Galilee involves accelerated urbanization while maintaining the demographic balance between Jews and Arabs, by improving the quality of housing for Jews, providing a wide range of employment possibilities and ameliorating the welfare services. Another plan for the development of Galilee called for the establishment of some 30 top-sites. The goal of that plan was to occupy areas earmarked for Jewish settlement in the future and thus prevent the local Arabs from creating faits accomplis. The plan also called for the occupation of State land for which no plans had as yet been formulated, thus making possible the concentration of land areas in the future for settlement purposes.

THE TOPSITES – A NEW SETTLEMENT CHALLENGE

Israel's response to the geopolitical problem that has arisen in central Galilee is the establishment of new Jewish settlement blocs with a large number of topsites, the addition of an industrial zone, and a zone for science-based industry in Karmi'el. The overall plan for the settlement of Galilee envisages 62 settlements, 33 of them topsites. To date 28 have been set up, and the others are in various stages of planning or construction. The land concentration and road blazing is being done by the Jewish National Fund, which is also preparing 25,000 acres of land for agriculture and 42,500 acres for grazing.

The topsites have been established on State land, mostly in rocky areas. Their locations have been selected so they have the greatest possible control of their surroundings and any alteration in land utilization can be observed from them. Most of the topsites are situated along two axes: in eastern Galilee, between Ma'alot, the Tefen bloc, and the Segev bloc up to the Shefaram hills; and in central Galilee between the Segev bloc, the Tzalmon bloc, and Qadarim up to eastern Galilee. Each topsite is to contain 100–200 families. The topsite has the organizational form of a community type settlement with most people working away from home. The topsites are included in three blocs – Tefen, Segev and Tzalmon – plus a fourth smaller one called Nahal Zipori (Figure 31).

The Segev bloc has an area of 7,500 acres, mostly uncultivable. Land preparation there was begun in the mid-1970s. Ya'ad was the first settlement in the bloc to become permanent in 1978. Since then, another 12 topsites have been set up, as well as the Misgav service centre and the Teradyon industrial zone. Plans for the bloc include an industrial park to be based on enterprises owned by the topsite residents. Its object is to enhance the development of Galilee by the

FIGURE 31

NEW SETTLEMENTS AND TOPSITES IN GALILEE

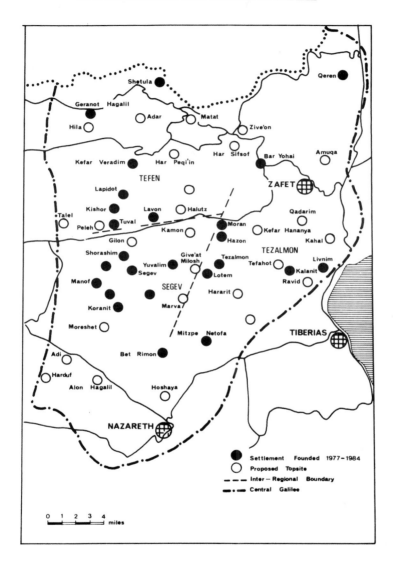

establishing of science-based industry in pollution-free places, using the human potential populating the topsites which cannot support itself from agriculture.

The conflict between Jews and Arabs was especially serious in this bloc because both claimed a right to the land. The installation of 'Nahal' groups at Atzmon and Givat Qered, which had been a military area, showed the Arabs that a new period was starting in the settlement of the region. They began to express their opposition every time any land preparation was undertaken near their villages. As a result the authorities decided to accelerate the establishment of the topsites that had been planned. In addition, as noted above, the Arabs voiced serious objections to the establishment of the Misgav regional council for such an extensive jurisdictional area that touched on their land. The situation is unusual because these topsites, inhabited by very few Jews, consist of large tracts of land, much larger than they can make use of. Protests, petitions, and continued attempts to cultivate this land are the main measures being taken by the Arabs.

The Tefen bloc includes 9,000 acres south of Ma'alot. The accelerated development of the area began in the mid-1970s, and comprised two combined projects, an industrial zone of 300 acres south of Ma'alot, and several industrial villages. The industrial zone was designed to solve the development difficulties in Ma'alot. The enterprises in the Tefen bloc are owned by private individuals or public companies. In 1981 there were already six settlements in the bloc, including the topsites Kishor, Lavon and Toval.

The Tzalmon bloc is east of the Segev bloc, and designed to connect the Segev bloc and Karmiel with the area north of Lake Kinneret. It is a settlement barrier in central Galilee on the east–west axis, intended among other things to prevent the expansion of the villages of Elabun, Araba and Merar, and of the Bedouin concentrations in the neighbourhood. The availability of agricultural land in this bloc led to a decision to establish the topsites of Zviya and Qadarim as well as four moshavim and four community-type settlements. The agriculture to be developed there is to include orchards, flowers and vegetables in greenhouses, poultry coops, and grazing cattle for meat. The bloc is not encircled by Arab villages and therefore no conflict between Jews and Arabs is likely to arise.

The Nahal Zipori bloc in eastern Galilee has a sparse Jewish population and a wide scattering of Bedouin settlements. It is expected to limit that expansion and stop it in the vicinity of

Nazareth. Its geopolitical importance is greater than that of the other blocs, and the attempt of the government and settlement institutions to safeguard State land at all costs is obvious here. Eight topsites are planned for this bloc, two of them of the community type, two kibbutzim and one moshav. The bloc today contains 20,000 Arabs, 11,000 Bedouin in 13 concentrations and 28 tribes, and 3,000 Druze, while the Jewish population numbers only about one thousand.

The entire topsite plan when implemented provides for 6,000 Jews, but it is doubtful whether they will be able to improve the demographic balance in central Galilee. The topsite solution, which has recently become so popular, is thus of questionable effectiveness. The political and settlement importance of the development regions of Tefen, Segev, Tzalmon and Nahal Zipori, and the dozens of topsites that have been built should not be minimized, however. The topsites can perhaps be viewed as a modern version of the 'Stockade and Tower' settlements, based this time on crafts and sophisticated industry rather than agriculture. The alignment of topsites may succeed in stopping Arab occupancy of State land, but it can hardly improve the demographic balance in Galilee in favour of the Jews.

THE FUTURE OF GALILEE

While there is no comprehensive plan in existence for the Judaization of Galilee, all the present plans aim at attaining a Jewish majority, a stable population, and a settlement distribution that will not leave large areas without a Jewish presence. The shared goal of all the plans is accelerated growth of population which will stop the demographic retreat of the Jews in comparison with the Arabs. From the quantitative viewpoint this can perhaps be done through the cities, but then the spatial effect is weakened; and if scattering throughout the area is promoted, the quantitative effect is reduced. The plans also stress the need for a solid economic base for the various settlement types, so that opportunities in Galilee should not be worse than those in other more developed parts of the country. The goal is especially difficult to achieve because Galilee lacks natural economic advantages and opportunities for development through private initiative.

As to the future of Galilee, its inferior point of departure will continue to affect it. The unsystematic development of both rural and urban settlement, the constant cultivation of State land, the negative Jewish demographic situation, the declining attraction of development towns and the absence of integration on the practical level – all these are not easily remedied or corrected. Consequently, not much hope can be placed in the topsites as a means of Judaizing Galilee. Improvement can only be achieved if the government and settlement institutions start viewing Galilee as a region of vital importance and are prepared to invest in it most of the available resources, effecting a fundamental change in the urban and rural picture and in the regional infrastructure.

CHAPTER THIRTEEN

The Minorities – some Geopolitical Aspects

The political conflict between Jews and Arabs as expressed in the competition for the land of central Galilee raises a crucial problem relating to the development and advancement of the minorities in Israel. Old-time Israel, which did so much to absorb hundreds of thousands of newcomers in the 1950s and 1960s, created a physical, economic and social infrastructure for them, integrated them into the life of the country and succeeded to a considerable extent in providing what was called the 'Second Israel' (the mass immigration of the 1950s) with a solid foundation, did too little for its non-Jewish minorities, the 'Third Israel'.

CHARACTERISTICS OF THE ARAB POPULATION

The minorities in Israel numbered 770,000 in 1986, 17 per cent of the total population. Mostly Muslim, they live in 130 settlements, a quarter in the mixed towns of Jerusalem, Jaffa, Lod, Ramla and Acre. Of the rest, two-thirds live in the Galilee villages and a quarter east of the coastal plain and in the Iron valley. There are also 57,000 Bedouin in the Negev and the Judean desert. In the northern district the minorities constitute half the population, their villages scattered from the Nazareth hills in the south to the Lebanese border in the north, an area of about 250,000 acres. In parts of Galilee the minorities form a majority. In the eastern coastal plain is a narrow strip, from the Iron valley to the Modi'im region in the south, with a substantial rural population, once part of a larger Arab rural area, stretching toward the 'large triangle' formed by Nablus–Tulkarm–Qalqilya. This strip in Israel sovereign territory at present has an Arab population of about 100,000. It contains the villages of Um el-Fahm, Tira and Taiybe with several thousand inhabitants each. In this strip, and in other Arab villages in Galilee, homogeneous regional complexes of villages are developing along main roads, and around large villages with 5,000 or more inhabitants. About two-thirds of the non-urban Arab population of Israel live in such areas, which are acquiring the characteristics of Arab enclaves in the Israel expanse.

The minorities have greatly increased in number since the establishment of the State of Israel in 1948, when they numbered as few as 156,000. In the last two decades their rate of natural increase was more than 4 per cent per annum, one of the highest in the world. The birth rate declined during that period, but so did the death rate. More than 75 per cent of the Arabs in Israel were born after the establishment of the State. Furthermore, there is little emigration among the Arabs of Israel. The official population forecast confirmed by the government envisages a minority population of 820,000 by the end of the century, with many settlements having a population of more than 10,000: Kafr Qara – 12,000; Baqa el-Garbiya – 16,000; Taiybe – 23,000; Um el-Fahm – 22,000; and in Galilee villages such as Tamra, Sakhnin, Merar, Yafia and many others will also be in this category. The two towns Nazareth and Shefaram will together have over 100,000 residents; thus in another few years the minority population in Israel will be greater than the entire present Jewish population of development towns.

It should be noted that the minority population is at present undergoing considerable changes. Before the establishment of the State, the Arab economy was mainly autarkic, and based on small tracts of land, but the situation has since changed; a new type of agriculture has developed within Israel's new sovereign borders, integrated into a modern economy that has provided agricultural guidance and increasing yields, and has raised the standard of living in Arab villages. As a result of contacts with the cities, economic and social relations have become closer, traditional patterns in Arab villages have been modified, jobs outside the village have become more common and agricultural work has been reduced to the extent that today half the manpower of the villages is employed outside them. This has resulted in considerable economic progress among the villagers, a higher cash income, the division of households, the establishment of new core families, a desire for more luxurious housing, the expansion of built-up areas, an increased need for public institutions, and pressure on agricultural land for building homes. Recently industrialization too has come to the Arab village, the first sign of semi-urbanization. With government encouragement local government too has been introduced in the Arab sector. All these developments indicate a portentous demographic, economic and social situation that is evolving before our eyes and requires profound, far reaching attention.

WHAT ARE THE AUTHORITIES DOING?

It is very doubtful whether, in view of these trends in the Arab sector, sufficiently constructive steps have been taken to meet the new situation. District and regional planning does not concern itself to the same extent with the Jewish and Arab sectors, resulting in considerable differences in residential areas, infrastructure for roads, land for public institutions and industrial zones, in regard to both location and the acreage allotted. The planning of the Arab village as a professional matter still lags far behind urban and rural planning in the Jewish sector. No conception has as yet been evolved of what a modern Arab village should look like, with its particular building styles, the way of life of its inhabitants, and the economic and social changes taking place in it. There are not yet many Arab planners known to be engaged in improving their villages in collaboration with the residents. Most of the villages do not yet have approved local outline schemes, and most have not yet developed consciousness in regard to planning. Modernization in rural construction has not yet reached them, although rural construction has made great advances elsewhere in the world and found interesting solutions for populations of various types.

The government is grappling with development problems in the minorities sector on two levels, local and national. On the local level it is striving to improve housing and the rural infrastructure, to diversify employment, and raise the inhabitants' standard of living, while on the national level it is striving to prevent the Arabs from expanding onto State land, and to maintain a demographic balance between Jews and Arabs. The first plane is supposedly constructive, but involves limiting the building area in the villages, with legal measures threatened for any deviation, while the overcrowding in the villages, the demographic and economic changes, and the internal pressures confronting the Arab population compel them to break building laws, turn agricultural land into building sites, and clash with the authorities. The political approach to the problems does not solve the real problems that exist in the sector, so that in the absence of a positive concern about them, any practical steps are valueless. Although the government has tried to promote the development of the Arab village, what is salient is the constant fight against its inhabitants, whether through demolition orders in the villages, the struggle against Arab utilization of State land in Galilee, or conflict with Bedouin and their flocks in the Negev. On the other plane, the national one, no institutional approach to the problem of the minorities is visible, and to the extent that one emerges, it takes the form of restrictive measures in the physical, spatial and demographic domains.

The confiscation of land is among the crucial causes of unrest, if not the most serious of all. 'Land Day' would never have been initiated were it not for the confiscation of land from Arabs. The situation is entirely different from that prevailing in the occupied territories. Of course the residents of the territories object to the confiscation of land, but their main objection is to Jewish settlement aimed at establishing faits accomplis; the Arabs of Israel, on the other hand, have become reconciled to their status as a minority in a Jewish State, and do not object to Jews settling in Galilee or any other region of the country so long as that settlement does not require the confiscation of land. What is essential is an immediate, thorough investigation of the national and settlement land needs for the coming decade to ascertain whether they can be met without confiscating land from Arabs, and a government decision explicitly stipulating that no more land shall be confiscated from Arabs. A survey conducted in the past showed that there are enough land reserves to meet security and settlement needs, so it is clear that the government can make a bold, historic decision and effect the immediate placation of the large Arab population.

THE NEED FOR A CHANGE OF ATTITUDE

The problem of the integration of the Arabs of Israel into the life of the country is not one of legislation or governmental decisions but involves overcoming anxiety and psychological blocks, prejudices, and rigid thinking on both the decision-making and implementing levels as well as in most of the Jewish population. Anyone interested in grappling with the problems of the Jewish–Arab conflict must recognize the existence of some basic facts, even if they are not to his liking from the geopolitical viewpoint. A sixth of the country's population, occupying several hundred thousand acres of land, is disadvantaged in regard to the planning and development of its physical infrastructure. This population is rapidly becoming urbanized, does not emigrate, and demands a proper physical infrastructure for life in modern conditions. This population is continually growing in level of education, economic power and social welfare requirements. This population constitutes a nationalistic potential that may not accord with the policies and goals of Israel. And this population, located at the Iron valley, on the eastern coastal plain, in the Negev and in northern Galilee, is close to the borders or the former 'Green Line', and ought to be viewed as a non-Jewish border population with all the security implications deriving from such a status.

Consequently, in order to prevent the eruption of pressures caused by discrimination, there is no escape from addressing the matter seriously and constructively. That means the preparation of a national physical, economic and settlement plan for the entire sector, taking into account its specific geographical characteristics; developing a settlement hierarchy in the regional Arab village complexes already in existence, with centres of a size and standard capable of providing services to their surroundings; creating, as needed, a new Arab townlet or town to absorb rural population unable to locate in the existing place; developing models of modern rural construction and adopting them as a basis of future development even if that means encroaching on agricultural land for housing purposes; promoting, in the large villages, the semi-urban elements such as public institutions, roads, industrial and craft zones, multi-storey construction, public areas, etc; facilitating the expansion of construction in the villages with dense populations and inadequate infrastructures, and integrating them into the national and regional system.

The formulation of a policy in regard to the Arabs of Israel is not so difficult, for an agreed policy exists. It is not a matter involving the solution of a nationalist conflict, but one of granting equality to citizens of the country. An examination of all party platforms shows that there is no disagreement among them on this point. The problem is only one of implementation and application. As the 'Second Israel' is gradually becoming well established and integrated the time has come to direct more resources to the 'Third Israel' as well. Such a step is likely to avert superfluous political tensions in the future, expressed in 'Land Days' and memorial days, and reflecting the frustration of the minorities who wish to live in a democratic country.

CHAPTER FOURTEEN

The Negev Vision and Settlement Reality

Is the dream of settling the Negev an impossible one? Does it stand the test of geography? Or is the effort to settle the Negev simply a geopolitical measure taken to prove the justice of Israeli sovereignty over the arid areas it captured in the War of Independence? In order to reply to these questions we must compare the geographical features of the Negev with those of other arid or semi-arid regions in the world, highlight their characteristics, the similar and dissimilar in them, and on that basis evaluate the potential in the Negev and its prospects for future settlement.

THE NEGEV AS SPACE FOR JEWISH SETTLEMENT

The Negev, which is south of the Beersheba valley, and the Judean desert northeast of it, are not areas of the kind whose geographical features encourage population and settlement, because they are below the 10 inch annual rainfall line that marks the division between wasteland and pasture. An arid or semi-arid region will not naturally lead to the development of an extensive settlement complex as would happen in regions with temperate or Mediterranean climates.

Life in a desert is difficult physiologically because the temperature is high in summer, the night cold, and dryness, dust and sandstorms endemic. The desert is also far from settlement centres, and the geographical remoteness results in social difficulties as well. Thus the settlement possibilities are limited to begin with, so that in order to ensure population in a desert beyond the pioneering and experimental stage, it must be provided with good basic conditions with regard to housing, accessibility and economy.

Surprisingly although the Negev is today sparsely settled, we have considerable information about a relatively great well-being and prosperity in the past. The Negev has developed an unfavourable image, which a survey of its settlement in earlier periods may well contradict. The Negev previously contained cities and border fortresses. The central Negev was an important crossroads for the whole region. In the Israelite period it was inhabited up to Sinai and Qadesh Barne'a. In the Nabatean period, the first century B.C., there were six towns in the Negev: Advat, Shivta, Halutza, Rehovot, Mamshit, and Nitzana. Under the Romans and Byzantines, the Negev reached a pinnacle of prosperity, and contained tens of thousands of people. Religious elements were interested in the Negev as well, and churches and other religious sites were located in its towns. In the Arab period, from the seventh century on, this settlement complex collapsed and the region was visited by a destruction which lasted almost a millenium.

The key to the settlement and development of the Negev was water, without which life was impossible in that arid region. And indeed, in the Nabatean, Roman and Byzantine periods, that desert had technologically unusual irrigation and water-collecting installations, including networks of canals, pits and diversion dams. These supplied water to the inhabitants of the time according to their needs and standard of living, which was of course infinitely lower than those of the present. Wars and the destruction of the water sources later put an end to the ancient settlement.

The Negev has not changed in basic geographical features in the past centuries. The changes that did take place were the result of political and cultural developments that affected its settlement. They took the form of additional semi-urban locations, villages, roads, railway lines, and a number of enterprises for the exploitation of minerals.

For many years the Negev was controlled by the Turks and the British. Neither of them considered the region especially important. Toward the end of the Ottoman period, the region acquired some strategic value after the opening of the Suez Canal (1869), and the demarcation of the boundary between the Land of Israel and Egypt (1906); consequently toward World War I the Turks invested some efforts there to meet the danger of a British invasion from the south. The British did not view the Negev as special either, and wished to hold it without making any great changes in it.

The acquisition of Negev land by Jews, as a political-settlement measure, continued from the start of the century up to the establishment of Israel. It encountered difficulties; conditions of land ownership were complicated; both the Turks who were in control in the early years and the British who succeeded them put obstacles in the way of Jews wishing to purchase land in the region; the region itself, which was semi-arid, was different from all the regions where land had previously been bought by Jews.

The Jews learned quite rapidly that populating the Negev was a difficult matter that would not succeed in the absence of scientific experiments. The Jewish National Fund took a generally unfavourable attitude regarding the Negev, preferring to concentrate its limited resources on other parts of the country. The scanty rainfall and water sources and the consequent impossibility of developing intensive agriculture in the Negev discouraged any practical measures.

The 1929 disturbances were followed by the Passfield 'White Paper' which among other things assessed the economic absorption capacity of the country. The disturbances set in motion a wave of land purchases in the Negev, mainly by private authorities, and by the mid-1930s Jews owned about 25,000 acres there. The 1936–9 disturbances led to even greater political polarization between Jews and Arabs. Again British inquiry commissions were formed, and one of them, the Peel Commission, in 1937 came to the conclusion that the British Mandate should be terminated and the country partitioned into an Arab state and a Jewish state under the aegis of Britain. According to that proposal the entire Negev was excluded from the future Jewish State – a stipulation which only intensified Jewish desire to hold on to the Negev.

Between the 1936–9 disturbances and the end of World War II (1945), a great upswing had taken place in Jewish efforts to purchase land in the Negev and establish new settlements there. During those years there was little fuss about the areas purchased, since political considerations were paramount, so that the quality or location of the land was hardly ever taken into account in decisions to purchase land. During the 'Stockade and Tower' period, when 50 new settlements were set up within three years in order to hold various parts of the country, Kefar Menahem, Kefar Warburg and Negba were established in the northern Negev. During World War II settlement in the Negev was still sparse, the available manpower being engaged in the war effort, but Dorot was founded in 1941 and Ruhama two years later. Their locations were determined on the basis of plans for drilling for water and supplying it. They were, however, north of the aridity line. The settlement of Gat and Gevar'am in 1941, and Nir Am and Be'erot Yitzhaq in 1942–3, moved the settlement area southwards to the Gaza–Dorot line. The number of Jews in all the southern and Negev settlement did not then exceed 1,600.

In that period a new settlement initiative was adopted by the Jewish National Fund, the establishment of topsites. Each was to contain about a dozen people to carry out agricultural experiments, grapple with the Negev climatic conditions and water scarcity, and test the reactions of the British and the local Bedouin to these settlement projects. Three such topsites were established in 1943 – Gevulot, Revivim and Bet Eshel. The idea of these sites proved itself and led to the establishment of additional settlements in the Negev in the following years. For political and economic reasons the settlement authorities believed that they should content themselves with the Gaza–Dorot line as the boundary of Jewish settlement in the south, and not go further south.

After World War II a more vigorous Jewish opposition was undertaken against the British, who made use of considerable military forces to combat it. The British government came to realize that it had reached an impasse on the Jewish question in the Land of Israel. An inquiry commission in 1946 recommended providing 1,000 immigration certificates for Jews in the displaced persons' camps of Europe, repealing the land laws, and establishing a British trusteeship in the Land of Israel. According to the Morrison–Grady plan, the country was to be divided into three parts, 17 per cent for a Jewish State, 40 per cent for an Arab State, and 43 per cent, mainly in the Negev, as British territory. The plan was rejected by all, even by some of the British themselves. In response, an extensive settlement project was carried out in 1946, with 11 settlements being set up in one night, the night of Yom Kippur. This operation surpassed all previous ones in scope, as regards the number of sites, the number of departure points, and the drama of settlement in the arid Negev.

In 1947 the political situation in the country became quite delicate, and the British decided to submit the problem to the UN. In view of this, the settlement authorities decided to consolidate and extend Jewish settlement in the Negev so that that region would remain primarily Jewish. The principal problem at the time was the transfer of water from the north to the Negev. The alternatives were the utilization of water from drillings near the Negev or the transfer of water from the Yarqon and Jordan and other northern streams, on the assumption that the water would be needed for some 30 Negev settlements on about 140,000 acres. Earlier the Jewish National Fund had reduced land purchasing in the northern Negev because of the fear of a lack of water, but wells had been dug at the experimental sites that indicated that with a reasonable quantity of water that area could be settled. At that time the American engineer Walter Clay Lowdermilk proposed a plan for carrying water from the north of the country to the south. However, the immediate water projects carried out included two pipelines from the Nir Am drillings, the eastern one going to Dorot, Ruhama, Shoval, Mishmar HaNegev, Bet Eshel and Nevatim, and the western one to Be'erot Yitzhaq, Urim and Nirim, with branches to Tequma and Be'eri. The need to protect these important pipelines led to the establishment of Tze'elim and Gevim. And just before the establishment of the State of Israel, the last three sites – Alumim, Halutza and Mishmar HaNegev – were set up.

The UN resolution of 29 November 1947 included the Negev in the Jewish State whose establishment it declared, arousing sharp objections from both the Arabs and the British as the Negev had been seen as a buffer between Jordan and Egypt. An area amounting to 62 per cent of the mandatory Land of Israel, including most of the Negev, was assigned to the Jewish State. When the War of Independence broke out, there were 30 Jewish settlements in the Negev with a total of 3,000 inhabitants. They had to defend the region during the war, blaze roads, and face the Egyptian army coming from the south.

It can thus be seen that from the turn of the century to the establishment of Israel, the Negev experienced many settlement variations characterized on the one hand by a political struggle and on the other by trial and error regarding the possibility of achieving well-established settlement there. The Turks had little interest in the Negev, although they established Beersheba in 1900 and during World War I felt it was important in pre-venting the penetration of the British through the Suez Canal south of the country. The British viewed the region as a buffer between Sinai and the Lands of Israel and stressed its military and transport value. The Jewish community, for its part, was hesitant about settling it and until World War II made few attempts to do so, most of them marked by unsystematic land purchases, generally dictated by their low cost.

THE NEGEV POPULATION POTENTIAL

The assessment of a region's natural population potential can be made in several ways. We shall adopt one of them, perhaps the simplest and most reasonable: comparison with regions like the Negev in similar geographical conditions.

Let us bound the Negev by its natural climatic boundaries and encompass all sovereign territory in the southern part of Israel which is below the 10 inches rain line separating the wasteland from the cultivated. Arid and semi-arid zones of the Middle East and North Africa which have a long settlement history and geographical conditions similar to those of the Negev include western Jordan, the southern Atlas mountain in Algeria, the Tripoli–Bengazi axis in Libya, western Syria, northern Iraq and central Iran between Tehran and Isfahan. If we examine their population density and settlement picture, we will find the following:

a. The average rainfall in all of them is less than 10 inches per annum, and they are arid or semi-arid.
b. They have sparse populations, the density ranging from 5 to 50 per square mile.
c. The population concentrations are located in selected places with local advantages in water, transportation, topography, land or climate, generally at oases, crossroads, and intermediate points between geographical subdivisions.
d. The population extends along main traffic routes.
e. The agricultural population is small, mostly nomadic.
f. If there are urban concentrations, they contain between 50,000 and 100,000 people, mostly on the desert margins. Such population concentrations are exemplified by Tlemken in Algeria, Bengazi in Libya, Kirkuk in Iraq, and Kum and Kashan in Iran.

It is interesting to note that Israel's Negev has similar characteristics. The annual rainfall averages less than 10 inches, climatically it is semi-arid, its population density from Beersheba southwards is 30 per square mile, its main population concentrations are in towns like Dimona, Arad, Yeruham, Mitzpe Ramon and Elat, all of them scattered along main roads, and its largest urban centre, Beersheba, has a population of 120,000 and is located at the northern edge of the desert. As to the agricultural population, it is very small, about 7,000, while the nomadic Bedouin population there numbers some 57,000.

If all the regions listed above developed a similar settlement pattern and population density under similar geographical conditions, and if in their long settlement history they arrived at a certain population size and placement of cities and villages, it may be assumed that Israel's Negev, which has similar physical features, is likely to develop in similar fashion. Applying the average desert population density of 37.5 per sq. mile to the Negev area of 5,024 sq. miles including the northern extension toward the Judean desert, we get a natural population potential of 188,400. In fact, in 1977 the Negev had a Jewish population of 182,300, and today has reached about 230,000. There are 63 settlements of various types in the northern Negev and the Negev south of Beersheba, but they account for only 13 per cent of the total population of the region.

If the Negev resembles arid and semi-arid regions in other parts of the world, and if its population potential and settlement deployment are subject to the same dominant geographical factors, perhaps it can be said that the potential physical attributes of the Negev have already been exhausted, and there is not much likelihood of its absorbing more population in the future.

THE GEOPOLITICAL STRUGGLE TO SETTLE THE NEGEV

In view of the above conclusion, it may be assumed that no account was ever taken of the natural potential or population capacity of the Negev. The Negev was a goal for the scattering of the country's population, the aim being to cancel out the inequality between the densely populated regions on the coastal plain and the empty southern spaces. The first decade after the establishment of the State was characterized by continued settlement in the Negev and persistent efforts to develop that arid region. Up to the establishment of the State there were 30 settlements in the Negev, all kibbutzim, which among other things had served as bases for military operations and the conquest of the Negev all the way to Elat in the south. After the War of Independence, however, the Negev became rather static and little agricultural settlement was initiated there. There were a few attempts in the wake of the Suez campaign (1957), but they were shortly abandoned.

An unusual project was the establishment of five 'Nahal' settlements across from the Nitzana demilitarized zone and opposite the Rafah area. These were Diqla and Kerem Shalom near Rafah, Ashalim–Pequ'a, Mevo Shivta and Shadmot Shezaf opposite Bir Asluj–Auja, and they joined the two settlements already located in the Nitzana demilitarized zone – Be'erotayim and Qetziot. This was a reinforcement of settlements to meet the danger of a military conflagration in the area. After the Suez Campaign, when UN observers were stationed at the border with Egypt, the settlements were dismantled, except for Kerem Shalom.

The settlement form fashionable in the 1950s in the Negev was the development town. When the large waves of immigration arrived in the country, the abandoned Arab towns in the centre of the country began to fill up, while there were few such in the Negev – only Beersheba, Yavne and Majdal. In order to attract new population to the Negev, development towns were established between 1951 and 1956 that were not built on an earlier infrastructure. The Negev was opened to urban settlement in the mid-1950s after the paving of roads had been accelerated and the first development plants installed. Yeruham, Dimona and Mitzpe Ramon were set up to function as 'caravan towns' to provide services for passers-by.

Yeruham started as a transit camp for newcomers on the British 'oil road' between Beersheba and the 'Big Crater', 22 miles south of Beersheba. Dimona too was originally a transit camp on the Beersheba–Sedom road. Its development was promoted by local industrial enterprises, the atomic pile on the Rotem plain, and others. Mitzpe Ramon was founded in the wake of the Suez Campaign as a camp for people working on the Mitzpe Ramon–Elat road in the central Negev. The opening of Ma'ale Ha'atzma'ut turned this axis into the main road to Elat. Because of the absence of sufficient employment opportunities this town developed very slowly, and later found itself far from the main road when the Sedom–Elat road was opened to traffic. Arad, on the other hand, was established only in the 1960s, a kind of second generation development town. Its economy is based on the exploitation of environmental resources and on providing housing for people working at Sedom.

The remoteness and isolation of the urban settlements in the Negev led to a separate urban complex based on Beersheba as the main city. That city accounts for 54% of the urban population of the Negev while the others constitute: Dimona – 13%; Elat – 9%; Ofaqim – 6%; Arad – 6%; Sederot – 4%; Netivot – 4%; Yeruham – 3%; and Mitze Ramon – 1%. Most of the development towns were founded in the 1950s, and all were populated by newcomers. Since the 1960s the pace of populating the towns has slowed, and at the end of 1985, the situation was as shown in Table 12. Beersheba is unusual in its size and serves as the capital of the Negev. Only one town, Dimona, has more than 20,000 people, while the others remain small towns. This urban complex also lacks a rural hinterland since it is located in a desert region. Each of the towns is in fact an isolated locality in its surroundings, although some of those in the northern Negev were supposed to be service centres for agricultural surroundings. Most were established as service and industrial towns,

GPI—M

TABLE 12
POPULATION OF NEGEV TOWNS, 1985

Town	Population
Beersheba	114,300
Dimona	26,600
Elat	18,800
Ofaqim	13,100
Arad	13,600
Sederot	9,300
Netivot	8,400
Yeruham	6,100
Mitzpe Ramon	2,500

based on minerals, chemical plants or textile manufacture. They have grown for three reasons: natural increase, the arrival of newcomers, and a favourable immigration balance. In recent years, their growth has slowed somewhat, and most of them have an unfavourable immigration balance. On the other hand Beersheba is today a large urban concentration by general Israeli standards and is growing faster than any other new town in the country.

When the IDF withdrew from Sinai in 1957, the Negev enjoyed an economic spirit, investments were made in infrastructure and industry, the Elat area was developed, and enterprises were established in Dimona. Newcomers gradually settled in the development towns, 20 per cent of the 240,000 that arrived during that period going to towns in the south, yet the pace was still slow given the population needs of the Negev. In the mid-1960s, a sluggish economy heralded a general depression and the Negev suffered from population instability reflecting departures from the towns and a considerable decrease in newcomers to them. Apart from the towns large enterprises were installed in the Negev such as the potash plant at Sedom, the phosphates plant at Oron, and the copper operation at Timna. Of the 800,000 newcomers to Israel, only 10 per cent went to the Negev, and only 9 per cent of the resources for infrastructure were channelled southwards. Security was a difficult matter in those years, the infiltration of terrorists from the Gaza Strip and Sinai upsetting the stability of development and settlement.

Water from the Yarqon–Negev pipeline to the western Negev, supplying a hundred million cubic metres of water annually, the Na'an–Beersheba railway line, and the improvement of the roads added a great deal to the development potential of the region. Yet despite the varied development opportunities the Negev population remained small, constituting in 1965 no more than 5.3 per cent of the Israeli total.

The Six Day War pushed the western boundary of the Negev 188 miles away to the bank of the Suez Canal. The economic prosperity the country then experienced had no particular effect on the Negev. Certain development projects were initiated, such as the extension of the railway to Mount Tzefa, the operation of the 'land bridge' for cargo as a substitute for the Suez Canal, the construction of a university at Beersheba, etc. However the post-war waves of immigration, which included many newcomers from affluent countries, were not directed to the Negev, and the hope for population integration did not take place. Many investments made in Sinai and Judea–Samaria led to a moratorium on development in the Negev, and the departure of many of its residents for more densely populated regions.

After the Yom Kippur War, the Suez Canal was reopened, and the land bridge lost much of its economic value. The Elat–Ashqelon oil pipeline likewise remained functionally static. The Arava region, from Ne'ot Hakikar on the Dead Sea coast to Elat in the south, was given no serious development thrust. The Yamit region was established in northern Sinai as a new settlement region, reducing considerably the importance of Negev development at the time.

The Negev, which constitutes half of Israel's territory, is inhabited only in parts, and the process of populating it is hindered by natural, financial and manpower difficulties. Nevertheless the settlement policy implemented succeeded in getting it settled by Jews. In 1948 there were 3,000 Jews in the Negev, none at all in Beersheba. At the end of 1987 the Negev population was 289,600, of whom 232,000 were Jewish. Most of this growth took place between 1948 and 1965, due mainly to the settlements founded after Israel was established. While the first ones were located mainly in the northern Negev, in the course of time settlements were scattered further south to the central Negev, the Arava and Elat. Population density in the Negev moved from 0.3 per sq. mile in 1948 to 27.5 in 1961 and 45 in 1987. Despite the increased population and increased density there are still many uninhabited areas in the Negev. For half the 232,000 Jewish inhabitants of the Negev live in Beersheba, and south of that city – half the territory of the country – contains only 3 per cent of its people. And if we extend the northern boundary of the

Negev to the Beersheba–Gaza–Sederot line, we will be adding 6 per cent to the territory but only 4 per cent to the population. As to the rural settlements in the Negev, when Israel was established there were twelve kibbutzim and three moshavim. Nine of the 28 kibbutzim there at present were founded in pre-State days between 1943 and 1947. Thirteen others were established in the 1948–54 period, and only four since 1964. Of the 40 moshavim in the Negev, only one is a survival from mandatory times, 27 were founded in the 1948–54 period, and only six since 1961. Most of the rural settlements have 100 to 500 inhabitants. Most of the kibbutzim founded in pre-State days are smaller. The number of rural settlements in the Negev has risen from 15 in 1942 to about 80 in 1987, but whereas in the past the entire Negev population was rural, today only 13 per cent of it is, due mainly to the growing urbanization in the Negev (Figure 32).

HAS THE DREAM OF SETTLING THE NEGEV BEEN REALIZED?

Arid and semi-arid zones are areas naturally rejected by man. However, since more than half of Israel's territory falls into that category, the settlement institutions have no alternative but to utilize it as much as possible, since it is the country's largest reservoir of settlement areas. After 40 years of government development of the Negev, the population total there is 289,600. Of these, 57,600 are Bedouin, the Jewish population in the development towns totals about 210,000, the Jewish rural population in the central and southern Negev is only 7,000, while that in the northern Negev is 25,000. As we noted above, compared with arid and semi-arid zones elsewhere, the natural potential population capacity of the Negev is 188,400. Thus what has been achieved after decades of investment and Zionist aspirations is that the natural potential has been exceeded by 100,000, half of whom are Bedouin. The net 'profit' is therefore 50,000 Jews, by no means a negligible amount for semi-desert regions, but of doubtful value compared with the investment up to now.

A disproportion has evolved between the investments in industry, construction and services, and the rate at which the Negev has been populated. A lot of money has been invested in its infrastructure, but very few people live there. The fact that the Negev comprises about 60 per cent of Israel's territory, but only 13 per cent of its population points to a serious regional inequality. Before 1948 there were many potential settlement groups and no Negev land to settle;

FIGURE 32
SETTLEMENTS IN THE NEGEV

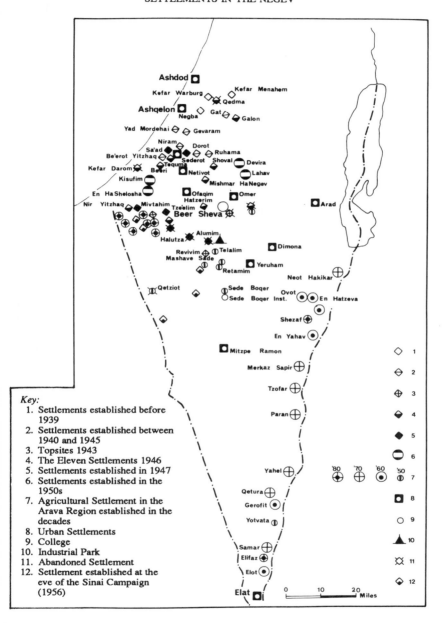

Key:
1. Settlements established before
   1939
2. Settlements established between
   1940 and 1945
3. Topsites 1943
4. The Eleven Settlements 1946
5. Settlements established in 1947
6. Settlements established in the
   1950s
7. Agricultural Settlement in the
   Arava Region established in the
   decades
8. Urban Settlements
9. College
10. Industrial Park
11. Abandoned Settlement
12. Settlement established at the
    eve of the Sinai Campaign
    (1956)

now there is land but a paucity of manpower. Since the establishment of Israel, the kibbutz movements have not been able to found
many new settlements. Most of the new ones have been 'Nahal'
groups which settled in border regions or joined existing settlements
that were suffering from social problems.

While after the establishment of Israel regional settlement complexes developed in various parts of the country, such as the Lakhish
region, the Ta'anakh region, and settlement under the Merhavim
regional council, no such hierarchy developed in the central Negev.
The settlements there are linked directly to Beersheba, and are not
self-sufficient.

The water resources of the Negev are today being used almost in
entirety, so that in the future it will be necessary to use desalinated
water, purified sewage water, or artesian water found in the Nubian
sandstone deposits of the Negev. The pipeline laid in the Negev in
1955, and the larger one laid in 1968, carried water only to the
western Negev, thus contributing to the development of the Eshkol
region, while in the other parts of the Negev settlement could only
develop selectively. It is no wonder that from time to time proposals
are made for projects such as conveying water from the Nile to Sinai
and the Negev, or utilizing the salty aquifer located between Urim
and Mashave Sade. The soil of the Negev also presents a difficulty
for most of it is loess, which requires constant harrowing to prepare
it for agriculture. Two thirds of the country's water resources are in
the north, a region which actually does not need all the water. On the
other hand, the Negev in the south, which includes about two thirds
of Israel's land, has no water resources at all, and therefore cannot
be cultivated. While water and land are the two main means of
production, a geographical inequality exists.

The development of transportation in the Negev has not been
regular either. Before the State, there were just two roads there,
from Beersheba to Gaza and from Beersheba to Nitzana and
Ismailiya. The main road to the Negev passed from the Givati
crossroads to Nir Am, and from there to Sa'ad and the Beersheba–
Gaza road. Jewish settlement before 1948 was located mainly in the
northwestern Negev, and relied on dirt roads. Afterwards the road
to Elat proceeded along the Beersheba–Kefar Yeruham–Big
Crater–Oron–Ma'ale Aqrabim–Ein Husub line through the Arava
to Elat. In the 1950s roads were surfaced from the Gilat crossroads
to Magen and Kerem Shalom, and from Beersheba to Dimona and
Sedom. It was only in the 1960s that a road to Elat through Sedom
and Be'er Menuha was completed. The Negev road network is

inadequate even today, despite the additional roads built as a result of the IDF redeployment in the Negev.

The settlement of this region is a most complicated challenge that requires the concentration of potential resources and a comprehensive planning approach. Certainly, a great deal has been invested and accomplished in the Negev, yet in the mid-1980s it is still in an undeveloped state. It is no wonder then that as the century draws to an end new visions are emerging for accelerating the development of the Negev including, among other things, sophisticated agriculture in hothouses, new methods of irrigating sandy soil, greater exploitation of sewage water, the lavation of saline soil in the Sedom area, the use of fossil water in the Arava, the establishment of a large industrial zone at Ramat Hovav, the utilization of an atomic pile to desalinate water at the Halutza sands, and urban settlement in the Lahav–Yatir area. There is no doubt that the cost of investment in the Negev is rising, and the dream of settling the desert has become extremely expensive. That is the price man must pay for fighting the dominance of a disadvantaged region and its sensitive natural ecological balance.

CHAPTER FIFTEEN

Land and Security in Border Settlements

Border settlement as a geographical phenomenon is the installation of people in peripheral areas of the country, generally near an international border, or at the edge of an area that cannot be settled because of climatic, political, physical or other reasons. Such settlement is generally motivated by ideological, pioneer, economic or political factors impelling the population to live its life in new regions. Border settlement involves human endeavours to adapt to new geographical conditions, the adoption of a way of life different from the conventional type, constant trial and error as regards means of livelihood, and also a more than negligible amount of danger. Border regions are far from the country's large urban concentrations and densely populated areas, their population is sparse and scattered and subject to frequent replacement. There are border regions that remain in their frozen state for a long period, and others whose economic and settlement success results in their naturally integrating into the country's settled space to the point where their having ever been marginal or 'unsettlable' simply becomes ancient history.

We shall endeavour to analyze the development of border settlement in Israel, characterizing its typical patterns against the background of the security and political motives that led to their creation.

PRE-STATE BORDER SETTLEMENT; THE SINGLE POINT MODEL

Between the first modern immigrants (1882) and World War I, the settlements of Metulla, Tel Hai and Kefar Giladi can be described as border settlements planned and organized as such by the Zionist Organization. There were settlements in Galilee and on the coastal plain founded before these, but by structure and location they were not border settlements.

The special feature of Metulla, which was founded in 1896, is its geographical location at the northern extremity of the Land of Israel. In its early years, Metulla suffered repeated attacks by Druze, but its inhabitants defended themselves and did not abandon the site. After World War I, during the struggle for control of the region by the French and the Arabs, Metulla was taken alternately by both.

Although it was linked to the villages of Hatzbiya and Jedida in southern Lebanon, and its land was in the Ayun valley, Metulla managed to be included in the area of the British Mandate and within the boundaries of the 'National Home', and thus established an important political fact for the Jewish people in the Land of Israel. Tel Hai and Kefar Giladi were definitely border settlements of the security type, meant to secure the northern border. Tel Hai's land was acquired in 1893 by Baron Rothschild in order to supplement the land held by the Metulla farmers. Because of its distance from Metulla, only a few farmers settled there; they were constantly harassed by the Arabs, were more than once reinforced by new settlers, the last time in 1918. The site was finally abandoned in 1920 after the attack during which Joseph Trumpeldor and his comrades were killed.

Kefar Giladi was established in 1916. Its members engaged in farming and mounting guard. The Kefar Giladi people were well aware of the security and political importance of their settling on the site, which required constant fighting and self-defence. The struggle between the Arabs and the French for control of Upper Galilee did not bypass Kefar Giladi, which experienced the same problems as Metulla.

Another border settlement initiative outstanding in dimensions and geographical extent took place during the 1930s. That was a period in which international tensions and economic crises provoked disturbance among the Arabs of the Land of Israel, who had never been reconciled to Jewish settlement in the country and had even imperilled the continued existence of the 'National Home'. The restrictions the mandatory authorities placed on Jewish settlement, the publication of the White Paper, the con-traction of the area open to Jewish settlement, the danger that the country would gradually become a Palestinian State with a Jewish minority, and the concern regarding the partitioning of the country aroused by the Peel Commission impelled the Jewish community to undertake massive settlement activity to occupy the 'internal periphery', the areas without a Jewish population.

The type of settlement called 'Stockade and Tower' was used

between 1936 and 1939 in various parts of the country, particularly in sectors mainly populated by Arabs. The function of these settlements was to ensure the possession of the lands purchased, extend to settled areas, and demonstrate steadfastness in the face of Arab aggression that derived from the uncertain situation in the country. As a rule they were constructed in such a way as to be able to defend themselves immediately. The practice was to build an observation tower, wooden fence and cabins in a not too distant locality, and secretly transport them dismantled to the spot chosen for the new settlement. This instant construction was unusual anywhere in the world. During those three or four tumultuous years, 50 new settlements were established, most of them by this pre-fabrication method. The most widely celebrated of them was Hanita, which symbolized border settlement, as it was located near the country's northern border, where there had been no Jewish settlement since the Metulla, Tel Hai and Kefar Giladi period.

The 'Stockade and Tower' settlement was very dynamic; it was spread over the entire country, but for the most part was focused on the Bet She'an Valley and Galilee. At the time comparisons were made between that innovation and the tank. The appearance of the latter in World War I put an end to wearying static trench warfare, and the former, in a time of disturbances, made possible the rapid advance into border regions and uninhabited areas.

The 1940s were marked by border settlement in the northern Negev. In 1943 the national institutions began to view the settlement of the Negev as particularly important, because of the impending partition of the country and the danger that the Negev might be excluded from the area of Jewish settlement. As know-how about settlement in arid zones was then very scanty, it was decided to set up a number of observation points where for three years the possibilities of desert agriculture would be investigated. The Jewish National Fund programme at the time stipulated that wherever in the Negev there was a possibility of buying land, such an observation point with ten or twelve workers should be established to systematically study the local soil, climate, flora and water conditions. Each of these points was to have a courtyard surrounded by a fence, a two-storey security tower, a dining room and kitchen, two residential rooms, a weapons storeroom and sheds. Points were set up at Bet Eshel, Revivim and Gevulot, which had differing soil and climatic conditions; these represented the first border-type settlements in the southern part of the country. Some time later construction was begun on permanent buildings in these observation points, designed somewhat like castles. Planned for 25 people, they also had a storeroom for arms, and a surrounding wall. Until 1947, the residents did not go outside the walls to expand the farming operation. The isolation of the points persisted until 1946 when 11 new settlements were established in the northern Negev in order to reinforce the border settlement in that region. In 1947 another seven settlements were founded. In the secret operation to set up the new localities in the northern Negev, more than 1,000 people and 200 vehicles were involved. The placement of the settlements was determined by the areas where land had been acquired by the Jewish National Fund. It had made its purchases wherever possible, without taking into account the quality of the land, the proximity of water sources or roads. Contact between settlements was effected by signalling, radio, or field telephone. Many found themselves isolated when rain fell, since their centre for services, supplies, mail, etc. was Rehovot or Tel Aviv. Each settlement was built on the highest ground of the land assigned to it, and had a water tower in the middle. Generally at their inception the settlements comprised three huts, an observation tower that eventually became the security building, and tents. Its area did not usually exceed 25 acres. The pre-State border settlement described above was carried out in the changing security and political conditions then prevailing, and had the following characteristics (Figure 33).

a. Land was occupied and rural settlements set up at disparate points selected by settlement institutions.
b. The number of points and the size of the area settled depended on the resources then at the disposal of the settlement institutions and on the seriousness of the prevailing political situation.
c. The purpose of the border settlement was to solve domestic problems reflected in a conflict between Jews and Arabs that had international repercussions.
d. The 'Stockade and Tower' type settlement was the most common, and the establishment of the northern Negev settlements was the most during one-time settlement operation.
e. The pre-State border type settlement was characterized by fortuitous locations, small units, simple unsophisticated defence measures, and by the pioneer spirit, courage and readiness to make sacrifices of the settlers.
f. Examination of this border settlement along a time axis shows

FIGURE 33
BORDER SETTLEMENTS IN THE LAND OF ISRAEL 1896–1947

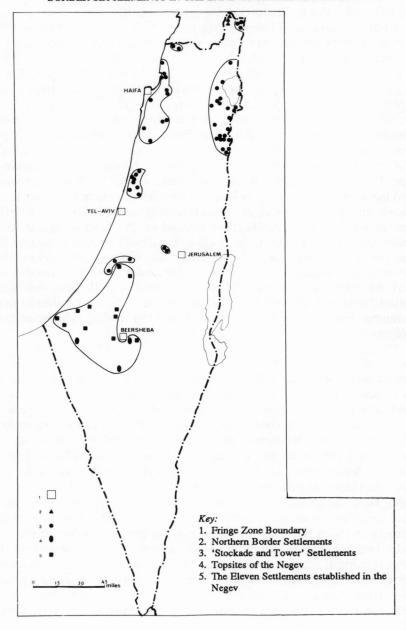

Key:
1. Fringe Zone Boundary
2. Northern Border Settlements
3. 'Stockade and Tower' Settlements
4. Topsites of the Negev
5. The Eleven Settlements established in the
   Negev

that in the 1930s it consisted of widely scattered isolated points while in the 1940s regional border settlement was begun.

g. The absence of regional border settlement elsewhere in the Land of Israel may provide the background for the development of the 'Green Line' after the War of Independence and of the subsequent border settlement.

BORDER SETTLEMENT IN ISRAEL UP TO THE SIX DAY WAR;
THE REGIONAL MODEL

Border settlement in the State of Israel derived from the need to fortify its borders, whether international or of the 'Green Line' variety which emerged from the 1949 armistice agreements between Israel and the Arab countries. The establishment of the State produced a new situation compelling Israel to set up border settlements along hostile frontiers with the confronting enemy countries that in 1947–8 had waged open war against it. The border was 665 miles long. On the other hand, most of the 'border' settlement inside the country diminished in importance because a large part of the Arab population left the villages during the War of Independence, and the 8,017 square miles area within the new borders became Israel sovereign territory. Thereafter border settlement was concentrated at external borders, most of them in difficult topography inconvenient for settlement.

The nature of the new 'periphery' is reflected in the ratio between the length of the land borders and the area, which was 1:12. In other words, every mile of border has an average 'land depth' of 12 sq. miles, quite a small area both in absolute terms and in comparison with other 'confrontation states' in the world.

If we accept as the definition of a border area a strip of land adjacent to an international border or armistice line meant to serve as a security buffer between what is on the other side and the settled parts of the country, we will find that a strip one mile wide on the average runs along those borders. The actual width varies with the topography, the extent of the danger across the border, the hinterland area and its suitability for settlement, and the settlement density in the hinterland.

In order to determine the periphery in Israel we can use as indicator the list of Israeli localities whose population figures were not given in official government statistics for security reasons. The 134 such settlements can demarcate the Israeli periphery by indicating a settlement continuum opposite Lebanon and Syria, a settlement deployment opposite Judea–Samaria in strips of varying length, the location of Jerusalem as a divided border city, the absence of any settlement continuity south of Mount Hebron, at the Dead Sea, and most of the border with Sinai, and on the other hand the 'thickening' border at the Gaza Strip. This peripheral area totalled 850 sq. miles, or about 10 per cent of Israel's territory. The population can be estimated at 36,000, but the urban settlements in the periphery – East Jersualem, Qiryat Shemona, Bet She'an and Elat – number about 100,000 (Figure 34).

The type of border settlement characteristic of the early years of the State was strongholds occupied first by the army and then by 'Nahal' units trained for agricultural and security settlement. These strongholds were organized by the Ministry of Defence and the army to occupy uninhabited border areas, examine agricultural settlement conditions in new areas, serve as observation posts for areas across the border, and constitute a dissuasive force against infiltrators in those uninhabited areas. The strongholds were set in localities with difficult topography, were sometimes isolated and in places where ordinary people would not readily settle. A border settlement of that kind included military and agricultural equipment, was populated by young people, and could be transformed into a permanent settlement if economic and agricultural conditions permitted. The authorities' approach was that settlements along the borders, whose residents would cultivate fields right up to the armistice line, would guarantee the security of the country.

Before the Six Day War, there were two main waves of 'Nahal' settlement. The first, between 1950 and 1956, closed the dangerous gaps in the periphery: in the northwestern corner of the country, in the Hula valley below the Golan Heights, east of the Jordan's effluence from Lake Kinneret, in the eastern part of the Sharon lowland, and in areas opposite the Latrun enclave, the Mount Hebron slopes and the Gaza Strip. During that period 26 such strongholds were set up. During the second period, between 1957 and 1967, nine more were founded to complete the task where the security problem was especially sensitive: where the Jordan flows into Lake Kinneret, opposite the Gilbo'a mountains, in the Modi'im district and through the Arava. This settlement deployment still followed the isolated point pattern, with each locality capable of independent existence and therefore able to be placed in almost any geographical conditions. This isolated point pattern differed from the pre-State type in being linearly distributed along security borders.

FIGURE 34
BORDER SETTLEMENTS AND DEVELOPMENT REGIONS IN ISRAEL 1948–1966

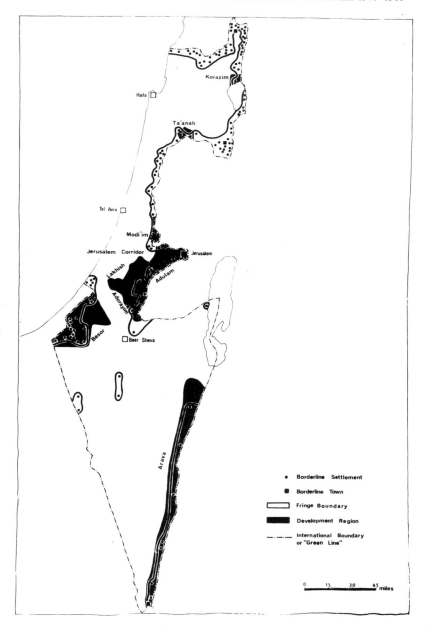

By the mid-1950s it became clear that a long narrow border strip did not ensure security of the space behind it, even if manned by 'Nahal' personnel. The problem of strategic depth in a long, narrow, sparsely populated country was resoundingly to the fore, with disquiet along the borders and the infiltration of terrorists who committed robbery and murder. The need to 'deepen' the periphery, the availability of uninhabited land, and a potential population from among the mass immigration to Israel in those early years – all these joined to inspire the idea of development districts to solve the new problems of the borders. The organization of a development district was meant to create a hinterland for the periphery where settlement would be carried out on a regional level through a large number of localities having economic and cultural ties arranged by the settlement institutions, among which centres would be located to provide services and organization for life in the region. In the course of a decade and a half nine development regions were founded whose features are shown in Table 13.

TABLE 13

DEVELOPMENT REGIONS – AREA, RURAL LOCALITIES AND CENTRES

Name of Region	Area in sq. miles	No. of Rural Localities	No. of Centres
Korazim	20.8	2	
Ta'anakh	26.0	13	3 (Ya'el, Omen, Hever)
Modi'im	38.8	2	
Jerusalem Corridor	111.2	28	1 (Bet Shemesh)
Adulam	36.4	6	1 (Neve Mikha'el)
Lakhish	246.8	30	3 (Qiryat Gat, Nehora, Even Shemuel)
Adoryaim	14.8	2	
Besor	260.0	38	1 (Ofaqim)
HaArava	166.4	12	2 (Hatzeva, Merkaz Sapir)

The table shows the following:

a. The overall area of the development districts came to 921.2 sq. miles, 11.4 per cent of the area of Israel. That is quite a large proportion and indicates the importance of the periphery in the settlement deployment. This is in addition to the peripheral strip described above, which constituted 10 per cent of Israel territory.

b. There were more development regions in the southern part of the country than in the north, and the southern regions were also larger. The concentration of development regions is in positive correlation with the sparsity of population, which was greater in the south than in the north.

c. Towns developed in only three of these regions – Lakhish, Besor and the Jerusalem Corridor. In Ta'anakh, Adulam and HaArava only bloc centres evolved, and in Korazim, Modi'im and Adorayim, none at all.

d. The number of localities varies from region to region. They are numerous in Lakhish, Besor and Jerusalem Corridor, fewer in Ta'anach and HaArava, and very few in the rest. Thus a complete settlement hierarchy evolved in selected regions only, while the rest remained in a kind of experimental stage of regional settlement that was not fully realized.

As noted, the sparse population in southern Israel, the desire to spread it over uninhabited sectors, and the availability of new tracts of land made it possible to enlarge the hinterland of the southern border strip more than that of the northern one, and even establish new towns as service centres for those regions. The special feature of this border settlement is that it exemplifies a regional hierarchical pattern carried out by new immigrant settlements with no special defensive or security structure, which by their mere distribution in the region created a certain state of affairs behind the border line. As this settlement endeavour was based on a new type of population with no ideological or military background, it could not be built of settlements in the isolated point pattern. The cultural level of the population, its social background and agricultural know-how required regional settlement and the constant help of the settlement categories from village to regional town. The emphasis was however on rural development, although in a few places priority was given to the establishment of agricultural industry and the improvement of services, contributing to the growth of the various bloc centres, but as a background for agriculture. Before 1967 no attempt was made to develop an urban periphery as a regional solution. In the case of Jerusalem we have witnessed the result of the unplanned appearance of an urban periphery in a divided city, while Elat, Bet She'an or Qiryat Shemona were founded as development towns as part of a national programme for distributing the population, but not as part of a planned urban periphery.

BORDER SETTLEMENT AFTER THE SIX DAY WAR; THE
REGIONAL–URBAN PATTERN

The border-region map of Israel changed drastically after the Six
Day War. The chief changes derived from the cancellation of the
border region at the 'Green Line' around Judea–Samaria and the
Gaza Strip. The border region in eastern Upper Galilee lost its
importance as did that at East Jerusalem. The border region near
the Lebanese border retained its importance and so did the one near
the Arava. Israel's border regions moved eastwards and southwards
for geopolitical reasons, so that four new border regions evolved:
the Golan Heights, the Jordan valley, and northern and eastern
Sinai (Figure 35).

While the previous border areas were within the recognized
borders of Israel and were meant to safeguard the lives of the
residents there, the new border areas were beyond the accepted
borders, and intended to protect long-range interests of security and
settlement in the 'Greater Land of Israel'. These new border regions
were populated principally by old-timers preferring to settle in new
spaces open for economic development, by establishing 'Nahal'
villages, kibbutzim and urban centres of various kinds. The data on
those border regions is given in Table 14, which indicates:

TABLE 14

BORDER REGIONS SINCE 1967 – AREA, LOCALITIES AND CENTRES

Region	Area (in sq. miles)	Rural Settlements	Centres
Golan Heights	444	31	3 (Qatzrin, Hispin, Bene Yehuda)
Jordan Valley	412	27	3 (Ma'ale Efrayim, Hamra, Shelomziyyon)
Yamit (before evacuation)	196	15	2 (Yamit, Avshalom)
Eastern Sinai (before evacuation)	200	2	1 (Ofira)

a. The new border regions are larger than the pre-Six Day War
    ones, the total area being 1,252 sq. miles.

b. These border regions contain regional centres planned
    according to a hierarchical pattern more advanced than the
    earlier one.

c. A multiplicity of rural settlements on the Golan Heights, in the
    Jordan Valley and the erstwhile Yamit region. 'Nahal' localities
    were very important and popular during the first 19 years of

FIGURE 35

BORDER REGIONS IN ISRAEL AND IN THE 'OCCUPIED TERRITORIES' 1967–1979

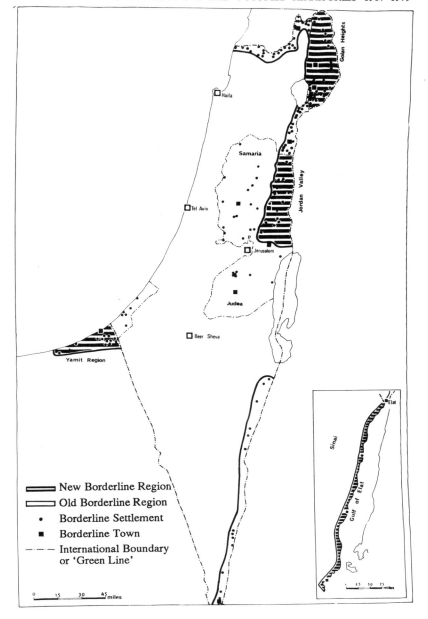

New Borderline Region
Old Borderline Region
• Borderline Settlement
■ Borderline Town
—·—· International Boundary
    or 'Green Line'

Israel's statehood, between its establishment and the Six Day War (1948–1967), because the armistice line (the 'Green Line') was a very complicated one. One could consider them as a very good solution in their time. But after the Six Day War this type of settlement was again used by the military authorities as a means to protect the new borderlines, mainly during the six years between the Six Day War and the Yom Kippur War (1967–1973). This third wave of 'Nahal' settlement includes 20 sites on the Golan Heights, 12 in the Jordan Valley, and seven in the Yamit region.

d.   Outstanding in this more recent settlement is the urban element. Within a short time the town of Qatzrin and the bloc centres of Hispin and Bene Yehuda were established on the Golan Heights, the regional centre Ma'ale Efrayim and the bloc centre Hamra and Shelomziyyon in the Jordan Valley, and the town of Yamit in the region of Yamit. These urban settlements were quickly integrated into the economic and social organization in their regions.

e.   An innovation is discernible in the placement of the settlement within each region. On the Golan Heights, for instance, three lines of settlements are distinguishable: an eastern one near the Syrian border, more interior sites on the central Golan Heights, and another in the south eastern corner across from the Syrian and Jordanian border. In the Jordan Valley there was one line of settlements on the east along the river and another at the edge of the Judean desert. In the Yamit region there were three clusters of two or three settlements each, which filled the space between the Gaza Strip on the east and El-Arish on the west.

f.   Especially outstanding were the exceptional developments in eastern Sinai – the construction of the town of Ofira at the most remote southern end of the region, and the various resorts and recreational sites between Elat and Sharm esh-Sheikh at Di-Zahav and Nevi'ot.

All in all, after the Six Day War the most advanced and comprehensive type of political border settlement ever undertaken in Israel was developed. Its main feature was the prominence of the urban element, accompanied by comprehensive regional settlement that also developed sophisticated agriculture and new methods of cultivation when needed. In desert regions like the Yamit and Eastern Sinai the cities were a dominant border manifestation. When the agricultural basis of the district is better, as in the Jordan Valley and

Golan Heights, a more inclusive settlement hierarchy develops that includes a town plus secondary urban centres.

BORDER SETTLEMENTS IN JUDEA–SAMARIA; THE MIXED PATTERN

Whereas after the Six Day War most border settlement was carried out in areas with little or no population, this was not the case in Judea–Samaria. There a new phenomenon appeared, intra-regional border settlement for the purpose of holding districts populated by Arabs, maintaining internal security in the area, and making possible sovereignty over new ones. No 'exterior periphery' was created here as in the regions described above, but rather an 'interior periphery', and the settlements here had some of the quality of the 'Stockade and Tower' model, though more advanced and improved, aiming at installation within an Arab-populated area. This applied also to a number of places in the Gaza Strip.

The settlement here took the form of strongholds, 'Nahal' sites and industrial villages, at a later stage gradually achieving a permanent status. Many were built on unoccupied State land, on land inferior for agricultural purposes and sometimes far from existing roads, and those places still lack a good infrastructure and supply of services. Amounting to many dozens of sites, this settlement in certain cases exemplifies location along roads, and at crossroads, but lacks a planned complex showing a clear pattern, a hierarchical structure or any regional conception at all. Except for the cluster of settlements in the Etzion bloc which are supposed to constitute a unit, and the settlement in the Jordan Valley, all the rest seem quite scattered and unsuitable for a border structure. These strongholds are for the most part located in the eastern parts of Samaria, and in the Jerusalem area. They were set up there because of the land available and to cause minimal detriment to the existing population.

Another approach to the settlement of the region is urban settlement, which is reflected in three places: in Qiryat Arba, whose construction is connected with religious and nationalist ideology regarding renewed Jewish residence in Hebron; the Jerusalem environs for the purpose of creating a metropolitan urban space around the capital; and in Judea–Samaria, with the intention of setting up a network of larger than usual non-agricultural settlements that would be able to develop on stony soil, such as Qarne Shomron, Ari'el, Emmanu'el, Ma'ale Edumim, Giv'on and Efrat.

Smaller places planned as industrial villages are expected to 'thicken' the area and fill it up.

To sum up, border settlement in Israel actually reflects a political reality in constant flux, the resources available for it at any one time, the geographical features of the region in question, and past settlement experience. It is very obvious that a gradual transition has been taking place from the rural agricultural approach to the community-urban approach, for the border regions and the country as a whole. Since within the State of Israel border settlement of whatever pattern has always had an effect on the boundaries of sovereignty, presumably today too the facts of the new settlement will have an impact on political and territorial decisions made in the future.

CHAPTER SIXTEEN

Land Use for New Political Settlement

The pre-State form of settlement suited the population structure, the demographic components, and the economic and political goals. The kibbutz was designed for a young, idealistic, pioneering population that sought challenges reflected in border settlement and the 'conquest' of new regions. The moshav structure was a framework for an agricultural population interested in developing a farm economy with a degree of cooperation in the area of marketing, mechanized equipment and public services; anyone who was inclined to agriculture but had no political or youth movement background, and was not prepared for the total collectivity of the kibbutz lifestyle, found the moshav a perfect solution. The moshava, or colony, provided an agricultural base for the lower-middle-class sector of the population that was interested in suburban living based on private farming. The rest of the population which had no interest in any form of agricultural settlement gathered in the cities where the main occupations were services, crafts and industry.

When Israel was established, those traditional types of settlement were the basis for absorbing the mass immigration, each having its own absorption potential. The potential of the kibbutz was minimal because it was based on a political and ideological background that did not suit most of the newcomers. The colonies did not absorb many newcomers because they were based on private farms that most of the newcomers could not afford, so transit camps grew up around them, later becoming newcomers' neighbourhoods, whose residents were employed in part-time farm work. The moshav was the form of settlement adopted by most of the newcomers inclined to agriculture, to the point where hundreds of newcomer moshavim were set up in the pattern of the classic moshav structure. The rest of the newcomers settled in the development towns then established as a new urban form of settlement.

The social and economic changes that took place in Israel as a result of the mass immigration, and the consequent large-scale agricultural settlement, led to a search for new spatial solutions. The existence of 'occupied territories', the creation of a dense network of settlements within the 'Green Line', the change to new crops, the development of specialist farms, and the changed relationship of the village to its surroundings as regards farm services, industrial installations, and agricultural service, produced new approaches that were reflected in regional planning, new uses of land, and settlement farms adapted to changing political conditions.

We shall concentrate below on the new political forms of settlement – especially the industrial villages, the Galilee topsites, the community centres, the 'inanimate centres' and exurbs (see below) – which have evolved in Israel in recent years out of the need to solve new population problems. These problems are related to the goal of scattering the population and to the desire to settle new regions which, as noted, could not be settled in the traditional settlement hopes of kibbutz, colony or moshav (Newman, 1984). We shall also consider two main problems: How do the settlement institutions view these new types today, and what land uses will they find for them?

THE INDUSTRIAL VILLAGE

The industrial village is a rural cooperative unit whose main source of livelihood is not agriculture but rather industry and services. Most of the industrial villages are located in zones poor in means of production, mainly land and water. Thus most are on the Golan Heights, in central Galilee, in Samaria and in the Jordan Valley. The current conception is that industrial villages should be established in blocs of five to eight units, with the addition of two 'inanimate centres'. That is necessary because new industrial production generally requires a large manpower reservoir and area. The location of several industrial villages in a bloc makes it possible to concentrate a number of plants in an area and thus also allow for variety. The bloc arrangement also makes for a larger total population than scattered industrial villages would, and thus justifies a higher level of public services.

The hope is to locate the industrial villages in spots that provide advantages in climate, scenery and accessibility. Generally about 50 acres of State land is allotted to each, 25 acres to the 'inanimate centres' near them, and 250 acres for areas between the villages. The space is so planned that one or two villages with attached industry are constructed in the first stage, and a bloc service centre plus two or three additional villages and the industrial infrastructure in the second stage. The entire complex including the industrial centre is completed in the third stage. The need for such a settlement element was felt both by the population and the settlement organizations. Groups of potential settlements seeking a new framework, were formed in the late 1960s. The settlement organizations were at the time faced with the need to settle areas that were land- and water-poor, and had few Jewish inhabitants, and after the Six Day War these areas were joined by the occupied territories. The need to find a solution for the second generation from the rural agricultural areas also led to the idea of the industrial villages. The moshav structure allows for only a limited number of residents to be engaged in non-agricultural pursuits, no more than a quarter of the local population. Actual membership is the exclusive privilege of the holders of the land allotments and the one child expected to carry on. Consequently the other children have problems settling in the moshav and raising their families there. Most of the moshav areas, it should be added, are populated by people of African and Asian descent whose traditional way of life is patriarchal. They are therefore reluctant to leave their moshavim even if they cannot earn their living from agriculture. The industrial village can also provide a solution for the social absorption of newcomers from affluent countries who encounter problems in their contact with competing cultures and Israeli culture. An industrial village with a community that is homogeneous in culture, way of life and occupation may provide a suitable solution to this problem and for newcomers in the 1980s as well; it is a way of setting up a social type of settlement adapted to the professional structure and educational level of the newcomers.

There are today in Israel, including Judea–Samaria, some 80 industrial villages, most of them of the community type, and a few cooperative moshavim. While their organization is not uniform, they share a number of features: the land is owned by the State, the work is done by the people themselves, the cooperative and workers jointly own the means of production, the services and the public property, and the residents act together in regard to purchasing, supply and maintenance, education, culture, health and local government. The industrial villages that are moshavim are designed eventually to include 150–200 families, and the community type even 300. Every resident gets a house and some land for a garden; all the houses are the same size.

While the idea of the industrial villages was proposed in the Jewish Agency Settlement Department in 1973, they are still in a formative stage and it is too early to draw any conclusion regarding how well they suit their stated purpose.

THE COMMUNITY-TYPE SETTLEMENT

The community-type settlement, which in its final stage contains 200–300 families, enjoys great independence despite the co-operative of which all residents are members. The economic system is based on independent family units joined together whose employment and means of production are within the settlement. The by-laws of the association ensure the preservation of the character of the place and define the relationship between the association and its members. Most of the Gush Emunim settlements were established as community-type units. Most are concentrated today in Judea–Samaria.

The need for community-type settlements derives from Gush Emunim's ideological and political pressure to settle in Judea–Samaria and from the desire of some city people to live in a country area. While this community-type settlement is an independent unit in its social structure, it is not isolated. The tendency is to establish several such localities in geographical proximity, so that they form a cluster and can enjoy a higher level of services than can be provided to a single locality of 300 families; the region will also have a larger number of wage-earners, and greater security. In the final developmental stage an 'inanimate' regional centre will be set up within the cluster for industry and services, to reduce the amount of commuting for the residents. What has been learned to date is that placing culturally homogeneous groups in a locality and involving the people in the planning process ensures better adjustment. The community-type settlement is likely to assume a variety of forms, according to the residents' desire. Today it is a settlement type that serves the desire to populate sites in Judea–Samaria, but can in the future be applied in setting up clusters of localities around 'inanimate centres' and populating new regions.

TOPSITES

In the 1940s three strongholds, termed 'topsites', were set up in the Negev to investigate agricultural possibilities there. In the 1950s topsites were set up that were watch-towers to prevent forest fires, and they also served as observation points for tourists. These topsites were constructed in many places in Galilee and the Jerusalem

Corridor. In only one place, Yodfat, did an agricultural settlement develop around the topsite. In the late 1970s a considerable number were scheduled for Galilee and designed to develop into permanent settlements that would add population to Galilee.

The topsite complex in Galilee, 28 units in all, is distributed in six geographical concentrations: along the northern border, in the Tefen bloc, in the Tzalmon bloc and the Sakhnin valley, in western Galilee, in the Segev bloc and in the Nahal Zipori bloc. Most of the topsites are in advanced stages of construction and some are already occupied. Examination of their locations indicates the principles applied. They are located on State land, mostly stony or grazing areas difficult to traverse, or on hilltops unsuitable for agriculture. They occupy elevated sites that overlook areas not likely to be settled by Jews, and can observe what is happening around them. Their function is also to hold points that might be the sites of settlements in the future.

Some view the topsite programme as a political means of hastening the solution of the difficult problems of settling Galilee. Today that settlement is new in its means, but very similar to its predecessor in its principles. Presumably the topsites programme will solve the problem of holding the land, but it is doubtful whether it can change the demographic balance in Galilee appreciably. When the topsites are fully populated, however, they may very well evolve a new life style heretofore unknown.

THE INANIMATE CENTRES

The inanimate service centre is an uninhabited complex located between villages whose function is to supply educational, public, personal and other services and employment in industry and crafts. The 50 such centres in Israel are distributed as follows: 15 in the Negev, four in the Jerusalem Corridor, nine in the coastal plain, 14 in the northern valleys and eight in Galilee. The inanimate centre serves the rural settlements, and is therefore generally located in regions where rural settlement is predominant and has not yet become urbanized. Typical are the Hamra and Patza'el blocs in the Jordan Valley, each of which has its own inanimate centre: the Segev bloc has one under construction. The inanimate centre integrates well with the industrial village, and consequently one can be found in every cluster of such villages.

Underlying the idea of regional cooperation is the assumption that the potential of each settlement cannot be fully utilized within its own boundaries, while the association of several makes possible the use of that potential within a general framework that has its own capacity for activity and creativity. Such cooperation also makes possible a reasonable standard of cultural life. Such a unit is called an 'inter-village centre', and is a site in a rural area where various plants and installations are concentrated, generally owned by institutions established jointly by the settlements in the area.

The development of inanimate centres began in the early 1960s in kibbutz areas, then spread to mixed areas, and also areas of new moshavim. They were designed to concentrate various enterprises and the joint projects of several settlements, and are generally operated by people from the settlements that are partners in the enterprises. There are also inanimate centres that attract non-economic activity such as education, health, culture, etc. A distinction can thus be made between an inanimate centre for community services and one for industry. The inanimate centre constitutes a focal point for the regional cooperation frameworks in a limited area. It is characterized by a broad range of cooperation, a small number of participants, and by organizational centralization. These characteristics explain why the inanimate centres evolved in undeveloped homogeneous areas. On the need for inanimate centres supplying community services, there is no difference of opinion, and it may be assumed that such will in the future take root. In regard to the inanimate industrial centres, some are of the opinion that they are less likely to succeed because, except in kibbutz areas, the settlements cannot provide enough manpower to operate the industrial installations. If they must have recourse to the population of a large city for that purpose, it would be better to locate them in the city itself.

THE EXURB

This is an open settlement of rural character serving mainly as a residential quarter for a larger urban concentration. The population is likely to range between 500 and 2,000 families, so that local services of a reasonable standard can be provided, and a decent social fabric evolved. Construction is on land purchased by the resident. Characteristic today of private settlement on the margins of the 'Green Line', the exurb supplies the demand of considerable strata of the citizenry for relatively spacious dwellings at low cost.

This type of settlement is suitable for populating extensive areas with limited and difficult terrain located within convenient commuting distance from existing urban employment centres. It thus appears that the settlement authorities adopted new forms in order to meet the demand for the scattering of the population, and for settlement with political motives in new regions where land is not plentiful. Characteristic of these settlement forms is the change to industry and services and to forms of cooperation different from those usual in the past. These types of settlement do not require very large areas of land, and not always agricultural land, and scattering them is not too difficult. However, they are still in the trial and error stage, and only in the 1990s will it be possible to ascertain the extent to which they are adapted to Israel's new settlement fabric.

CHAPTER SEVENTEEN

Land and Development Policy in the Future

The 1980s and 1990s are likely to be critical years for Israel as regards land use as a basis for rational development. The time dimension, which is the future, and the space dimension, which is land, present planning and political problems involving the possible and optimal land uses in the space that will be at Israel's disposal in the future.

WHAT WILL HAPPEN IN THE FUTURE?

We shall attempt to estimate to what extent and in what areas we will have land for development in the 1990s for the basic purposes we will wish to advance at that time. In doing so we make a number of assumptions:

a. Israel's borders will include territory not much larger than it was before the Six Day War, with perhaps a marginal addition, a total area of about 10,000 sq. miles.

b. Development will not be evenly spread. In the future too there will be geographical inequality, with certain regions getting priority because of their past and their preferential geographical conditions, while others on hills or desert edges will remain underdeveloped and never match the general pace of development in the country as a whole.

c. The Israeli population will grow moderately. There will not be any mass waves of immigration bringing hundreds of thousands of newcomers within a short time. Natural increase plus some immigration will result in the addition of a million to the present population.

d. The State will have to provide dwellings for the growing population and will do so in selected places in accordance with the principle of scattering the population.

e. There will be increased economic activity along with the inhabitants' aspiration for a standard of development and living resembling those of western Europe.

f.   The three urban concentrations – Tel Aviv, Haifa and its suburbs, and Jerusalem and its environs – will continue to grow and constitute greater attractions than other places in the country.

g.   A certain pressure will be exerted on the margins of the central part of the country. Sections such as the northern Negev, the southern lowland, and certain mountainous parts of Galilee and the Jerusalem vicinity will, for security and political reasons, enjoy a greater development of infrastructure.

h.   In the near future we will witness a transition to new forms of settlement and construction, in each locality as well as in their positioning.

These assumptions are not particularly fanciful, indeed they are quite reasonable. They do indicate, however, that in the 1980s and 1990s the pressure to obtain land, especially for housing, industry, transportation, and engineering infrastructure, will continue, so that the trend towards changing the use of agricultural land will prevail.

WILL ISRAEL HAVE LAND FOR THE POPULATION AND SETTLEMENTS?

The population of Israel today is more than four million, and approximately another million is added every decade. Thus by the early 1990s Israel will have five million people, and by the end of the century five and a half. Such a large population will need a great deal of land for dwellings, economic activity and circulation, especially since it will be more and more difficult to spread it over new areas in the Negev and Galilee. To scatter the population becomes harder every year; the trend is towards crowding more and more, mainly in the coastal plain and the areas which were historically the first settlement areas in the country. To the extent that it does scatter, it locates on the Golan Heights, and Judea–Samaria. Although there will be increased population in the Negev, it must be recognized that the coastal plain, where all fear overpopulation, will continue to absorb people, and become more and more densely populated. To maintain the situation of a third of the population in the Tel Aviv conurbation, would mean a third of five and a half million, or a million and a half to two million people, in the central part of the country.

Israel is a country where the pressure of urbanization on agricultural land is extremely great. There are several reasons for this situation: (a) Israel is highly urbanized, with 89 per cent of the population living in cities or urban settlements, and that leads to a demand for additional land for dwellings, industry, services and commerce. (b) The rates of natural increase and immigration to Israel are high. The population grew by 90 per cent between 1961 and 1987, or about 3.5 per cent per annum, a high percentage compared to other countries. The urban population during those years grew by 96 per cent or 3.6 per cent per annum. (c) From the Beersheba Valley northwards, and particularly in the coastal plain, the population density in Israel is extremely high, close to 1,000 per sq. mile, which is higher than the density in Japan or Holland. (d) The territory of Israel is small, the distances short, and most villages are close to the cities, a proximity which naturally increases the pressure of urbanization on the rural sector, leading to a rise in the price of agricultural land and its sale for purposes of urban construction. It should be kept in mind, however, that because of the urbanization pressure, the agricultural areas of Israel also increased. In the first decade after the establishment of the State, the cultivated area grew by 625,000 acres, to 1,025,000 acres. Thereafter the rate of increase declined and today the area under cultivation totals 1,067,500 acres. The location of the land is also very important so far as urbanization is concerned. There is a great demand for urban land, while the supply of building lots in the towns is limited. Consequently urban land can exert a powerful influence on the price and uses of agricultural land. Increased demand for land for urban needs confronts the farmer with an economic dilemma, for if the agricultural use of the land is retained, he loses the added income he would have earned from the urbanization of the land. Still, in Israel land is not negotiable in completely open market conditions. Great importance is attached to national land and its uses are supervised by government institutions.

The demand for land in the vicinity of the towns derives from the increase in the urban population, from the resultant overcrowding, from the rise in real income enabling the citizens to seek larger dwellings in the suburbs, and also from inflationary pressures impelling people to invest in land. Urban pressure on agricultural land will constantly increase within each town's limits, and subsequently extend to the periphery.

The coastal plain is the most intensive urbanized region in Israel and also the most definitely agricultural one. The effect of urbanization on the land occurs in stages through its market value. When urban land prices are so high that the citizen cannot afford them, there is a movement toward purchases beyond the urban periphery, in areas where there is generally agricultural land. As the land in the coastal plain is suitable for both urbanization and agriculture, the competition for its use is fierce.

The extension of construction onto agricultural land took place in particular in the Tel Aviv area, and was effected in ever-expanding circles whose centre is the big city. The Tel Aviv extended circle and area of urban influence were once quite close, reaching the Yarqon River to the north, Holon and Bat Yam to the south, and Ramat Gan and Bene Beraq to the east. Today they are approaching Netanya to the north, Rehovot to the south, and Petah Tqiva to the east. The intensity with which agricultural land is being transformed for other uses is spreading radially, as the urban demands of the city grow. In the wake of the continual dwindling of the land reserves for residential purposes, for industrial plants, and other uses in the large cities, there is a tendency today to convert agricultural land in the medium-sized and smaller towns as well, which include 40–50 per cent of the urban jurisdictional areas in the country. The presence of large areas of agricultural land within the city limits of the smaller localities is a result of their development from beginnings as agricultural colonies. Most of the medium-sized towns in the coastal plain – Rishon le-Zion, Rehovot, Petah Tiqva, Kefar Sava – began as colonies whose main means of livelihood was agriculture. In the course of time their populations increased, most of the residents began to engage in non-agricultural pursuits, until the localities became towns containing agricultural areas such as orchards and vineyards within their municipal boundaries. In the small and medium-sized towns of the coastal plain, such agricultural land may total anywhere from 30 per cent to 80 per cent of the jurisdictional area. In most of these places there is no vacant urban reserve, and therefore the pressure builds up to convert agricultural land to other uses.

The government is unequivocally opposed to the conversion of agricultural land to other uses. The ability of agriculture to resist urbanization derives from the institutional structure dealing with land matters. It must be borne in mind that all agricultural land in the country is state-owned; the planning and building law gives the highest priority to the preservation of agricultural land through committees; the cooperative structure of the rural sector is able organizationally to withstand urbanization pressures; the existence of national and regional plans goes a long way to prevent creeping urbanization, for no city plan can be approved unless it accords with a more inclusive higher level plan; and the 1967 agricultural settlement law does not allow the use of agricultural land for non-agricultural purposes. Thus the State has gradually developed a set of laws to preserve agricultural land and prevent its conversion, as far as possible, for other uses.

WILL ANY LAND REMAIN FOR ROADS?

It may be assumed that the increase in the number of cars of 15 per cent per annum will continue in the future as well, despite the restrictions. This means a persistent increase in private cars, an increasing burden on the roads, and a need to add highways, railway lines, roundabouts and modern transport and safety facilities. The roads will be wider and better, and will therefore need to use more land.

The pressure of various transport needs in towns and outside them will continue, and it is doubtful whether Israel will be able to cope with the intensive development that characterizes all countries in advanced stages of development. It will be necessary to allot more and more areas for parking, for widening roads and roundabouts even at the cost of good land. If in the past one or two lanes sufficed in each direction, today three or four are a minimum. Israel has not yet reached a saturation point in private cars, so that it can look forward to several decades of increasing car ownership and the development of the necessary facilities at the expense of the little land available.

If we exclude the possibility of unconventional means of transport we will in the 1990s need another 950 miles of roads, 220 miles of railway lines, ten domestic airfields, and enough area for a hundred filling stations. Urban transport will become more difficult as regards the conveyance of goods and the provision of facilities for commuters. Transport requires level, open areas, in residential neighbourhoods and city outskirts, and these conflict with farming, landscape, and many other land uses.

However, economic development is inconceivable without transport developments, so that a clash with other vital uses is inevitable unless unused land is sacrificed for this function.

WILL THESE BE THE ONLY DEMANDS FOR LAND?

It is superfluous to point out that land will be needed for purposes other than settlements, population and transport. There is no doubt that the rising standard of living will be reflected in a demand for recreational areas, suburban dwellings, public institutions, parks, nature reserves, bathing beaches, etc. As the population has not yet reached the saturation point in affluence and standard of living, there will be a demand for land for these purposes, and many of the installations required are located physically within the settlements and on their edges.

The construction of power stations for energy is also a great consumer of land. Today there are five, some conventional and some unconventional, in the planning stage and each will require an area of hundreds of acres as a security radius. The demand for land for that purpose will certainly conflict with the land uses of agricultural populations, dwellings, recreational facilities and other open areas. The controversy that will arise in deciding on the location of power stations is already evident today. If some technology is developed to locate them in the interior, that will be a boon, but if not, and they have to be located along the shore, damage to the land will be very great. The public debates around the power stations at Ashqelon and Hadera indicate what can be expected in the future.

As to industry, even greater industrialization is in the offing. Most of the industrial zones in the populated settlements are filling up. There is little reserve land for this purpose in the big cities, but more in the Negev and Galilee. However, because of the economic advantages of the coastal plain, industry will prefer to locate there, and create pressures on land use of an intensity heretofore unknown. Industry is gradually emerging into the inter-city areas, and causing a significant loss of agricultural land. It will be difficult to counter the industrialists when they prove that their contribution to the economy is considerable, greater than that of agriculture.

Faced with demand for land for such important uses as dwellings, settlements, population, transport, industry, recreation, energy, etc. in the future, the question is whether Israel will have enough land, and if not, what is to be done.

LAND USES IN ORDER OF PRIORITY

It is reasonable to suppose that there will certainly not be enough land for all the demands made upon it. Even today not enough is available and that will continue to be the case. The State cannot afford to meet the demands of every development body, as it judges its own needs. There is simply not enough land for optimal transport facilities, for all power stations in the coastal plain, for all suburbs and all industrial plants interested in locating in the centre of the country. There will be no recourse but to establish an order of priorities for the physical development of the country in the 1980s and 1990s, taking into account that only items with the highest priority will be able to obtain land for their uses.

Underlying the establishment of the order of priorities in land use are a series of important questions. Should industry be developed at the expense of agricultural land? Are roads preferable to dwellings? Is it more desirable to allocate room for energy facilities or for nature reserves and recreational areas? Should new urban areas be designated for newcomer housing, or should the newcomers be directed to peripheral regions at the risk of their departure from the country? Should airfields be expanded or should the land concerned be used for agricultural settlements? The determination of the order of priorities and decision-making on the fundamental aspects of the development of the country will engage planners and policy-makers in the future.

LAND USES UNDER COMPULSION

In addition to all these concerns, Israel will also be confronting an actual situation of compulsion, for the planning and administrative system cannot always resist coercive situations that contradict planning logic. Such compulsions are generally determined outside the normal professional framework, and derive mainly from political changes that are an unknown factor so far as conventional planning goes. The world energy crisis and the need to withdraw from Sinai were events that led to considerable spatial changes. All aspects of these matters are not always taken into account, and what if there is suddenly a mass immigration, or far-reaching political and military changes in the region?

In the future, every trend in land use will be subject to radical change. The agricultural sector under constant pressure will move toward even more intensive exploitation of the land as regards choice of crops and improvement of the soil, and may reduce the areas under extensive cultivation. In urban construction greater use will be made of the dimension of height and depth; buildings will be taller and many of the engineering uses of land will become subterranean, as is already indicated in the centres of the larger cities. The urban landscape will change beyond recognition. The agricultural colonies will become more urbanized, land uses there more citified as the big urban concentrations expand, to the point where the colonies turn into medium-sized towns. Engineering installations connected with communication, transport, industry, security and urban services will occupy large areas with access roads. The development towns will undoubtedly experience a new building phase with a greater degree of crowding, high-rise buildings and improved infrastructure, changing their urban profile and absorbing a larger population. They will each attain 30,000 to 50,000 inhabitants and some will attract even more. New settlement forms will develop to compensate for the paucity of land and water, and there will be a tendency to reinforce border areas and utilize more efficiently unoccupied areas skirting desert and mountain.

As regards possibilities for land development Israel will be in no better situation in the late 1980s and 1990s than it is today. To the extent that the needs of building, transport, industry, energy, recreation, etc. can be adapted to the objective situation of the land potential, and to the extent that the sectorial demands for land can be restrained, Israel will be able to more or less preserve the condition that prevails at present, and that is the reasonable optimum. If that is not done, if we do not use land intensively, if we succumb to various pressures and convert agricultural land to other uses, we shall gradually lose the land basis on which the State of Israel was established, and it will turn into a country of concrete, installations and accessories.

Glossary of Terms

Alignment – The Israeli Labour party, composed of a combination of the Labour Party (Mapai) and a number of other Social Democratic groups on the left of the political spectrum.

Allon Plan – A regional settlement plan for the Jordan Valley proposed after the Six Day War by Yigal Allon, a government minister and later deputy prime minister.

Amana Movement – The operational arm of the Likud and the Gush Emunim movement engaged in the establishment and construction of settlements in Judea–Samaria.

Arava – The region between the Dead Sea to the north and the Gulf of Elat to the south, part of the rift valley of Israel, characterized by its dry climate.

Betar Movement – The youth movement of the Revisionist Zionist Party, founded in 1923 by Ze'ev Jabotinsky who then headed it. It was named after Joseph Trumpeldor: the word Betar includes the three consonants B, T and R. B is short for Brith (covenant), T and R are the first and last letters of Trumpeldor.

Big Crater – A morphological depression in the central Negev, formed by the erosive action of gullies.

Development town – A city or town founded after 1948 for the purpose of absorbing new immigrants, within the framework of the programme for distributing the population throughout the country.

Effendi – A landlord in the Arab community and owner of property.

Eretz Yisrael – see Land of Israel

Exurb – A settlement of rural character serving mainly as a residential quarter for a larger urban concentration. See pp. 206–7

Good Fence – A fence with a gate between Israel and Lebanon, put up in 1982 to make it possible for residents of south Lebanon to obtain help in Israel in the areas of security, medicine and work.

Greater Land of Israel – A political term used mainly by Israeli nationalists, who claim Judea, Samaria and the Gaza Strip as an integral part of the State of Israel. See *Land of Israel*.

Green Line – The border between Israel and Jordan established after the War of Independence in 1949, which separates Judea–Samaria from the rest of Israeli territory. The line also separated Israel from the Gaza Strip.

Gush Emunim – A pioneer, religious and fanatical group founded in the mid-1970s for the purpose of settling Judea–Samaria in dozens of new sites (*Gush* – bloc, *Emunim* – confidence).

HaKibbutz HaArtzi – The national federation of Hashomer Hatsair kibbutzim, established in 1927. It is a party body requiring ideological conformity. It adopted the orthodox Marxist creed and added Zionism to it.

HaKibbutz HaMe'uchad – A kibbutz federation founded in 1927, connected with a large kibbutz movement led by the Mapai Party.

Hapo'el Hasmizrahi – A union of religious nationalist workers in Israel who aspire to a lifestyle based on the Torah and work.

Hashomer Hatsair – A socialist youth movement, established in Poland before World War I. It became a Zionist movement in the 1920s and presented socialism in its orthodox Marxist version. This movement created many kibbutzim in the Land of Israel, and after 1948 became a political party which strove for a Jewish–Arab bi-national state.

Histadrut – The General Federation of Hebrew Workers in the Land of Israel. Founded in 1920, it is the largest labour organization in Israel.

IDF – The Israel Defence Force, established in 1948 during Israel's War of Independence.

Kibbutz (pl. kibbutzim) – A collective settlement in Israel whose members believe in doing their work, and personal pioneering in work and defence. It is based on complete collectivism in production and consumption and absolute equality among its members.

Knesset – Israel's 120-member parliament, elected every four years in free, democratic elections on the basis of parties or political factions.

Land Day – One day in the year (March 30th) during which the Arab citizens of Israel conduct demonstrations protesting over dispossession from their land.

Land of Israel (*Eretz Yisrael*) – According to the Old Testament, the land which was promised by God to the Children of Israel. Today it comprises the territory between Syria in the north, Egypt in the south and Jordan in the East. See *Greater Land of Israel*

Large Triangle – The area between the Arab towns of Nablus, Tulkarm and Jenin.

Likud – A union of the rightist parties in Israel – Herut, the Revisionists and the Liberals. The name means 'unity' or 'consolidation'.

Med–Dead Canal – A proposed canal to connect the Mediterranean and Dead Sea in order to produce hydro-electric energy created by the waterfall between the Judean hills and the Dead Sea.

Moshav (pl. moshavim) – An agricultural village based on personal labour and cooperation in supply and marketing, and on mutual help between individual farmers. The production is handled cooperatively, but the means of production are bought and the crops are sold by a jointly owned company.

Mountain Road – A historic road from Beersheba north to the Judea–Samaria hills through Jerusalem and Nablus.

Mukhtar – The head of a tribe, a sect or a village among the Arab population.

Nahal – An army unit combining security and military training with agricultural work and border settlement.

National Kibbutz Organization – A self-contained economic organization founded by the kibbutzim in Israel in order to supply them with all their needs in food, products, seeds, building material and even with education, entertainment, vehicles etc.

Peel Commission – A British Royal Commission headed by Lord Peel which in 1936–7 investigated the situation in Palestine and recommended the partition of the country between Arabs and Jews.

Small Triangle – The area between the Arab towns of Um-el Fahm, Taybe and Tulkarm.

Stockade and tower – The term applied to agricultural settlements each set up in the course of a single night during the 1936–39 disturbances, with the settlers bringing pre-fabricated sections of an observation tower and fence to the site, as well as tents.

Topsite – A settlement in Galilee established in a region disputed by Jews and Arabs in order to prevent the illegal exploitation of State land.

Torah – The holiest book, in which according to Jewish belief Moses recorded God's words and gave them to the Jewish people. It contains annals from the creation to Abraham, and precepts which Jews are enjoined to fulfil.

White Paper – The terms applied to the British government's 1939 declaration of its policy on Palestine which deals with the partition of the country, places where Jews are forbidden to purchase land, and the restriction of Jewish immigration.

Yeshiva – A school for orthodox Jewish students who dedicate their life to the learning and the teaching of Holy Scriptures.

Yom Kippur – The most sacred day of the year for Jews, a day of remorse, forgiveness and atonement. It is also a fast day. The Yom Kippur War between Israel, Egypt and Syria broke out on that day in 1973.

Selected Bibliography

Akzin, B. and Y. Dror (1966), *Israel: High-Pressure Planning*, Syracuse, N.Y., Syracuse University Press.

Allon, Y. (1976), 'The Case for Defensible Borders', *Foreign Affairs*, 55 (1), pp. 38–53.

Arkadie, B. V. (1977), *Benefits and Burdens: A Report on the West Bank and Gaza Strip Economics since 1967*, Carnegie Endowment for Peace, Washington, DC.

Bahiri, S. (1987), 'Industrialization in the West Bank and Gaza', The West Bank Data Base Project, *The Jerusalem Post*.

Benvenisti, M. (1984), *The West Bank Data Project – A Survey of Israel's Policies*, American Enterprise Institute of Public Policy Research, Washington and London.

Benvenisti, M. (1987), 'The West Bank Data Base Project – 1987 Report: Demographic, Economic, Legal, Social and Political Development in the West Bank', *The Jerusalem Post*.

Borokhov, E. (1979), *Land Policy in Israel*, Working Paper 2, Centre of Urban and Regional Studies, Tel Aviv University.

Brawer, M. (1978), 'The Impact of Boundaries on Patterns of Rural Settlement: The Case of Samaria, Israel', *GeoJournal*, 2, 6, pp. 539–48.

Brecher, M. (1972), *The Foreign Policy System of Israel: Setting, Image and Process*, Yale University Press, New Haven.

Brichta, A. and G. Ben-Dor (1974), 'Representation and Misrepresentation of Political Elites: The Case of Israel', *Jewish Social Studies*, vol. 36, pp. 234–52.

Cohen, A. (1965), *Arab Border Villages in Israel*, Manchester University Press.

Cohen, A. (1983), *West Bank Agriculture 1968–1980*, The Institute of Arabic Studies, Givat Haviva, Israel.

Cohen, E. (1974), 'The Power Structure of Israel Development Towns', in T. N. Clark (ed.), *Comparative Community Politics*, New York, Sage & Wiley, pp. 179–201.

Dan. J. (1968), *The Soils in the Judean and Samarian Mountains*, Vulkani Institute for Agricultural Research, Rehovot.

Dehter, A. (1987), 'How Expensive are West Bank Settlements', The West Bank Data Base Project, *The Jerusalem Post*.

Efrat, E. (1984), *Urbanization in Israel*, Croom Helm, Kent, England and St. Martin's Press, N.Y.

– (1982), 'Spatial Patterns of Jewish and Arab Settlements in Judea and Samaria', in D. J. Elazar (ed.), *Judea, Samaria and Gaza: Views on the Present and Future*, American Enterprise Institute for Public Policy

Research, Washington, pp.9–43.
- (1978), 'Optimum versus Reality in Israel's Town System', *GeoJournal*, vol. 2, 6, pp.507–20.
- (1977), 'Changes in the Settlement Pattern of Judea and Samaria during Jordanian Rule, *Middle Eastern Studies*, Vol. 13, No. 1, pp.97–111.
- (1976) 'Changes in the Settlement Pattern of the Gaza Strip 1945–1975', *Asian Affairs*, London, vol. 63, pp.168–77.
- (1971) 'Changes in the Town Planning Concepts of Jerusalem 1919–1969' *Environmental Planning*, The Israeli Association for Environmental Planning Quarterly, pp.53–65.
Elazar, D.J. (ed.) (1982), *Judea, Samaria and Gaza: Views on the Present and Future*, American Enterprise Institute for Public Policy Research, Washington.
- (1978), *Israel, From Ideological to Territorial Democracy*, General Learning Press, New York.
Falah, G. (1985), 'Recent Jewish Colonization in Hebron', in: D. Newman (ed.), *The Impact of Gush Emunim: Politics and Settlement in the West Bank*, Croom Helm, London.
Gharaibeh, F. (1985), *The Economics of the West Bank and Gaza Strip*, Boulder, Colorado.
Gradus, Y. (1984), 'The Emergence of Regionalism in a Centralized System: The Case of Israel', *Environment and Planning*, D: 'Society and Space', pp.87–100.
- (1983), 'The Role of Politics in Regional Inequality: The Israeli Case', *Annals of the Association of American Geographers*, 73 (3), pp.388–403.
- (1982), *Power Relations in Space and Regional Inequalities – The Israeli Case*, University of Haifa.
- and Y. Einy (1981), 'Trends in Core–Periphery Industrialization: Gaps in Israel', *Geographical Research Forum*, 3, Beersheba, pp.25–37.
- and S. Krakover (1977), 'The Effect of Government Policy on the Spatial Structure of Manufacturing in Israel', *Journal of Developing Areas*, 11, pp.393–409.
- and E. Stern (1980), 'Changing Strategies of Development: Toward a Regiopolis in the Negev Desert', *Journal of the American Planning Association*, 46, pp.410–23.
- and E. Stern (1977), 'New Perspectives on the Negev Continental Bridge', *Geoforum*, 8, pp.311–18.
Harris, W.W. (1980), *Taking Root: Israeli Settlement in the West Bank, Golan, Gaza and Sinai, 1967–1980*, John Wiley & Sons, N.Y.
Hasson, S. (1981), 'Social and Spatial Conflicts: The Settlement Process in Israel during the 1950s and 1960s', *L'Espace Géographique*, 3, pp.169–79.
- and N. Gosenfeld (1980), 'Israeli Frontier Settlement: a Cross-Temporal

Analysis', *Geoforum*, 11, pp.315–34.

Horowitz, D. (1975), *Israel's Concept of Defensible Borders*, Leonard David Institute of International Relations, The Hebrew University of Jerusalem, Papers on Peace Problems, 16.

Isaac, R.J. (1976), *Israel Divided: Ideological Politics in the Jewish State*, Johns Hopkins University Press, Baltimore.

Kahan, D. (1987), 'Agriculture and Water Resources in the West Bank and Gaza (1967–1987)', The West Bank Data Base Project, *The Jerusalem Post*.

Kimhi, I., S. Reichman and J. Schweid (1984), *The Metropolitan Area of Jerusalem*, The Jerusalem Institute for Israel Studies, Jerusalem.

Kimmerling, B. (1983), *Zionism and Territory*, Institute of International Studies, University of California, Berkeley.

– (1979), *A Conceptual Framework for the Analysis of Behaviour in a Territorial Conflict: The Generalization of the Israeli Case*, Leonard Davis Institute of International Relations, The Hebrew University of Jerusalem, Papers on Peace Problems, 25.

– (1976), *Conflict and Nation Building: A Sociological Study of the Territorial Factors in the Jewish–Arab Conflict*, The Hebrew University of Jerusalem, Department of Sociology.

Kingdom of Jordan (1986), *A Programme for Economic and Social Development in the Occupied Territories 1986–1990: Profile of the Development Projects*, Amman.

Kliot, N. and S. Waterman (eds.) (1983), *Pluralism and Political Geography, People, Territory and State*, Croom Helm, London.

Landau, J. (1969), *The Arabs in Israel: A Political Study*, Oxford University Press.

Lisak, M. (1969), *Social Mobility in Israeli Society*, Israel University Press, Jerusalem.

Lustick, I. (1980), *Arabs in the Jewish State*, University of Texas Press, Austin.

Lynch, K. (1968), 'The Pattern of Metropolis', in C.E. Elias Jr., J. Gillis and S. Riemer, *Metropolis: Values in Conflict*, Wadsworth Publ., Belmont, California, pp.95–106.

Nakhleh, K. and E. Zureik (eds.) (1980), *The Sociology of the Palestinians*, St. Martin's Press, N.Y.

Newman, D. (1984), 'Ideological and Political Influences on Israeli Urban Colonization: The West Bank and Galilee Mountains', *Canadian Geographer*, 23, 2, pp.142–55.

– (1982), 'The Development of the Yishuv Kehillati in Judea and Samaria: Political Process and Settlement Form', *Tijdschrift voor Economische en Sociale Geografie*, 75 (2), pp.140–50.

– (1982), *Jewish Settlement in the West Bank: The Role of Gush Emunim*, Occasional Paper, 16, Centre of Middle Eastern Studies, University of Durham.

– (1981), 'Gush Emunim and Settlement Type in the West Bank', *Bulletin of the British Society for Middle Eastern Studies*, 8, 1, pp.33–7.

– (1980), 'The Political Interest Group Factor in Planning: The Case of Gush Emunim', *Durham University Geographical Journal*, 22.

Peres, Y. (1971), 'Ethnic Relations in Israel', *American Journal of Sociology*, 76, pp.1021–47.

Peretz, D. (1979), *The Government and Politics of Israel*, Westview Press, Colorado.

Pohoryles, S. (1976), *Development of Agriculture in the Administrative Areas: Accelerated Patterns of Economic Growth*, Ministry of Agriculture, Jerusalem.

Romann, M. (1986), 'Jewish Kiryat Arba versus Arab Hebron', The West Bank Data Base Project, *The Jerusalem Post*.

Romann, M. (1978), 'Jerusalem since 1967: a Profile of a Reunited City', *GeoJournal*, 6, 2, pp.499–506.

Roy, S. (1986), 'The Gaza Strip Survey', The West Bank Data Base Project, *The Jerusalem Post*.

Samouha, S. (1978), *Israel: Pluralism and Conflict*, Routledge & Kegan Paul, London and New York.

Shachar, A. and G. Lipshitz (1980), 'Regional Inequalities in Israel', *Environment and Planning*, A13, pp.463–73.

Sharon, A., *Planning Jerusalem, The Old City and its Environs*, Weidenfeld & Nicolson, Jerusalem.

Shimshoni, D. (1982), *Israeli Democracy*, Free Press, N.Y.

Shinar, D. and Rubinstein, D. (1987), 'Palestinian Press in the West Bank: The Political Dimension', The West Bank Data Base Project, *The Jerusalem Post*.

Sinai, A. and A. Pollack (1977), *The Hashemite Kingdom of Jordan and the West Bank, a Handbook*, American Academic Association for Peace in the Middle East, New York.

Sofer, A. and Y. Bar-Gal (1976), 'Urban Elements in Non-Jewish Villages in the North of Israel', *Geography in Israel*, The Israel National Committee, Jerusalem, pp.275–96.

Stern, E. and Y. Hayuth (1984), '12 Developmental Effects of Geopolitically Located Ports', in B.S. Hoyle and D. Hilling (eds.), *Seaport Systems and Spatial Change*, John Wiley & Sons, N.Y., pp.239–55.

Waterman, S. (1979), 'Ideology and Events in Israeli Human Landscapes', *Geography*, 64, pp.171–81.

Weingrod, A. (1979), 'Recent Trends in Israel's Ethnicity', *Ethnic and Racial Studies*, 2, pp.55–65.

Weitz, R. (1975), *Agriculture in the Gaza Strip and West Bank 1974*, Ministry of Agriculture, Tel Aviv.

Zohar, D.M. (1974), *Political Parties in Israel: The Evolution of Israel's Democracy*, Praeger, New York.

Index